Alan Bryden, Vincenza Scherrer (Eds)

Disarmament, Demobilization and Reintegration and Security Sector Reform

Geneva Centre for the
Democratic Control of Armed Forces
(DCAF)

LIT

Alan Bryden, Vincenza Scherrer (Eds)

Disarmament, Demobilization and Reintegration and Security Sector Reform

Insights from UN Experience in Afghanistan, Burundi, the Central African Republic and the Democratic Republic of the Congo

LIT

Gedruckt auf alterungsbeständigem Werkdruckpapier entsprechend
ANSI Z3948 DIN ISO 9706

Bibliographic information published by the Deutsche Nationalbibliothek
The Deutsche Nationalbibliothek lists this publication in the Deutsche Nationalbibliografie; detailed bibliographic data are available in the Internet at http://dnb.d-nb.de.

ISBN 978-3-643-80132-6

A catalogue record for this book is available from the British Library

Klosbachstr. 107
CH-8032 Zürich
Tel. +41 (0) 44-251 75 05
Fax +41 (0) 44-251 75 06
e-Mail: zuerich@lit-verlag.ch
http://www.lit-verlag.ch

LIT VERLAG Dr. W. Hopf
Berlin 2012
Fresnostr. 2
D-48159 Münster
Tel. +49 (0) 2 51-620 320
Fax +49 (0) 2 51-23 19 72
e-Mail: lit@lit-verlag.de
http://www.lit-verlag.de

Distribution:
In Germany: LIT Verlag Fresnostr. 2, D-48159 Münster
Tel. +49 (0) 2 51-620 32 22, Fax +49 (0) 2 51-922 60 99, e-mail: vertrieb@lit-verlag.de

In Austria: Medienlogistik Pichler-ÖBZ, e-mail: mlo@medien-logistik.at

In Switzerland: B + M Buch- und Medienvertrieb, e-mail: order@buch-medien.ch

In the UK: Global Book Marketing, e-mail: mo@centralbooks.com

Contents

Foreword

The United Nations is increasingly called upon to support post-conflict societies in their efforts to end conflict, stabilise, consolidate peace and commence recovery. Disarmament, demobilization and reintegration (DDR) and security sector reform (SSR) processes are critical elements of such efforts. As the authors of this publication observe, the conceptual linkages between DDR and SSR are already recognised widely by Member States, practitioners and other actors. Yet the implementation of mutually supportive DDR and SSR initiatives has often been elusive. DDR is a discrete conceptual and operational process that has been undertaken by the United Nations over the last twenty years in direct support of national partners, while SSR, as recently noted by the Security Council, is a much broader and newer concept. In the words of Secretary-General Ban Ki-moon, 'We have come a long way from simply being ceasefire monitors. Today we are expected to keep, enforce and build peace.'

Both approaches are evolving in a very dynamic manner, and there is a need to establish close inter-linkages between DDR and SSR. To some extent, this reflects the operational nature of DDR – a time-bound and quantifiable process – while SSR aims at transforming institutions of government and even concepts of security. The book is a product of a close working relationship between the UN Department of Peacekeeping Operations and the Geneva Centre for the Democratic Control of Armed Forces, and it provides a timely and much-needed contribution to enhance our understanding about the topic. I hope it will stimulate further research in this very important emerging area.

In a time of global economic challenges, efficiency, adaptability, innovation and vision are needed in all areas of post-conflict management. Unity of purpose and coherence are also vital. Actors must think beyond organisational boundaries and play to different strengths of peace operations, special political missions or UN agencies, funds and programmes. Synergy and coherence, together with delivering as one, are essential. Viewed from this perspective, DDR and SSR offer opportunities for designing mutually reinforcing early peacebuilding interventions that increase our capacity to achieve more with less.

The book provides an impressive panorama of different contexts in which DDR and SSR intersect. The case studies on Afghanistan, Burundi, Central African Republic and the Democratic Republic of the Congo highlight the politically charged and inter-linked nature of DDR and SSR. While it should also be noted that the new concept of SSR will continue to evolve, these examples provide useful historical and practical references. We believe that the lessons offered in this publication will prove valuable for the many tasks lying ahead for the international community. They also remind us that no two conflicts are the same. It is therefore safe to say that the success of the international community's engagement in conflict-torn countries will continue to rest on the ability to contextualise, adapt and re-evaluate current approaches.

Dmitry Titov
Assistant Secretary-General for Rule of Law and Security Institutions
Department of Peacekeeping Operations
United Nations

Preface

The UN has a long track record in the field of disarmament, demobilization and reintegration (DDR). Although also involved in supporting security sector reform (SSR) in member states over a number of years, translating these efforts into a common UN approach to SSR policy and practice is a more recent endeavour. The distinct trajectories of UN engagement in DDR and SSR underline that the activities often involve different objectives, timelines and stakeholders. Yet at the same time, both share a common goal of helping states emerging from conflict move towards recovery and longer term development. As a result, the need to exploit positive synergies but also to 'do no harm' in designing and implementing UN support for DDR and SSR has become increasingly evident.

In order to understand the nexus between DDR and SSR and its implications for UN policy and practice, a requirement was identified by the UN Inter-Agency Working Group on DDR (IAWG-DDR) for additional guidance on DDR and SSR. Under the leadership of the United Nations Development Programme (UNDP) and the Department for Peacekeeping Operations (DPKO), DCAF was engaged to develop a new module for the UN Integrated Disarmament, Demobilization and Reintegration Standards (IDDRS) on this topic. The resulting IDDRS Module 6.10 on *Disarmament, Demobilization and Reintegration and Security Sector Reform* was officially launched at an IAWG-DDR Principals meeting on 14 December 2009.[1] This volume reflects the key insights developed through this project and, in particular, showcases the country case studies developed as part of this work.

We hope that this volume provides a useful point of reference for academics, policy makers and practitioners involved in the challenging fields of DDR and SSR. It is important to acknowledge that the four cases studies on Afghanistan, Burundi, the Central African Republic and the Democratic Republic of the Congo reflect the prevailing political and security situation at their time of writing. Much has certainly evolved since the field research was undertaken between September 2008 and January 2009. What has not changed is the need for international engagements in DDR, SSR and related fields to be contextually-grounded. Programmes must be responsive to the needs and interests of different national actors. Without understanding the dynamic political processes that shape the origins, parameters and outcomes

---

1 The module is available at: www.unddr.org

of both processes, DDR and SSR may address security deficits, but will be unfit to support sustainable transitions towards national recovery and development.

The successful completion of the DDR-SSR project would not have been possible without the engagement of a number of people. The initial concept for the IDDRS module was developed by Kelvin Ong, now with the UN Department for Political Affairs. The process was guided on the UN side by Ayaka Suzuki and Simon Yazgi from the DPKO DDR Unit as well as Sophie da Camara, Luc Lafrenière and Dean Piedmont from UNDP's Bureau for Crisis Prevention and Recovery. Valuable input was received from members of the IAWG-DDR and the Inter-Agency SSR Task Force as well as from many representatives of UN field missions and country offices. Conceptualization and drafting was supported by an advisory board of independent experts which included Jeremy Brickhill, Michael Brzoska, Mark Downes, Mark Knight, Robert Muggah and Edward Rees. Finally, the case study authors Boubacar N'Diaye, Serge Rumin, Vincenza Scherrer and Mark Sedra gave unsparingly of their time and knowledge to deliver against a complex and demanding set of requirements.

The editors would like to thank sincerely all those who contributed to this process. The views expressed in this volume are those of the authors and do not in any way reflect the views of either the institutions or their representatives involved in this process.

The Editors
Geneva, March 2012

Abbreviations

AMF	Afghan Military Force
AMIB	African Union Mission in Burundi
ANA	Afghan National Army
ANBP	Afghan New Beginnings Programme
ANP	Afghan National Police
APPM	Armed Political Parties and Movements
AU	African Union
BINUB	*Bureau Intégré des Nations Unies au Burundi*, UN Integrated Office in Burundi
BONUCA	*Bureau politique d'observation des Nations Unies en Centrafrique*, United Nations Peace-building Office in the Central African Republic
CAR	Central African Republic
CC	*Cellule de concertation*, consultation unit
CEMAC	*Communauté Économique et Monétaire de l'Afrique Centrale*, Economic and Monetary Community of Central Africa
CFA franc	African Financial Community franc
CivPol	Civilian police
CONADER	*Commission Nationale de la Démobilization et Réinsertion*, National Commision for Demobilization and Reintegration, DRC
CNDD/FDD	*Conseil National pour la Défense et la Démocratie/Forces pour la Défense de la Démocratie*, National Council for Defence and Democracy / Forces for the Defence of Democracy, Burundi
CNDDR	*Commission Nationale de Désarmement, Démobilization, et Réinsertion*, National Commission for Disarmamant, Demobilization and Reintegration, CAR
CNDP	*Congrès national pour la défense du peuple*, National Congress for the Defence of the People, DRC
CSTC-A	Combined Security Transition Command Afghanistan
DAC	Development Assistance Committee (of the OECD)
DCR	Disarmament and community reintegration
DDR	Disarmament, demobilization and reintegration

DDR-RR	Disarmament, demobilization, repatriation, reintegration and resettlement
DIAG	Disbandment of illegal armed groups
DFC	Defence and Security Corps, Burundi
DPA	Department of Political Affairs (UN)
DPI	Department of Public Information (UN)
DPKO	Department for Peacekeeping Operations
DRC	Democratic Republic of the Congo
DRR	Demobilization, reinsertion and reintegration
DRRP	Demobilization, reinsertion and reintegration programme
DSRSG	Deputy Special Representative of the Secretary-General (UN)
ECOWAS	Economic Community of West African States
EU	European Union
EUPOL	European Union Police Mission, DRC
EUSEC	European Union Security Sector Reform Mission
FAB	*Forces Armées Burundaises,* Burundian Armed Forces
FACA	*Forces Armées de Centrafrique,* Central African Armed Forces
FAR	*Forces Armées Rwandaises,* Rwandan Armed Forces
FARDC	*Forces Armées de la République Démocratique du Congo*, Armed Forces of the Democratic Republic of Congo
FDD	Focused District Development (of ANP)
FDLR	*Forces Democratiques de Liberation du Rwanda,* Democratic Liberation Forces of Rwanda
FDN	*Force de Défense Nationale,* National Defence Force, Burundi
FNL	*Forces Nationales de Libération*, National Liberation Forces, Burundi
FOMUC	*Force Multinationale en Centrafrique,* Multinational Force in Central Africa
FRODEBU	*Front pour la démocratie au Burundi,* Democratic Front in Burundi
Frolina	*Front Libération National,* National Liberation Front, Burundi
G8	Group of Eight (Canada, France, Germany, Italy, Japan, Russia, UK, USA)
GCP	Coordination Group of Partners, Burundi
HLP	Housing, land and property
IASSRTF	Inter-Agency SSR Task Force

IAWG-DDR	Inter-Agency Working Group on DDR
IDDRS	Integrated Disarmament, Demobilization and Reintegration Standards
IDP	Internally displaced person
ILO	International Labour Organization
IMC	Implementation Monitoring Committee, Burundi
IMF	International Monetary Fund
IOM	International Organization for Migration
ISAF	International Security Assistance Force, Afghanistan
JCC	Joint Ceasefire Commission, Burundi
MDRP	Multi-Country Demobilization and Reintegration Program
MESAN	*Mouvement pour l'Evolution Sociale de l'Afrique Noire,* Movement for the Social Evolution of Black Africa, CAR
MICOPAX	*Mission de consolidation de la paix en République Centrafricaine,* Mission for the Consolidation of Peace in the Central African Republic
MINURCA	*Mission des Nations Unies en République centrafricaine,* UN Mission in the Central African Republic
MINURCAT	*Mission des Nations Unies en République centrafricaine et au Tchad,* UN Mission in the Central African Republic and Chad
MINUSTAH	*Mission des Nations Unies pour la stabilisation en Haïti,* United Nations Stabilization Mission in Haiti
MIS	Management information system
MISAB	*Mission Interafricaine de Surveillance des Accords de Bangui,* Inter-African Monitoring Mission of the Bangui Accords, CAR
MoJ	Ministry of Justice
MONUC	*Mission des Nations Unies en République démocratique du Congo,* United Nations Mission in the Democratic Republic of Congo
MONUSCO	*Mission de l'Organization des Nations Unies pour la stabilisation en République démocratique du Congo,* United Nations Organization Stabilization Mission in the Democratic Republic of the Congo
MoPS	Ministry of Public Security, Burundi
NATO	North Atlantic Treaty Organization
NCDDR	National Commission on Demobilization, Reinsertion and Reintegration, Burundi
NDF	National Defence Force

NPDDR	National Programme on Demobilization, Reinsertion and Reintegration, Burundi
ODA	Office for Disarmament Affairs (UN)
OECD DAC	Organization for Economic Cooperation and Development's Development Assistance Committee
OHCHR	United Nations Office of the High Commissioner for Human Rights
OIOS	UN Office of Internal Oversight Services
ONSC	Office of the National Security Council, Afghanistan
ONUB	*Opération des Nations Unies au Burundi*, United Nations Operation in Burundi
OSAA	Office of the Special Advisor on Africa
PBC	UN Peacebuilding Commission
PBF	UN Peacebuilding Fund
PBSO	Peacebuilding Support Office (UN)
PID	Political Inclusive Dialogue, Burundi
PNB	Police Nationale du Burundi
PNC	Police Nationale Congolaise
PNDDR	*Programme Nationale de DDR*, National DDR Programme, CAR
PRAC	*Projet de Réinsertion des ex-combattants et d'Appui aux Communautés,* Project for the Reintegration of ex-combatants and Community Support, CAR
PSC	Private security company
SALW	Small arms and light weapons
SAPSD	South African Protection Service Detachment
SMI	Integrated Military Structure, DRC
SRSG	Special Representative of the Secretary-General (UN)
SRSG-CAAC	Office of the Special Representative of the Secretary-General for Children and Armed Conflict (UN)
SSG	Security sector governance
SSR	Security sector reform
STP	*Secrétariat Technique Permanent,* Permanent Technical Secretariat, CAR
TRC	Truth and Reconciliation Commission
UE-PNDDR	*Unité d'Execution du Programme Nationale de DDR,* Implementation Unit of the National DDR Programme, CAR
UN	United Nations
UNAIDS	Joint United Nations Programme on HIV/AIDS

UNAMA	UN Assistance Mission in Afghanistan
UNAMSIL	United Nations Mission in Sierra Leone
UNDP	United Nations Development Programme
UNICEF	United Nations Children's Fund
UNIDIR	United Nations Institute for Disarmament Research
UNFPA	United Nations Population Fund
UNHCR	United Nations High Commissioner for Refugees
UNITAR	United Nations Institute for Training and Research
UNMIL	United Nations Mission in Liberia
UNOCI	United Nations Operation in Côte d'Ivoire
UNODC	United Nations Office on Drugs and Crime
UNPOL	United Nations Police
UPRONA	*Union pour le Progrès National,* Union for National Progress, Burundi
UN Women	United Nations Entity for Gender Equality and the Empowerment of Women
WFP	World Food Programme
WHO	World Health Organization

PART I

INTRODUCTION

Chapter 1

The DDR-SSR Nexus: Concepts and Policies

Alan Bryden and Vincenza Scherrer

Introduction

Disarmament, demobilization and reintegration (DDR) and security sector reform (SSR) are today acknowledged pillars of the international community's commitment to post-conflict peacebuilding and sustainable development. While a growing community of experts and academics have emerged to support and promote both activities, the policy and programming linkages between DDR and SSR remain under-developed. This is partly because both sets of initiatives are frequently pursued autonomously, independent of one another. As a result, artificial epistemic and bureaucratic silos have emerged that frustrate productive exchange. Opportunities to build on synergies and strengthen positive outcomes in both sets of activities are therefore often missed.

This volume sets out to break down these stove-pipes and identify positive associations between DDR and SSR. Drawing on case studies from selected post-conflict settings, it demonstrates the potential and reality of improved collaboration between both endeavours. Enhanced cooperation could avoid negative outcomes. These may include former-combatants dropping out of programmes, trust undermined in security institutions and the creation of security vacuums that jeopardise the safety of individuals and communities. A central claim of this volume is that a failure to account for the nexus between DDR and SSR can yield negative consequences for security more generally.

The admittedly nascent policy literature considering the relationships between DDR and SSR tends to be dislocated from practitioner experiences of supporting DDR and SSR. This runs the risk of under-estimating the frequently dynamic political processes that fundamentally influence the origins, parameters and outcomes of both processes. Indeed, power relations that are reflected in the structure of post-conflict settlements are complex, fast-changing and frequently difficult to understand. Yet a major finding of this volume is that interventions must engage with these diverse constituencies from the national to the local levels. At a minimum, it requires durable partnerships between international supporters and the range of formal and informal actors at the national level involved in security provision, management and oversight. It may also require actively promoting the involvement of different entities – from parliament or civil society bodies to the leadership of armed groups – so that they play a more central role in DDR and SSR.

In any post-conflict setting, proponents of DDR and SSR are required to sensitively balance the expectations and interests of different stakeholders. Specifically, international donors and agencies may require quick wins and clear exit strategies. Likewise, local authorities, elites, former combatants and affected communities will require protracted engagement to avoid the reconstitution of old networks of power, authority and patronage. To succeed, practitioners will need to avoid overtly prescriptive approaches, learn to read the terrain and demonstrate flexibility.

This volume stems from a wider project designed to clarify the policy and programming issues associated with the DDR-SSR nexus. Its main output has been a new module on DDR and SSR as part of the UN's Integrated Disarmament, Demobilization and Reintegration Standards (IDDRS).[1] A particular focus is reserved for the United Nations (UN) and its partners that are involved in post-conflict peacebuilding. Whilst the target audience for this volume includes UN practitioners, it is important to recall that they are not the only actors involved in these processes. The volume also accounts for the interests and functions of national and local authorities who are most closely affected by DDR and SSR success or failure.

This chapter begins by reviewing the objectives of and approaches to DDR and SSR. Drawing on a security sector governance perspective, the chapter then analyses some of the key elements of the DDR-SSR nexus. It also reflects on UN approaches to the design and implementation of DDR and SSR. The chapter concludes by introducing the case studies from Afghanistan, Burundi, the Central African Republic (CAR) and the Democratic Republic of the Congo (DRC) that are examined in Part II of this volume.

Conceptualizing DDR and SSR

A number of policy studies have attempted to better illuminate the real and potential linkages between DDR and SSR in countries emerging from war.[2] A common feature of this body of work is an emphasis on the need for policies and programmes informed by cogent and context-specific understandings of the character and dynamics of post-conflict settings. And while calling for more analysis of the political economy of post-war settings, there is still conceptual haziness on the form and function of DDR and SSR, much less the ways they interact. Confusion and in some cases contradiction arises when actors involved in DDR and SSR are forced to cooperate without understanding their respective roles. Thus, before embarking on a review of the 'nexus', this section first intends to promote clarity on the two concepts, including areas of mandate convergence and divergence.

Disarmament, Demobilization and Reintegration

A level of consensus has emerged around the anticipated goals and outcomes of DDR.[3] According to the IDDRS, DDR is intended to 'deal with the post-conflict security problem that arises when combatants are left without livelihoods and support networks during the vital period stretching from conflict to peace, recovery and development.'[4] The IDDRS describes DDR as 'a process that contributes to security and stability in a post-conflict recovery context by removing weapons from the hands of combatants, taking the combatants out of military structures and helping them to integrate socially and economically into society by finding civilian livelihoods.'[5] A UN definition of DDR[6] found in Table 1.1 succinctly explains the four phases to this process.

DDR emerged as a process intended to demilitarize, downsize, right size and/or professionalise erstwhile armies and non-statutory armed groups in the wake of a peace agreement and ceasefire. Due to its particular historical origins, DDR processes typically feature a clear primary target caseload including former combatants and their dependents. A number of other participants have been identified including children associated with armed groups, disabled ex-combatants and those associated with armed groups but not in combat roles.[7] In practice, DDR tends to draw on predominantly defence and security-related expertise during the disarmament and demobilization processes and more developmental approaches when it comes to reinsertion and reintegration.

Table 1.1: Disarmament, Demobilization, Reinsertion and Reintegration[8]

Disarmament
Disarmament is the collection, documentation, control and disposal of small arms, ammunition, explosives and light and heavy weapons of combatants and often also of the civilian population. Disarmament also includes the development of responsible arms management programmes.
Demobilization
Demobilization is the formal and controlled discharge of active combatants from armed forces or other armed groups. The first stage of demobilization may extend from the processing of individual combatants in temporary centres to the massing of troops in camps designated for this purpose (cantonment sites, encampments, assembly areas or barracks). The second stage of demobilization encompasses the support package provided to the demobilized, which is called reinsertion.
Reinsertion
Reinsertion is the assistance offered to ex-combatants during demobilization but prior to the longer-term process of reintegration. Reinsertion is a form of transitional assistance to help cover the basic needs of ex-combatants and their families and can include transitional safety allowances, food, clothes, shelter, medical services, short-term education, training, employment and tools. While reintegration is a long-term, continuous social and economic process of development, reinsertion is a short-term material and/or financial assistance to meet immediate needs, and can last up to one year.
Reintegration
Reintegration is the process by which ex-combatants acquire civilian status and gain sustainable employment and income. Reintegration is essentially a social and economic process with an open time-frame, primarily taking place in communities at the local level. It is part of the general development of a country and a national responsibility, and often necessitates long-term external assistance.

Depending on the configuration of the peace agreement or ceasefire arrangement and the political determination of the presiding national authorities, DDR commonly involves two parallel activities. In principle, a filtering process (typically involving profiling and screening) will often ensure that a certain proportion of the former combatants are diverted to the security services (e.g. reconstituted military, reformed police force, or other mechanisms). Meanwhile, those opting for voluntary retirement or considered unfit for service will be supported to assume civilian status through a combination of incentives and support packages. While a straightforward process in theory, the reality is often much more complicated and controversial.

International investment in DDR has grown significantly since the early 1990s. Normative developments have also taken place. For example, the *Stockholm Initiative on Disarmament, Demobilization and Reintegration*[9] and the IDDRS were each driven by the desire to translate practical experience into good practice. Both of these initiatives effectively brought practitioner, policy and research communities closer together in a productive exchange. There is some evidence to suggest that it has also generated more outcome-oriented approaches to DDR that stress the importance of specific, measurable indicators of achievement while also remaining attentive to the legitimacy and sustainability of the process.

In the meantime, a critical discourse has emerged that questions the attributed benefits of post-conflict peacebuilding activities (including both DDR and SSR), particularly when measured against the considerable financial investments by the aid community.[10] Likewise, many DDR programmes have been criticized for adopting overly technocratic approaches that fail to adequately account for the dynamics of the post-conflict setting and the perspectives of elites and erstwhile combatants.[11] Criticisms point to a lack of appreciation of the interests and actions of political and security elites as well as the marginalization of influential non-state actors and local nodes of resilience. In the process, interventions focus more on donor driven mandates than the needs of affected people (whether former-combatants or civilians).[12]

Increasingly, DDR practitioners have in fact been required to innovate and experiment in the design and execution of their interventions. Often the activities on the ground only marginally resemble the DDR programmes advocated from above. Indeed, innovative research on interim stabilization or 'second generation' DDR has demonstrated how programme staff and local authorities have developed bottom-up strategies that account for specific contextual factors.[13] These activities explicitly identify ways to promote security in the midst of political and security uncertainty found in fragile and contested societies. Examples of activities falling under this label include community violence reduction initiatives, transitional military integration arrangements or the establishment of local dialogue processes. At the centre of this new generation of activities is a strong commitment to engaging with local cultural norms and community-based participation and leadership.

Security Sector Reform

The UN Secretary-General's report on SSR describes this area as 'a process of assessment, review, and implementation as well as monitoring and evaluation led by national authorities that has as its goal the enhancement of effective and accountable security for the State [sic] and its peoples without discrimination and with full respect of human rights and the rule of law.'[14] In other words, SSR is motivated by the idea that an ineffective, inefficient and poorly governed security sector constitutes a decisive obstacle to security and development. Put succinctly, SSR includes a series of activities designed to facilitate the effective and efficient provision of state and human security within a framework of democratic governance.[15]

The SSR community is constituted by a wide range of multilateral agencies, governments, networks, civil society organizations and individual experts. Largely informed by a liberal democratic paradigm, SSR is intended to recalibrate the institutions of the security sector in line with accepted principles of democratic governance. A wide range of multilateral institutions have adopted this liberal framing of SSR including the African Union (AU), the Economic Community of West African States (ECOWAS), the European Union (EU), the Organization for Economic Cooperation and Development's Development Assistance Committee (OECD DAC) and the UN.[16]

The SSR approach is functionally ambitious because it seeks to integrate activities such as defence, intelligence, police and judicial reform that in the past were conceived and administered as separate activities. SSR has a strong norm-setting agenda with activities collectively intended to contribute to wider democratic security sector governance (SSG). What is more, SSR proponents have acknowledged the limitations of a top-down and state-centric focus by emphasizing the security of individuals and communities as a key criterion for success. Enhancing the performance of security providers without linking this to concerns of democratic control is insufficient and by itself does not constitute 'SSR'.

The scope of the SSR agenda is reflected in a wide range of actors involved in its formulation, execution and evaluation. SSR includes a multitude of entities playing a role in security provision, management and oversight (see Table 1.2). But it is important to recognize that SSR is not only focused on formal or governmental actors. Indeed, the UN Secretary-General's Report on SSR notes that 'other non-state actors that could be considered a part of the security sector include customary or informal

Table 1.2: Overview of SSR and related activities

<table>
<tr><td colspan="3">**1) The strategic framework**
(e.g. security sector reviews, needs assessments, development of SSR strategies and national security policies)</td></tr>
<tr><td>**2) Security and justice provision**</td><td>**3) Civilian management and democratic oversight**</td><td>**4) Related activities in post-conflict contexts**</td></tr>
<tr><td>Defence reform
Intelligence reform
Border security reform
Police reform
Justice reform[17]
Prison reform
Other activities</td><td>Executive management and control
Parliamentary oversight
Judicial review
Oversight by independent bodies
Civil society oversight</td><td>DDR
SALW control
Mine action
Transitional justice
Other activities</td></tr>
<tr><td colspan="3">**5) Cross-cutting issues** (e.g. gender equality, child protection)</td></tr>
</table>

Source: Heiner Hänggi and Vincenza Scherrer, eds., *Security Sector Reform and UN Integrated Missions: Experience from Burundi, the Democratic Republic of Congo, Haiti, and Kosovo* (Munster: Lit Verlag, 2008), 15.

authorities and private security services.'[18] As such, a broad understanding of the security sector recognises the particularly critical roles often played by armed non-state actors in societies emerging from conflict.

Having been introduced in the late 1990s, the SSR approach is relatively recent. In part due to this novelty, the concept has been subjected to a range of criticisms. First, there is as yet no comprehensive doctrine guiding SSR practice.[19] Instead, policy and practice are frequently guided by non-evidentiary policy prescriptions. Second, there are comparatively few scientific evaluations of SSR activities, much less agreement on metrics of success. As a result, estimations of outcomes continue to be anecdotal and subjective. Third, assessments of current donor practice point to a lack of emphasis on supporting the security sector governance dimension which is often matched by a lack of political will on the part of national authorities in this area;[20] the preponderance of external support remains focused on (re)building more effective security providers. Fourth, owing to its predominantly Anglo-Saxon origins,[21] SSR is routinely labelled as an externally generated agenda. As such, criticisms of SSR regularly point to their contested legitimacy and lack of genuine local ownership.[22] This 'ownership gap' tends to compound perceptions of SSR as military-technical assistance under another guise.

A security sector governance approach to the DDR/SSR relationship

The relationship between DDR and SSR was clearly acknowledged in the path-breaking *Brahimi Report.* The 1999 study described the impacts of DDR on SSR as 'an area in which peacebuilding makes a direct contribution to public security and law and order.'[23] Even so, translating the concept of a DDR-SSR nexus into programming synergies has proven more difficult. Part of the failure to identify opportunities to collaborate relates to disagreements between SSR and DDR specialists over their respective mandates and activities. For example, a lingering argument that DDR should be pursued as a subordinate component of SSR appears to be motivated more by narrow bureaucratic preoccupations than a genuine engagement with substance. Ultimately, more pragmatic experts tend to acknowledge the ways in which SSR and DDR comprise two separate but related activities (see Table 1.2 above) contributing to common peacebuilding and development aspirations. As noted in the OECD DAC Handbook on SSR, 'the two issues [DDR and SSR] are often best considered together as part of a comprehensive security and justice development programme.'[24]

This volume proposes that efforts to pursue SSR and DDR be guided by wider security sector governance concerns. Such a perspective seeks space for genuine engagement with civilian authorities and local populations about their legitimate security requirements in order to put community needs and vulnerabilities at the centre of the SSR process. It also provides a yardstick to scrutinise the values, objectives and feasibility of measures adopted by national actors and international partners. A security sector governance lens can thus potentially help bridge DDR and SSR programmes through pointing to mutually reinforcing activities (see Table 1.3).

Sequencing is one angle from which to examine the DDR-SSR nexus. In theory, DDR and SSR priorities should be taken into account at the beginning of the peace process in a rational and progressive manner. Ideally, the state, armed groups and mediators would articulate a coherent plan for the reconstitution of the security sector, the gradual standing down of armies and disarmament of rank and file as well as related concerns of civilian management and oversight. Of course in practice, this is rarely the case. Rather, complex peace negotiations and the arduous process leading to a peace agreement is marked by stop-start progress, political trade-offs, and lingering concerns about security dilemmas.

Table 1.3: The DDR-SSR nexus from a Security Sector Governance perspective

	DDR pillars		
	Disarmament	*Demobilization*	*Integration/ Reintegration*
SSR perspective	The state's ability to regulate and control the transfer, trafficking and use of weapons derived from the DDR process should be part of a broader approach to strengthening state regulation and management of weapons. Disarmament needs to be based on confidence fostered through targeted efforts to increase community security.	DDR decisions affecting force size and structure need to reflect an assessment of security sector reform objectives, priorities and absorption capacity. Demobilization should take into account implications for the security sector and the need to mitigate the risk of security vacuums.	Integration of demobilised ex-combatants into the security forces should reflect long-term sustainability and legitimacy concerns (e.g. rank harmonization, vetting, veterans rights etc.). SSR activities can complement reintegration through reinforcing community security.

Whether intended or not, DDR has immediate consequences for SSR in most conflict-affected environments. This is because disarmament and demobilization – the initial stages of DDR – are routinely undertaken before wider security sector interventions lift off. As a result, the disarming and demobilizing of a designated caseload of former combatants can shape the eventual size and shape of the future military, police and associated security organs. As such, DDR practitioners are frequently de facto engaging in SSR by re-configuring the security sector. At the same time, there is a possibility that confidence-building through SSR can also facilitate an enabling environment to kick-start a DDR programme. In other situations, DDR and SSR may move along parallel tracks. In all cases, the sequencing is less important than gauging the political as well as the technical consequences of these activities.

The influence of DDR on SSR is also evident in the frequent employment of ex-combatants in different parts of the formal or informal security sector. In such cases, DDR and SSR planners need to establish clear criteria to ensure that individuals with inappropriate backgrounds or skill-sets are not simply re-deployed since this would undermine both the effectiveness and credibility of future SSR activities. Profiling, vetting and re-training of former military personnel are clear examples of mutually reinforcing DDR and SSR processes.

Ultimately, the issue of legitimacy should be clearly thought through in policy directives for DDR and SSR. As a rule, the determination of which personnel will be disarmed, demobilised and reintegrated into society and wider decisions regarding retention in reformed security sectors will be fiercely contested by societal interest groups. A balance must be struck between the concerns and priorities of these different stakeholders. On the one hand, if critical decisions are left exclusively at the discretion of the leadership of former armed groups, this may well facilitate their engagement in a peace process. On the other hand, this can be counter-productive in the long term if decisions are seen to sustain their power base or reward allies rather than address real security needs.

If peace is to be sustainable and endure then there are clear pragmatic imperatives to better link DDR and SSR. Since conflict often results in the politicization of the state apparatus and the blurring of security providers' roles, DDR and SSR are uniquely positioned to clarify and re-define the mandate, structure and composition of the security sector and its governance system. It is essential that this restructuring is consistent with the absorptive capacity and resource base of the state. In order to contribute to durable security, it is critical that supporters of DDR and SSR ensure adequate negotiation over the architecture of the security sector (e.g. its size, shape and values). This will require flexibility and attention to process on the part of planners so that (previously) disenfranchised stakeholders are confident in the outcomes.

A security sector governance approach implies a more radical agenda than it may first appear. In essence, it envisions security as a public good rather than a partisan entitlement. Notwithstanding this large vision, the steps required to re-shape security sector governance must be pursued incrementally and with humility. Core goals may be advanced through support for management and oversight capacities amongst national stakeholders including government ministries, parliaments, the judiciary and civil society. Participatory approaches can enable actors at different levels of society to contribute to defining their own security needs and responses. An emphasis on capacity support and participation can foster trust and promote transparency and accountability – key factors in sustainable post-conflict stabilization and longer-term recovery and development.

UN Support for DDR and SSR

The UN has a lengthy track record in supporting DDR and a more recent and evolving experience in promoting SSR. In practice, the UN's approach to each activity area is quite distinct. There is a genuinely programmatic engagement with DDR that is often reflected in calls to support DDR 'programmes' understood as such across policy and operational levels. While by definition the UN understanding of SSR reflects a holistic understanding of the concept, in practice this is not necessarily translated into programmatic approaches. Instead, SSR support may be project-driven in response to a wide range of entry points – from police training to capacity building for civilian oversight. Thus, while strategic support to SSR may be offered to the field by the SSR Unit within DPKO, operational support in different thematic areas (e.g. justice, police, corrections etc.) will come from a range of different components and entities within the UN system.

The following section focuses on three important facets of the UN's role in both areas. First, it identifies core organizations involved in supporting aspects of DDR and SSR within the UN system. Second, it considers critical policy guidelines designed to inform UN support. Finally, the section reviews the mandates for different peacekeeping missions in order to determine how key agencies understand and prioritize DDR and SSR in these settings.

Organizations

The Department for Peacekeeping Operations (DPKO) and the United Nations Development Programme (UNDP) are prominent actors within the UN system engaged in both DDR and SSR.[25] Their activities are extensive and far-reaching and include tasks such as institutional capacity-building and operational assistance to police, defence and judicial reform, support to the development of action plans and implementation of DDR programmes, and overall financial management assistance and support to regulation and oversight mechanisms.[26] However, many other UN entities also play important roles. In response to the fragmented and uncoordinated approach undertaken by UN agencies to both DDR and SSR, a number of mechanisms

Table 1.4: Memberships of the IAWG-DDR and the IASSRTF[27]

Actors	IAWG-DDR	IASSRTF
Department of Peacekeeping Operations (DPKO)	x	x
Department of Political Affairs (DPA)	x	x
Department of Public Information (DPI)	x	
International Labour Organization (ILO)	x	
International Organization for Migration (IOM)	x	
Joint United Nations Programme on HIV/AIDS (UNAIDS)	x	
Office for Disarmament Affairs (ODA)	x	x
Office of the Special Advisor on Africa (OSAA)	x	x
Office of the Special Representative of the Secretary-General for Children and Armed Conflict (SRSG-CAAC)	x	
Peacebuilding Support Office (PBSO)	x	x
United Nations Children's Fund (UNICEF)	x	x
United Nations Development Programme (UNDP)	x	x
United Nations Entity for Gender Equality and the Empowerment of Women (UN Women)	x	x
United Nations Institute for Disarmament Research (UNIDIR)	x	
United Nations Institute for Training and Research (UNITAR)	x	
United Nations Office on Drugs and Crime (UNODC)		x
United Nations Population Fund (UNFPA)	x	x
United Nations High Commissioner for Refugees (UNHCR)	x	
United Nations Office of the High Commissioner for Human Rights (OHCHR)	x	x
World Food Programme (WFP)	x	
World Health Organization (WHO)	x	

were established to foster greater coherence. Specifically, the Inter-Agency Working Group on DDR (IAWG-DDR) was established in March 2005 with a mandate to improve UN performance in DDR. All 15 initial members jointly developed and approved the first edition of the IDDRS 'to provide the UN system with a set of policies, guidelines and procedures for the planning, implementation and monitoring of DDR programmes in a peacekeeping context.'[28] In the area of SSR, an Inter-Agency Working Group was created in 2006 and was replaced by an Inter-Agency SSR Task Force (IASSRTF) in 2007. The task force currently includes a total of 11 UN entities with a mandate to facilitate inter-agency consultation, elaborate standards and guidance on SSR, ensure their dissemination across the UN system and build capacities throughout the UN system.

With just ten of twenty-one entities present in both, the overlap is relatively small (see Table 1.4). And it is not necessarily the case that the same personnel are present on both bodies. While there was a DDR/SSR sub-group in the IAWG-DDR (intended to foster critical linkages during the development of the DDR-SSR module for the IDDRS), this was dissolved following the publication of the module. The sheer number of entities involved and the relatively limited overlap between the IAWG and the IASSRTF make coordination a challenge. If this is an issue at headquarters, it is even more important at the country level where joint planning, assessments, and programming are more the exception than the rule.

UN policies

The imperative to link DDR and SSR is noted in a number of UN policy documents. In the 2006 report of the Secretary-General on DDR, for example, it was recognised that 'disarmament, demobilization and reintegration programmes must be linked to security sector review and reform.'[29] This view is reflected in the IDDRS which states that 'DDR should also be linked to broader SSR, including judicial, police and military restructuring.'[30] Similarly, the Presidential Statement emerging from the 20 February 2007 Open Debate in the United Nations Security Council 'recognises the inter-linkages between security sector reform and other important factors of stabilization and reconstruction, such as transitional justice, disarmament, demobilization, repatriation, reintegration and rehabilitation of former combatants, small arms and light weapons control, as well as gender equality, children and armed conflict and human rights

Table 1.5: Common principles for UN DDR and SSR

DDR Principles	SSR Principles
People-centred and rights-based	Support development and contribute to the enjoyment of human rights by all Gender-sensitive
Flexible	Flexible and tailored to the country and/or region
Transparent and accountable	Effective, inclusive and accountable approach to security Need for a national decision, a Security Council mandate, and/or a General Assembly resolution
Nationally-owned	National ownership and commitment of involved states and societies
Integrated	Coordination of national and international partners efforts
Well-planned	SSR framework essential for post-conflict planning and implementation Clearly defined strategy, including the identification of priorities, indicative timelines and partnerships

Source: UN Inter-Agency Working Group on DDR. *Briefing Note for Senior Managers on the IDDRS*, 4, and, Secretary-General's report on SSR, S/2008/39.

issues.'[31] Thus, in policy terms it is clear that the UN acknowledges the DDR-SSR nexus and that this is one part of an integrated approach to the different elements of post-conflict peacebuilding.[32]

Differences notwithstanding, an approach founded on common principles represents an important conceptual bridge between DDR and SSR. Design principles for UN engagement in DDR are very similar to those contained in the Secretary-General's Report on SSR (see Table 1.5). Since they recur in approaches endorsed across the wider international community, shared principles should (at least in theory) facilitate improved linkages in practice.

The new IDDRS module on DDR and SSR represents a first attempt to articulate a common UN approach that moves from principles to operational linkages on the ground. Even so, considerable work needs to be done to translate new insights into coordinated, coherent and comprehensive interventions. As explored throughout this volume, challenging framing conditions and missed opportunities to foster synergies have combined to limit progress. A potentially significant step is the guidance development process driven by the Inter-Agency SSR Task Force. The topics being elaborated do not only focus on the technical aspects of SSR. They seek to develop new knowledge in areas such as peace processes or national security policy frameworks in which both DDR and SSR should feature prominently.[33] This process can therefore provide an opportunity to foster DDR-SSR synergies across a range of entry points for UN engagement.

Peacekeeping mission mandates

For at least two decades DPKO-led peace support operations have frequently supported DDR. DPKO is often requested to engage in all components of DDR although in some cases only in disarmament and demobilization.[34] UNDP has been a key actor in providing DDR support in both peace-keeping and non-peace-keeping contexts.[35] While SSR is also an increasing focus of UN activities, it has often been approached in an ad hoc manner and not necessarily understood as 'SSR' according to its holistic definition. Thus, certain UN peacekeeping mandates did not explicitly refer to SSR, but rather to one of its functional activities, in particular police, defence or judicial reform.[36]

Within peacekeeping missions, distinct operational responsibilities create natural stovepipes between DDR, SSR, justice, corrections, police and military components. The challenge is less structural than of fostering an integrated approach across actors and activities. For example, while there is a certain consistency in UN support for DDR processes, this is not necessarily the case in relation to SSR.[37] Inconsistency is evident in how mandates for DDR and SSR are framed within a given country. For example, in a 2003 report on Afghanistan, the Secretary-General included 'the rebuilding of a national army and police, the rehabilitation of the justice sector, the implementation of a disarmament, demobilization and reintegration programme and the curbing of the production and trafficking of illegal narcotics' in his understanding of SSR.[38] The report therefore applies a definition of SSR that encompasses DDR. In contrast, a 2005 Security Council Resolution on Afghanistan defines DDR and SSR as separate activities within a wider peacebuilding process. The latter resolution recognises the importance of the 'full completion of the disarmament,

Table 1.6: Security Council resolution mandates for DDR and SSR[39]

Mission	DDR terminology in mission mandates	SSR terminology in mission mandates
ONUB Burundi (2004-2007)	"Carry out the disarmament and demobilization portions of the national programme of disarmament, demobilization and reintegration" SCR 1545 (May 2004)	"Provide advice and assistance (for)…the constitution of the integrated national defence and internal security forces" SCR 1545 (May 2004)
UNOCI Cote d'Ivoire (2004-ongoing)	"Requests UNOCI to carry out its mandate…especially in the prevention of movements of arms and combatants across shared borders and the implementation of disarmament and demobilization programmes" SCR 1528 (Feb 2004)	"To assist the Government of National Reconciliation…in restoring a civilian policing presence throughout Côte d'Ivoire, and to advise the Government of National Reconciliation on the restructuring of the internal security services" SCR 1528 (Feb 2004)
MONUC DRC (1999-2010)	To develop an action plan... including "the comprehensive disarmament, demobilization, resettlement and reintegration of all members of all armed groups referred to in Annex A, Chapter 9.1 of the Ceasefire Agreement" SCR 1291 (Feb 2000)	To assist in the "Reform of security forces" (SCR 1493, 2003) "Security sector reform, including the integration of national defence and internal security forces together with disarmament, demobilization and reintegration and, in particular, the training and monitoring of the police, while ensuring that they are democratic and fully respect human rights and fundamental freedoms" SCR 1565 (Oct 2004)
MONUSCO DRC (2010 ongoing)	To support "the completion of activities of DDR of Congolese armed groups" To support "activities of DDRRR of foreign armed groups members…including repatriation, reinsertion or resettlement in other areas, or judicial prosecution as appropriate, with the help of all countries" SCR 1925 (May 2010)	To support "the efforts of the Congolese authorities to strengthen and reform security and judicial institutions;" To support "the reform of the police led by the Government of the Democratic Republic of the Congo, including by providing training to battalions of the Congolese National Police (PNC) and mobilizing donors to provide basic supplies" SCR 1925 (May 2010)

MINUSTAH Haiti (2004-ongoing)	To "assist the Transitional Government, particularly the Haitian National Police, with comprehensive and sustainable Disarmament, Demobilization and Reintegration (DDR) programmes for all armed groups, including women and children associated with such groups, as well as weapons control and public security measures" SCR 1542 (Apr 2004)	"To assist the Government in monitoring, restructuring and reforming the National Police, consistent with democratic policing standards" SCR 1542 (April 2004) To "further explore possibilities for greater support to reform, modernise and strengthen the judiciary and correctional systems, including through the provision of targeted technical assistance to rule of law institutions" SCR 1658 (Feb 2006)
UNMIL Liberia (2003-ongoing)	To "develop…an action plan for the overall implementation of a disarmament, demobilization, reintegration, and repatriation (DDRR) programme for all armed parties" SCR 1509 (Sep 2003)	"Support for security reform": (a) "to assist the transitional government of Liberia in monitoring and restructuring the police force of Liberia, consistent with democratic policing, to develop a civilian police training programme, and to otherwise assist in the training of civilian police; (b) "to assist the transitional government in the formation of a new and restructured Liberian military" SCR 1509 (Sep 2003)
UNAMSIL Sierra Leone (1999-2005)	"To assist the Government of Sierra Leone in the implementation of the disarmament, demobilization and reintegration plan" SCR 1270 (Oct 1999)	"To strengthen the operational effectiveness of the security sector" SCR 1436 (Sep 2002)

demobilization and reintegration process, of the disbandment of illegal armed groups, of justice sector reform, of security sector reform including reconstitution of the Afghan National Army and Police, and of combating narcotics trade and production.'[40]

The fact that SSR does not always figure explicitly or consistently in mandates has unintentionally impaired overall mission coherence. Specifically, it has hampered the ability of personnel to determine their exact role in SSR and, as a result, their relationship with those involved in pursuing DDR. Table 1.6 provides some examples of directives for supporting DDR and SSR in the initial mandates of integrated peacekeeping missions.[41] As the table demonstrates, earlier missions tended to first request support for DDR activities, while support for component SSR activities such as police and justice reform emerged only later in the missions' lifespan (e.g. UNAMSIL, MONUC). In more recent missions, with SSR terminology more widespread, provisions for DDR and SSR were introduced simultaneously in the mission mandates (e.g. UNMIL, MINUSTAH); however, there is often a lack of clarity on how they should relate to each another. This is why the UN has embarked on a programme to develop a common UN approach to SSR and to build system-wide capacities in this area.

In sum, the UN's engagement in DDR and SSR cuts across a wide range of programmes and agencies. As reflected in the different understandings found in peacekeeping mission mandates, this makes coherence a significant challenge. The new IDDRS module provides a means to embed principles and approaches within a common set of guidance. Positive effects can extend beyond the UN – the IDDRS is considered as the gold standard by many national SSR stakeholders, bilateral donors, international and regional organizations working in DDR. The growing phenomenon of communities of practice and expert networks involved in DDR and SSR provide new opportunities to reach out and influence the thinking of these wider sets of actors.[42]

DDR-SSR Challenges

In order to develop the new IDDRS module on DDR and SSR, it was recognised that insights from ongoing programmes would be essential.[43] The use of field based case studies was an innovation for IDDRS guidance development.[44] The four cases were selected on the basis of specific criteria:

- Significant UN engagement in supporting both DDR *and* SSR
- UN mission or country team presence on the ground in order to facilitate field research
- Relevance in terms of current UN priorities

This section draws on these cases to introduce some of the key implementation challenges in the different national contexts. The case studies on Afghanistan, Burundi, the Central African Republic and the Democratic Republic of the Congo were developed through a combination of desk analysis and in-country research.[45] Field research was in each case conducted by the authors over a two week period. Semi-structured interviews were conducted with a broad range of national and international stakeholders to ensure that diverse perspectives were taken into account. Inevitably, they offer a snapshot of wider security promotion processes that are in constant evolution. However, a security sector governance approach focuses on under-analysed political and security dynamics that can inform an understanding of DDR and SSR processes regardless of subsequent developments.

Afghanistan

In Afghanistan, DDR was recognised as inherently linked to SSR through its inclusion in the five-pillar SSR agenda (composed of military reform, police reform, judicial reform, DDR and counter-narcotics). The Commander Incentive Programme, developed to deal with commander obstructionism, is one example of an effort to address the DDR-SSR nexus in programming. However, in practice, the relationship was only partially addressed. As Mark Sedra (Chapter 2) points out challenges included numerous stakeholders involved but also weaknesses in the planning and assessment process. One consequence has been the de-legitimization of the Disbandment of Illegal Armed Groups Programme (successor to the DDR programme) which focused largely on the semi-formal militias of the former Northern Alliance. Indeed, the main instrument mandated to enforce the compliance of armed groups – the Afghan National Police – was unable to carry out this role due to capacity shortfalls and general mismanagement.

Burundi

Serge Rumin (Chapter 3) develops important insights through analysing DDR/SSR dynamics from the perspective of the individual ex-combatant. He demonstrates that if expectations are not managed, necessary short-term measures may exacerbate tensions in the long run. For example, disproportionate numbers of ex-combatants were integrated into armed and security forces as a deliberate strategy to 'buy the peace' with rightsizing left to a later stage. This double-trigger mechanism lacked transparency and the criteria used for assessing those to be demobilised have been questioned. Many angry ex-combatants subsequently rejected compulsory demobilization. The case of Burundi therefore underlines the need to strike a balance between efforts to build a sustainable, professionalised security sector and more immediate concerns of managing ex-combatants.

The Central African Republic

In the CAR, a dysfunctional and poorly governed security sector has been identified as one of the root causes of decades of conflict. Discussions on DDR have therefore been couched in the broader framework of SSR. Supporting a national dialogue process was identified as a first step in addressing dysfunctional relations between the state, security sector and citizens. The national seminar in April 2008 provided a framework for subsequent discussions and agreements, crystallizing in the minds of the various stakeholders the need to avoid thinking about the two activities separately. Nonetheless, as Boubacar N'Diaye (Chapter 4) indicates, the achievements of the national dialogue process need to be weighed against the difficulties experienced in linking DDR and SSR activities in practice.

The Democratic Republic of the Congo

The case of the DRC highlights the challenges of supporting DDR and SSR in a conspicuously non-enabling environment. Residual conflict, lack of basic infrastructure and ongoing security threats have resulted in shifting emphasis between DDR and SSR according to the key priorities of the moment. In practice, this generated short-term measures directed toward operational activities with immediate impact. Strategic analysis of the longer-term consequences that DDR may have on SSR and vice-versa has been lacking. Vincenza Scherrer (Chapter 5) demonstrates the consequences of *not* taking into account the relationship between DDR and SSR. This includes security vacuums in areas where police reform is not undertaken with the challenges of the DDR programme in mind and heightened tensions where ex-combatants have not been able to enter the DDR process due to funding gaps for army reform.

Conclusion

The need to foster synergies between DDR and SSR cannot be reduced to a simplistic sequential relationship. This is because both DDR and SSR involve a combination of activities – many of them overlapping – that entail highly distinct challenges depending on the specific context. In unpacking the relationship between DDR and SSR it is essential to take into account their different objectives, timelines, stakeholders and interests. However, informing wider DDR planning with insights and expertise from SSR can facilitate the wider 'design' of a society's future security sector. The security sector governance focus to DDR and SSR can enhance the legitimacy of programmes and their outcomes through emphasizing the need for transparent, nationally-driven decision making.

An important point of departure for this volume is the inherently political nature of both DDR and SSR. This reflects the sensitivity of issues that touch directly on sovereignty and national security as well as the fact that decisions in both areas necessarily generate 'winners' and 'losers.' At the heart of the DDR-SSR nexus is therefore the need to recognize and engage these sensitivities and carefully balance international assistance with respect for the principle of local ownership. Applying a security sector governance framework allows practitioners to better situate DDR-SSR activities within complex and often highly contested post-conflict transitions. This perspective is further developed in the concluding chapter of this volume.

Improving the effectiveness of DDR and SSR practice can have a significant, positive impact on states emerging from conflict. In order to design and implement programmes that contribute effectively to security and development goals, approaches need to be grounded in an informed understanding of specific political, socio-economic and security framing conditions. The ability to develop a nuanced and sophisticated understanding of 'what the market will bear' in distinct, challenging environments is therefore essential. This volume is intended to contribute to that important goal.

Notes

1 The development of a series of UN DDR standards was initiated in 2004. The three main aims of the IDDRS are 1) to set out clear, flexible and in-depth guidance for DDR practitioners; 2) to establish a shared basis for integrated operational planning; and, 3) to provide a training resource for the DDR community. An inter-agency working group on DDR (IAWG-DDR) was subsequently established by the Executive Committee on Peace and Security in March 2005 with the mandate to improve UN performance in DDR. The 26 modules comprising the first edition of the IDDRS were jointly developed and approved by the IAWG-DDR in July 2006 and formally launched in December 2006. As part of its commitment to review and update the IDDRS, the need for additional guidance was identified on the relationship between DDR and SSR as well as DDR and transitional justice. Based on discussions initiated in 2007, DCAF was engaged to develop this new module. The resulting IDDRS Module 6.10 on *Disarmament, Demobilisation and Reintegration and Security Sector Reform* was officially launched at an IAWG-DDR Principals meeting on 14 December 2009. The module is available at www.unddr.org.

2 See Alan Bryden, 'Understanding the DDR-SSR Nexus: Building Sustainable Peace in Africa' (2007). Available at: http://www.dcaf.ch/publications; W. Andy Knight, 'Linking DDR and SSR in Post-Conflict Peacebuilding: An Overview', *African Journal of Political Science and International Relations* 4, no. 1 (January 2010): 29-54; Michael Brzoska, 'Embedding DDR Programmes in Security Sector Reconstruction,' in *Security Governance in Post-Conflict Peacebuilding*, eds. Alan Bryden & Heiner Hänggi (Munster: Lit Verlag, 2005). The Department for International Development (DFID) also commissioned a study on DDR and SSR linkages within the context of a broader project on *DDR and Human Security: Post-Conflict Security Building in the Interests of the Poor*. See the project page at: http://www.ddr-humansecurity.org.uk/.

3 However, numerous variations on the term 'DDR' have emerged and are in use. See Robert Muggah, ed., *Security and Post-Conflict Reconstruction – Dealing with fighters in the aftermath of War* (London: Routledge, 2009), 6.

4 IDDRS Operational Guide, 24.

5 IDDRS 1.20 Glossary and Definitions.

6 As noted in the IDDRS, the UN "uses the concept and abbreviation 'DDR' as an all-inclusive term that includes related activities, such as repatriation, rehabilitation and reconciliation, that aim to achieve sustainable reintegration". IDDRS 1.10 Introduction to the IDDRS.

7 For the evolution of DDR approaches see Mats Berdal and David Ucko, eds., *Reintegration of Armed Groups After Conflict: War to Peace Transitions* (London: Routledge, 2009) and Robert Muggah, 'No Magic Bullet: A Critical perspective on Disarmament, Demobilisation and Reintegration and Weapons Reduction during Post-Conflict,' *The Commonwealth Journal of International Affairs* 94 (2005).

8 Note of the Secretary-General to the General Assembly on the administrative and budgetary aspects of the financing of the United Nations peacekeeping operations, A/C.5/59/31, 24 May 2005.

9 The Stockholm Initiative on Disarmament, Demobilisation and Reintegration (SIDDR) was launched by the Swedish Government in November 2004 to capture lessons from experience to date in DDR through drawing on the knowledge of a wide range of national and international experts. The final report of the SIDDR was issued in February 2006 and can be found at: www.sweden.gov.se/siddr.

10 See Cedric De Coning, 'Coherence and Coordination in United Nations Peacebuilding and Integrated Missions', *Security in Practice* 5, (Oslo: Norwegian Institute of International Affairs, 2007) and Robert Muggah, '(Dis)Integrated Missions: Reflections from Sudan and Haiti', *Humanitarian Practice Network*, 38. (London: Overseas Development Institute, 2007).

11 See Kathleen M. Jennings, 'Seeing DDR from Below: Challenges and Dilemmas Raised by the Experiences of Ex-Combatants in Liberia', FAFO Report (3) (Oslo: FAFO, 2008) and Muggah, ed., 2009.

12 The importance of contextual determinants is thoroughly explored in Nat J. Colletta and Robert Muggah, 'Context Matters: Interim Stabilisation and Second Generation Approaches to Security Promotion', *Conflict, Security and Development* 9, no. 4 (December 2009): 425-453.

13 See Nat J. Colletta, Jens Samuelsson Schjorlien and Hannes Berts, *Interim Stabilisation. Balancing Security and Development in Post-Conflict Peacebuilding* (Folke Bernadotte Academy: 2008); UN DPKO, *Second Generation Disarmament, Demobilisation and Reintegration Practices in Peace operations* (January 2010).

14 Report of the Secretary-General on 'Securing Peace and Development: the Role of the United Nations in Supporting Security Sector Reform', 23 January 2008, S/2008/39, para 17.

15 Heiner Hänggi, 'Security Sector Reform', in *Post-Conflict Peacebuilding – A Lexicon*, ed. Vincent Chetail (Oxford: Oxford University Press, 2009), 337.

16 'African Union policy on security sector reform – zero draft', presented at the AU-UN Security Sector Reform meeting to review the draft AU SSR policy document, Addis Ababa, 17-19 May 2010; ECOWAS conflict Prevention Framework, Regulation MSC/REG.1/01/08.; Council of the European Union, *EU Concept for ESDP Support to Security Sector Reform*, 12566/4/05 REV 4 (Brussels, 13 October 2005); European Commission, *A Concept for European Community Support for Security Sector Reform,* COM (2006)253 Final, (Brussels, 24 May 2006); Council of the European Union, *Council Conclusions on a Policy Framework for Security Sector Reform*, 2736th General Affairs Council Meeting (Luxembourg, 12 June 2006); OECD DAC, *Security System Reform and Governance*, DAC Guidelines and Reference Series (Paris: OECD DAC, 2004); OECD DAC, *OECD DAC Handbook on Security System Reform, Supporting Security and Justice* (Paris: OECD DAC, 2007); United Nations, 'Securing peace and development: The role of the United Nations in supporting security sector reform', report of UN Secretary-General, UN Doc. A/62/659-S/2008/39.

17 The Secretary-General's report on SSR includes judicial reform so far as this involves "elements of the judicial sector responsible for the adjudication of cases of alleged criminal conduct and misuse of force." S/2008/39, para 14.

18 S/2008/39, para 14.

19 The OECD-DAC Handbook on Security System Reform is generally considered to be the most complete policy guidance to date for internationally-supported SSR. OECD DAC, *OECD DAC Handbook on Security System Reform* (Paris: OECD DAC, 2007).

20 Dylan Hendrickson, 'Key Challenges for Security Sector Reform: A Case for Reframing the Donor Policy Debate', *GFN-SSR Working Paper* (Birmingham: University of Birmingham, 2009).

21 The term 'security sector reform' was coined by Claire Short, then UK Minister for International Development during a 1998 speech on 'Security, Development and Conflict Prevention' at the Royal College for Defence Studies. This augured a prominent UK role in SSR that remains to this day.

22 See Timothy Donais, ed., *Local Ownership and Security Sector Reform* (Munster: LIT Verlag, 2008). Available at: www.dcaf.ch/publications; Laurie Nathan, *No Ownership, No Commitment; A Guide to Local Ownership of Security Sector Reform*, 2nd ed. (Birmingham: University of Birmingham, 2007).

23 United Nations Report of the Panel on Peacekeeping Operations. UN doc. A/55/305S/2000/809 (2000), para 42.

24 OECD DAC, *OECD DAC Handbook on Security System Reform*; (Paris: OECD DAC, 2007), 105. Available online at: www.oecd.org/dac/conflict/if-ssr.

25 Although a prominent DDR actor within the DDR field, this project does not include the World Bank given its limited direct engagement in SSR.

26 For an overview of different UN entities' approaches to SSR see the UN SSR website: http://unssr.unlb.org/Actors.aspx.

27 This table is up to date as of 1 October 2011.

28 See "1.10: Introduction to Integrated DDR Standards": http://www.unddr.org/iddrs/01/#footnote.

29 SG report DDR 2006, paragraph 22.

30 IDDRS 2.10.

31 *Statement by the President of the Security Council* at the 5632nd meeting of the Security Council, held on 20 February 2007; S/PRST/2007/3 (21 February 2007).

32 See Bryden and Hänggi (2005).

33 The guidance notes under development as of July 2011 are Democratic Governance of the Security Sector; National Security Policies and Strategies; SSR and Peace Processes; and Coordination of UN SSR Assistance.

34 For example, the UNOCI (Cote d'Ivoire) and UNMIL (Liberia) mandates cover 'DDR' while the UNOMSIL (Sierra Leone) and UNMIN mandates (Nepal) only focus on 'DD'.

35 Central African Republic, Colombia, Comoros Islands, Indonesia (Aceh), Nepal, Niger, Philippines, Republic of Congo, Somalia, Solomon Islands and Uganda. See UNDP DDR webpage: http://www.undp.org/cpr/we_do/ddr.shtml.

36 SSR has been explicitly referred to in several mandates, including in those for the BINUB (Burundi), UNOCI, MONUC (Democratic Republic of Congo) and UNMIL missions. In these mission mandates, notably, DDR and SSR have both been called for explicitly. For more on SSR in mission mandates, see Heiner Hänggi and Vincenza Scherrer, eds., *Security Sector Reform and UN Integrated Missions: Experience from Burundi, the Democratic Republic of Congo, Haiti, and Kosovo* (Munster: LIT Verlag, 2008).

37 SCR 1542 (April 2004).

38 Report of the Secretary-General, 18 March 2003, 1-2.

39 The table considers the initial mandates of integrated peacekeeping missions established since 1999 that have been mandated to provide both DDR and SSR support. This table does not address the mandates of special political and peacebuilding missions which may also be mandated to support DDR and SSR (e.g. BINUB).

40 UN Security Council Resolution 1623 of 13 September 2005.

41 Hänggi and Scherrer define integrated missions as multidimensional peacekeeping operations with specific structure and command arrangements which seek to bring UN actors on the ground together within a common approach. Integration in this context is "the guiding principle for the design and implementation of complex UN operations in post-conflict situations and for linking the different dimensions (political, development, humanitarian, human rights, rule of law, social and security aspects) into a coherent support strategy". Hänggi and Scherrer (2008), 8.

42 Important examples include: the African Security Sector Network (ASSN) www.africansecuritynetwork.org; the Association for SSR Education and Training (ASSET) www.asset-ssr.org; the UN DDR Resource Centre www.unddr.org; and the community of practice established by DCAF's International Security Sector Advisory Team (ISSAT) http://issat.dcaf.ch.

43 The methodology for developing the new IDDRS module on DDR and SSR was designed jointly by DCAF and the UN lead agencies for this project (DPKO and UNDP).

44 In order to facilitate comparative analysis, the four case studies adopt the same structure and address common research questions. First, the case studies provide an overview of the political and security contexts that shape opportunities and constraints for DDR and SSR. The DDR-SSR nexus is then examined with particular regard to how far opportunities for linking DDR and SSR have been exploited. Finally, the chapters analyse context-specific challenges to operationalizing the relationship between DDR and SSR, as well as the lessons that can be drawn from them. Draft case studies underwent a thorough review

process involving feedback from headquarters and the field across the membership of the IAWG-DDR. The draft module, including boxes drawing on concrete insights from all four case studies was subsequently validated at a workshop linked by videoconference that was held simultaneously in Bukavu, Geneva, and New York.

[45] The field research took place between September 2008 and January 2009.

PART II

CASE STUDIES

Chapter 2

Afghanistan

Mark Sedra

Introduction

After the fall of the Taliban regime in the autumn of 2001, two of the initial priorities identified by the international community and nascent Afghan administration for the country's war-to-peace transition were the disarmament, demobilization and reintegration of ex-combatants (DDR) and security sector reform (SSR). There are few more difficult environments for the implementation of DDR and SSR than Afghanistan. The country faces high levels of insecurity in the form of the Taliban-led insurgency, warlordism, the narcotics trade and general criminality. A strong case can be made that Afghanistan has yet to enter the post-conflict phase and has merely entered a new stage of its three-decade-long civil war. Due to the present security crisis facing Afghanistan, DDR and SSR projects tend to be viewed by the international community and segments of the Afghan government not as elements of a broader peacebuilding and state-building process, but as instruments to address immediate security threats. This has tended to have the effect of imbuing these projects with a short-term focus.

Due to the perceived geo-strategic importance of Afghanistan, resources have not been the primary obstacle to DDR and SSR. Finding a common vision for the future of the Afghan security apparatus and settling on a strategy to achieve it have proven far more elusive. Coordination is a problem at every level of the DDR and SSR processes, and at the time of writing a coherent long-term strategy for the Afghan security sector did not exist. Afghan political will for reform has not kept pace with the growth of international engagement in the DDR and SSR processes. The deep ethnic and political divisions that characterise the Afghan administration are also omnipresent in the security sector. There is no consensus among the Afghan political elite concerning key issues such as DDR and SSR; as insecurity has grown, many Afghan actors have begun to resist demilitarization activities and, more worryingly, view them as a threat. Rampant corruption and clientelism at the highest levels of government have impeded and even paralysed reforms, particularly in the judicial sector. Even where political will is robust, chronic shortages of human and institutional capacity in the Afghan administration have made change grindingly slow and undercut genuine local ownership. Both activities were recognised as key elements of the state-building process and were included as part of the five-pillar Afghan SSR agenda outlined at two G8 security donors' meetings held in the spring of 2002 in Geneva. This recognition of the innate linkages between DDR and SSR did not, however, translate into integrated programming. The reality is that many years after the launch of Afghanistan's state-building process, DDR and SSR continue to face an uphill struggle in the Afghan context.

In the Afghan context, DDR must be understood within a broader framework of 'demilitarization'. Several interlinked initiatives have been undertaken under the auspices of a broader demilitarization process. They include a DDR programme focusing on the assemblage of militias that constituted the Northern Alliance, dubbed the Afghan Military Force (AMF); the Disbandment of Illegal Armed Groups (DIAG) programme targeting all armed groups in the country outside the AMF; the Heavy Weapons Cantonment Programme that sought to collect, deactivate and canton heavy weapons; and an ammunition and mine action programme mandated to collect, stockpile and destroy the estimated 100,000 tonnes of uncontrolled ammunition and explosive material littering the country.[1] Accordingly, this chapter will at times use the term 'demilitarization' when referring to DDR and its associated processes.

The United Nations is the key implementing agency for the Afghan DDR process. The Afghan New Beginnings Programme (ANBP) was established through a partnership between the UN Development Programme (UNDP) and the UN Assistance Mission in Afghanistan (UNAMA) to manage demilitarization activities. Although Japan was the lead funder of the process under the G8 lead-donor scheme and the Afghan government was intended to be the key policy-making instrument through the Demobilization and Reintegration Commission, the United Nations has in reality driven the process from its inception.

While the United Nations has played a key role in the elaboration of the DDR process, its involvement in SSR has been severely limited. UNDP has had some involvement in the police reform process via the Law and

Order Trust Fund for Afghanistan and is implementing some justice reform initiatives, largely funded by Italy and the European Commission. However, a lack of intensive involvement in the SSR agenda has contributed to a disconnect between the DDR and SSR processes. One of the principal obstacles encumbering the state-building agenda is the absence of a unified strategic vision. There are various conflicting interests at play among the external actors engaged in the security sector, and no overarching strategy or coordination body has emerged to provide the needed leadership in SSR implementation. It was widely hoped that Afghan bodies such as the Office of the National Security Council (ONSC) could assert an oversight and coordination role, but it has not demonstrated either the capacity or the willingness to do so.

The Afghan demilitarization process is one of the largest and most expensive in history. Its numerical achievements are impressive, but its long-term impact has yet to be assessed. The very issue of how to assess the sustainability of the programme remains unclear. These challenges therefore make Afghanistan a particularly instructive case study for DDR and SSR in the post-9/11 era.

Context for DDR and SSR

Security Sector Reform

The 2001 Bonn Agreement[2] addressed the security sector only superficially, with vague provisions for the extension of state authority over militias and the establishment of a judicial reform commission. By 2003, however, President Karzai referred to the SSR process as the 'basic pre-requisite to recreating the nation that today's parents hope to leave to future generations'.[3] Although the SSR concept was relatively well established in the international development and security communities by the time the Taliban fell in 2001, its influence over Afghanistan's SSR process has been short-lived, and over time the process has regressed into a Cold War-era train-and-equip programme. This has stemmed largely from the failure of international military forces to provide an adequate security buffer for the state-building project, compelling the government and donors to see the SSR process, particularly as it concerns the nascent Afghan security forces, as the principal mechanism to address immediate security threats. The resultant focus on improving the operational effectiveness of the security forces has drawn attention and resources away from judicial reform and initiatives to establish an effective system of democratic oversight. Many of the problems that confront the SSR process today can be traced back to this 'slide toward expediency' in its implementation.[4]

One of the principal obstacles to the SSR process was the initial framework established to support it.[5] At a G8 donors' conference in Geneva in April 2002, the SSR agenda was formally set with the establishment of the lead-nation system. The security sector was divided into five pillars, and a lead nation was appointed to oversee reforms in each.[6] The five pillars were military reform (the USA); police reform (Germany); judicial reform (Italy); disarmament, demobilization and reintegration of former combatants (Japan); and counternarcotics (the UK). By tying individual donors to specific areas of the reform agenda, the system was intended to ensure the balanced distribution of resources and durable donor engagement. However, no mechanism was established to harmonise the activities of the lead nations or build synergies between them, undercutting one of the core precepts of SSR, namely the need for a holistic and integrated approach. Some donors assumed that the Afghan government would take on this role, but acute shortfalls in capacity prevented it from doing so. While the system succeeded in firmly affixing the lead donors to their pillars, it also made them territorial. Donors were often more concerned with protecting their turf than advancing SSR more widely. Moreover, the system did not adequately consider differences between donors in competencies or resources. This contributed to significant imbalances and massive resource disparities between the pillars. As a result, the pace and achievements of reform have differed widely. It quickly became clear that, given the integrated nature of the security sector, such differentiation was counterproductive. Advances in deploying newly trained police, for instance, were being undermined by a lack of progress in the reform of the judicial system.

By the time of the London donor conference of January/February 2006, where the Afghanistan Compact and Interim Afghan National Development Strategy were endorsed by the Afghan government and donor community, the lead-nation system had effectively, although not formally, been jettisoned in favour of a focus on Afghan leadership and ownership. However, the legacy of the system continues to hang over the process, with coordination deficits and even clashes among key stakeholders a fact of life on the ground. The United Nations would have been well placed to fill the leadership vacuum in the process, but it lacked the capacity or political inclination to do so, particularly with the United States so heavily invested. Accordingly, it has maintained a role on the sidelines, only engaging the process in a superficial manner, primarily for internal monitoring and reporting. This deprived it of the ability to encourage and drive greater integration with demilitarization activities.

Demilitarization

In a 2003 speech, President Karzai asserted that 'achieving DDR answers the deepest aspirations of the Afghan people, who are eager to move away from war and violence toward a peaceful, safe and civil society'.[7] Karzai was speaking at a conference organised in Tokyo by the Japanese government to provide a forum for the Afghan government to present its plans for reforming the security sector. Although the original focus of the Japanese pillar was on establishing a DDR programme for the Afghan Military Force, it subsequently grew to encompass an initiative to disband illegal armed groups outside the AMF. Despite a slow start, by 2007 the demilitarization process was widely regarded as a success. Although the numerical achievements are certainly impressive, closer examination shows that the progress made has been tenuous.

The Disarmament, Demobilization and Reintegration of former combatants. The 2003 Tokyo conference was attended by more than 30 donor countries, as well as the EU and ten international organizations. Out of it came the Afghan New Beginnings Programme (ANBP), a DDR project implemented by UNDP on behalf of the Afghan government. Formally launched in April 2003, the stated objective of the ANBP, which focused solely on active units of the AMF, was:

> to decommission formations and units up to a total of 100,000 officers and soldiers and in the process to collect, store and deactivate weapons currently in their possession in order to be able to reconstruct the Afghan National Army (ANA) and return those not required to civilian life.[8]

While disarmament was explicitly stated as a central goal, in practice it was treated as a peripheral aspect. The two underlying goals of the process were 'to break the historic patriarchical [*sic*] chain of command existing between the former commanders and their men; and to provide the demobilised personnel with the ability to become economically independent'.[9] The Afghan government and the ANBP initially estimated that 100,000 combatants were eligible to enter the DDR process. This figure represented a compromise between the Afghan Defence Ministry, which initially claimed

Table 2.1: ANBP funding breakdown

Donor	Contribution (US$ million)
Japan	91.0
UK	19.0
Canada	16.0
USA	9.0
Netherlands	4.0
European Commission	1.9
Norway	0.8
Switzerland	0.5
Total	**142.2**

Source: Afghanistan New Beginnings Programme, 'Afghanistan New Beginnings Programme', brochure for second Tokyo conference on Consolidation of Peace in Afghanistan (Kabul: ANBP, 15 June 2006), 5.

that there were more than 250,000 AMF soldiers on duty, and UNAMA, which asserted that there were only 45,000–50,000.[10] No comprehensive assessment of the scale and nature of the problem was conducted to inform the programme's design, and ANBP officials were forced to rely on force figures provided by the defence ministry. However, the ministry and AMF commanders had an interest in overstating the number of troops under their command, as they could claim more resources from the central government to feed, house and remunerate them. After a year of operation, the ANBP lowered the operational target to approximately 60,000, concluding that a large proportion of the AMF personnel on the payroll of the Defence Ministry were in fact 'ghost soldiers'.

The minimum requirements for entry into the US$142 million programme (see Table 2.1) were eight months of military service and the submission of a functioning weapon, as determined by an ANBP weapons expert.[11] This prerequisite was largely symbolic, and intended to demonstrate the individual soldier's commitment to peace. The programme did not contain a mechanism to verify that individual soldiers or commanders were submitting all of their weapons stocks, or to compel them to do so.

After weapons collection in a particular area was completed, ex-soldiers were directed to the ANBP regional office for demobilization, where they were presented with a list of livelihood training opportunities. Ex-combatants were offered a choice of several reintegration packages devised by the ANBP in cooperation with the Afghan government and international partner organizations. If no immediate opportunities could be identified, or if an agricultural package could not begin for seasonal reasons, the ANBP offered temporary wage-labour positions until suitable alternatives could be made available.[12]

The main phase of the programme, launched in May 2004, proceeded slowly during its first three months of operation, primarily because of obstruction by commanders and insecurity. The process began to achieve tangible results in the latter part of 2004 due to two factors. Firstly, the Political Parties Law promulgated on 18 October 2003 provided a powerful incentive for armed factions with political ambitions to comply with the DDR process.[13] The law prohibits political parties from having 'military organizations or affiliations with armed forces' – a principle also enshrined in the constitution – and allows for the dissolution of parties that transgress the statute.[14] Intent on registering candidates in time for the October 2004 presidential elections, factional groups sought to demonstrate their support for the DDR process by demobilizing elements of their militias. The increased level of cooperation exhibited by all the main factional groups, although short of full compliance, was a product of their political ambitions and determination to avoid complications in the registration process.[15] Secondly, in the run-up to the presidential elections, the USA deepened its engagement in the process, applying pressure on recalcitrant commanders to comply. The shift in the US approach, which had previously been characterised by ambivalence and even obstructionism, was intended to boost Karzai's electoral fortunes and address deteriorating security conditions.

Commanders manipulated the process in particular regions, arbitrarily choosing candidates for entry into the programme and pilfering reintegration assistance.[16] In an attempt to address the dilemma of commander obstructionism, the ANBP launched the Commander Incentive Programme in 2004. The central component of the scheme was a financial redundancy package which provided commanders with a US$550–650 monthly cash stipend for a two-year period, in exchange for their cooperation with the ANBP. For commanders unlikely to be enticed by financial incentives alone, opportunities for travel and training overseas (primarily in Japan) and the prospect of a government posting were offered to suitable candidates, as determined by the government and the ANBP. The two-year, US$5 million programme, funded by Japan, targeted 550 militia commanders across the country. The redundancy payments continued until June 2007, with the programme reaching its conclusion in 2008.

The disarmament and demobilization phase of the process formally came to an end on 7 July 2005. It saw the demobilization of 63,380 ex-combatants and the collection of 57,629 light and medium weapons. The programme also led to the 'de-financing' of 100,000 soldiers – denoting the formal removal of soldiers, both real and 'ghost', from the state payroll – resulting in savings of US$120 million a year.[17] In the light of the challenges faced by the programme, its accomplishments are certainly impressive.

The fundamental goal of DDR was to break down military formations permanently, severing the patronage-based links between commanders and their militiamen. Reintegration programming, including vocational training, small-business support and agricultural packages,[18] may have provided the basic tools for former combatants to re-enter civilian life; however, it is unclear whether entry points into the civilian economy will exist to enable beneficiaries to exploit these tools over the medium and long-term. With economic activity in many areas of the country stagnant, unemployment hovering around 25–30 per cent and insecurity growing due to a reinvigorated insurgency, ex-combatants could be drawn back into militias.[19]

In an effort to gauge the impact of the reintegration process, the ANBP launched a client evaluation survey in 2006 that interviewed 5,000 programme beneficiaries who had received at least six to nine months of reintegration assistance.[20] The survey showed that 93 per cent of respondents were satisfied with the reintegration assistance they had received, and 90 per cent were still employed.[21] What the survey did not show was whether these positive results were sustainable, or whether the ex-combatants could withstand natural fluctuations in the economy. Most importantly, will they be able to endure the inevitable scaling down of international aid, which has provided a steady stream of labour-intensive projects to absorb ex-combatants? To ensure that former fighters do not fall back into previous patterns of military mobilization, continuous long-term support is required from a permanent government body. Plans have been discussed to build the capacity of key ministries, such as Labour and Social Affairs and Agriculture, to 'deliver reintegration services over the long-term' to former combatants.[22] One such plan envisages the integration of some of the structures of the ANBP into a special branch of the Ministry of Labour and Social Affairs.[23] However, as of autumn 2009, none of these ideas had been acted upon, with no long-term plan to provide services for DDR beneficiaries and military veterans.

The disbandment of illegal armed groups

Reflecting the provisions of the Bonn Agreement, the DDR programme focused squarely on officers and soldiers within the formal structure of the AMF. This ignored informal militia groups. Afghanistan's illegal armed groups range from tribal self-defence forces, primarily found in the southeast (known as *arbakai*), to criminal gangs.[24] The failure to target these groups from the outset of the process allowed them to solidify their power bases and consolidate their control over vital sources of revenue, such as the drug trade. Also, the success of many AMF commanders in shielding their units from the DDR process necessitated a further round of disarmament. As the DIAG strategy document affirms, 'several groups who entered the AMF and were formally demobilised through the DDR programme retained in many cases their core staff and a substantial amount of light weapons… [and] a number of commanders retained control of armed groups through their position as governors, chiefs of police and other local official positions'.[25] The threat these illegal armed groups pose to the state is multifaceted: they collect illegal taxes, obstructing government revenue collection; they are involved in the illegal exploitation of natural resources – oil, gas, coal and gemstones – and in some cases have assumed control of state-owned industries; they subvert reform processes and intimidate local government officials and security forces; and they drive the illegal economy, most notably the drug trade.[26]

In February 2005, as the formal DDR programme entered into its final phase, the ANBP was authorised, with funding from the Canadian government, to begin planning a programme to disband illegal armed groups. A planning cell was established within the ANBP to collect intelligence and, in conjunction with the government and a range of international stakeholders, devise an approach to address the problem. The planning cell estimated that there were 1,870 illegal armed groups[27] in the country, comprizing roughly 129,000 militiamen.[28] The government conservatively estimated that these groups possess 336,000 small arms and light weapons, 56,000 of which are believed to have been concealed from the DDR process by the AMF. The actual number is likely to be much higher, considering the scale of previous arms transfers into the country and the size of illegal weapons caches uncovered by coalition, ISAF

(International Security Assistance Force) and government security forces since 2001.

While the DDR process was internationally driven, the Disbandment of Illegal Armed Groups programme is government-led. The Demobilization and Reintegration Commission acts as the DIAG steering committee,[29] the high-level policy lead for the process, giving it strategic direction and coordinating the various actors engaged in it. The ANBP provides technical assistance and expertise to the joint secretariat and the DIAG provincial committees, the main Afghan bodies implementing the process.[30] The designated end state for the programme is the disarmament and disbanding of all 'identifiable illegal armed groups'. Although it was originally envisioned that the programme would reach its conclusion by the end of 2007, by the autumn of 2009 it was still in operation.

The process can be broken down into three phases: voluntary compliance, negotiated compliance and enforced compliance. The first phase involves fostering conditions conducive for voluntary compliance. Compliance is defined as the submission of 70 per cent of the estimated weapons of the illegally armed group being targeted.[31] However, unlike the DDR programme there is no prescription that the weapons submitted must meet a certain standard of functionality. Ex-combatants are informed of their legal obligations to disarm, and provided with a 30-day amnesty period to comply. Community and religious leaders are used as intermediaries to encourage commanders to cooperate with the process. The prospect of community development incentives in exchange for disarmament is introduced to local communities as a means of placing pressure on militiamen and their commanders. Compliant communities can receive up to US$300,000 in grants to undertake development projects. While many observers have likened the DIAG programme to a weapons-for-development scheme such as that pioneered in Albania, the Afghan government has sought to dispel this notion. The 'Guidelines for DIAG Development Activities' state that 'development projects shall not be considered as direct incentives to, or rewards for, disarmament, but may serve as a motivation for the community (*shuras*, leaders) to persuade the illegal armed groups to disarm and disband'.[32] The government is keen to avoid incentivizing the illegal possession of arms, opting instead to emphasise the obligation of armed groups to disarm under state law.

Phase two comes into effect after the designated period for voluntary compliance expires. It involves multitrack negotiations at the national and provincial levels as well as through local actors such as village mullahs and local *shuras*. Public information efforts will be intensified, with a focus on the implications of non-compliance, notably the denial of access to community development funds. When the negotiation period expires after 30 days, the enforcement phase comes into effect. The mandate for enforcing the process falls on the Interior Ministry and the Afghan National Police (ANP). In extreme circumstances, the Afghan National Army (ANA) and international security forces could be called in to assist.

The DIAG process was launched on a limited scale in autumn 2005. During its early stages the process targeted specific actors: government officials and national assembly and provincial council election candidates with links to illegal armed groups. The government sought to use the leverage provided by government positions and candidatures in the legislative elections to place pressure on militias to comply with the DIAG process. Although achieving only limited success,[33] these initiatives paved the way for the main stage of the process, launched on 1 May 2006 in Kapeesa province, where 38 commanders were issued notices instructing them to submit their weapons within the standard 30-day period. The process had an inauspicious beginning, foreshadowing future problems, as only seven weapons had been submitted by the end of the 30-day voluntary period. By the beginning of 2009 the programme had collected roughly 44,000 weapons; however, the bulk of these, a fraction of the estimated amount in circulation, were collected in *ad hoc* voluntary submissions prior to the launch of the main stage, and only 40 per cent were categorised as usable. Illegal armed groups were in fact giving the impression of cooperation by dumping their unserviceable equipment, while concealing their best weapons for use or sale on the illicit weapons market.

The DIAG process has failed to achieve its goals due in large part to a lack of political will from the government. The most conspicuous example of the government's fragile commitment to the process is the large number of government officials who have maintained links with illegal armed groups. High-profile government ministries, even those directly involved in the DIAG programme, have obstructed and even subverted the process. The executive branch, rather than championing the concept across the government, has sought to provide protection for government officials targeted by it. According to an official from the DIAG joint secretariat, the main implementing body for the programme, the government issued instructions not to pursue officials at the governor or cabinet level.[34] Several cabinet ministers, governors and parliamentarians appear on the list of the top ten illegal armed groups in the country compiled by the joint secretariat. Until serious attempts are made to persuade these figures to disarm, the process will remain paralysed.

The wholesale lack of compliance in many areas where the programme was applied shows how difficult it is to engage commanders effectively. The programme's designers erroneously assumed that the provision of development incentives would alienate communities from local commanders, thereby placing pressure on them to disarm. While this may be the case with community militias or self-defence forces, which are organic extensions of the local community, it is unlikely to affect criminal groups, whose interests diverge from those of local actors. Many militia groupings are already alienated from local communities due to their predatory behaviour, limiting the pressure that communities can bring to bear, and their involvement in the immensely profitable illicit economy makes community development projects unattractive. Weapons provide criminal groups with an entry ticket to the illicit economy; getting them to abandon their arms will require tailored individualised incentives, which the DIAG programme eschews. The same problem during the early stages of the DDR programme resulted in the establishment of the Commander Incentive Programme. Despite non-compliance by targeted groups during all stages of the process, the government had, as of early 2009, yet to employ force as dictated by the programme.

The DDR/SSR Nexus in Afghanistan

Experience from recent post-conflict reconstruction processes shows that the success of a SSR project is directly correlated with the efficacy of demilitarization activities. Without a process of demilitarization, SSR cannot achieve one of its main underlying goals: investing the state with a monopoly over the use of coercive force. The inverse is also accurate: demilitarization programmes will be hard pressed to succeed until people feel secure, have confidence that the security forces are competent and acting in their interest and have legal recourse if their rights are violated. Most donors engaged in SSR activities recognise the need to integrate demilitarization activities into the SSR agenda in post-conflict countries. However, as the Afghan case demonstrates, theory often fails to translate into practice.

The failure to exploit synergies between SSR and demilitarization programming can not only limit progress in state building and peacebuilding but can become a source of instability. Ineffective, repressive or corrupt security sectors can increase demand for militias, militants and weapons, and, conversely, the proliferation of armed individuals and groups can lead to the breakdown of state order and the militarization of security structures. Both phenomena can be detected in the Afghan case.

The Afghan demilitarization and SSR processes have largely been advanced in two parallel tracks. Although DDR has been framed as a pillar of the SSR process, it was designed and implemented as a stand-alone programme. Surprisingly little thinking was dedicated to the integration of DDR and SSR programming. One reason for this was the decision of the US military to turn down proposals to absorb former militiamen and *jihadi* fighters into the new ANA. This removed a natural link between the military reform process and DDR programme. Former combatants were not formally barred from enlisting in the ANA, but the age restriction of 18–28 naturally disqualified many from doing so. In creating a new army from the ground up the USA sought to build a new image and culture for the Afghan armed forces separate from that of the professional army under the communist regime or the *jihadi* militias of the Northern Alliance and Taliban, which most Afghans associate with repression and excess.

The Afghan government's 2005 'Millennium Development Goals Report' explicitly recognises the inextricable link between disarmament and SSR, and the importance of both enterprises in advancing security and stability. However, it tends to view disarmament as a distant or ancillary goal to be achieved only after meaningful reforms have been enacted in the security sector. The report argues that 'large scale civilian disarmament, without the strengthening and reform of the police and justice systems, is likely to be both difficult and may also increase peoples' vulnerability and perception of mistrust of the state'. It goes on to state that 'the registration and regulation of small arms may be a more viable option' when reforms in the security sector have reached a more advanced stage.[35] The report seemingly ignores the reciprocal importance of disarmament in facilitating SSR.

Some concrete links were established between the DDR and SSR processes around the issue of small arms and light weapons. Technical initiatives to transfer collected weapons from the DDR programme to the nascent Afghan security forces involved direct cooperation between the DDR and SSR programmes. Weapons transfers to the ANA from the DDR and DIAG programmes have been made but have failed to meet the expectations of the Combined Security Transition Command Afghanistan (CSTC-A), the US-led military body mandated to support the development of the Afghan security forces and Ministry of Defence. By the conclusion of the DDR programme in November 2005, the total number of weapons transferred by the ANBP to the Ministry of Defence was 20,993[36] (see Table

Table 2.2: Serviceable light and heavy weapons transferred to Ministry of Defence under the auspices of DDR

Weapons type	Number transferred
AK-47 assault rifle	17,144
PKM machine gun	663
RPK machine gun	780
RPG-7 rocket-propelled grenade	1,879
82 mm mortar	276
60 mm mortar	14
82 mm recoil	40
75 mm recoil	20
ZEGO (AA gun)	35
SPG-9 rifle	79
122 mm D-30	46
Tank RE	4
DShK machine gun	13
Total	**20,993**

Source: Michael Bhatia and Mark Sedra, *Afghanistan, Arms and Conflict: Armed Groups, Disarmament and Security in a Post-war Society* (London: Routledge, 2008), 166.

2.2 for breakdown of weapons transfers under the DDR programme). The UN-managed heavy weapons cantonment programme also handed over 530 pieces of weaponry to the government, primarily consisting of artillery, anti-aircraft and anti-tank systems as well as mortars.[37]

Weapons are transferred to the central weapons collection point at Pul-i Charkhi and are inspected by a team consisting of coalition and Afghan Ministry of Defence weapons specialists. The team determines whether a weapon is serviceable, repairable or unserviceable. Unserviceable weapons are cannibalised for usable parts, both for weapons repairs and to construct new weapons.

The Ministry of Interior and ANP have lobbied extensively in the DIAG forum and joint secretariat to gain access to weapons collected under the auspices of the DIAG programme; however, the Ministry of Defence, which is the Afghan agency responsible for the storage and management of all military weaponry, rebuffed those entreaties.[38] It has justified its rejection of the Ministry of Interior requests on the basis of its own weapons shortfalls.

The Ministry of Interior, however, will have more authority over the demilitarization process going forward, as the DIAG programme is currently being integrated into the ministry. In 2008 the government authorised the creation of a DIAG unit consisting of 187 personnel. The unit will comprise three sections: operations, private security company registration and individual weapons registration. The operations section manages all DIAG activities, including its field offices and personnel. As the country's nascent regulations on private security companies include strong provisions on weapons ownership and possession, the unit is responsible for the registration process. Finally, all individual weapon ownership under the country's weapons law is handled by the unit. A senior ANBP adviser is facilitating the establishment of the unit, the transfer of responsibility and expertise from the ANBP to it and general capacity building. The establishment of the unit should permit greater integration of police development and demilitarization activities. Over time it could lead to the development of new structures, expertise and protocols for stockpile management and community weapons collection. The ANBP has introduced plans to utilise the new unit, which will be one of the few government departments with detailed information on the country's militia structures, to support the vetting of candidates for the security services.

In 2009 the ANBP considered other strategies to link better with the police reform process. One approach discussed was to tie the DIAG programme to the Focused District Development (FDD) initiative for the ANP. Under the FDD programme, Afghan uniformed police are removed from their home districts and transferred to one of the country's five regional training centres to undergo eight weeks of training, after which they are equipped and returned to their districts under the guidance of police mentor teams. 52 districts had completed or were undergoing the programme, with 3,000 ANP having fully completed the training regimen by early 2009.[39] Although proceeding at a slower pace than originally envisaged, the programme has had good results. Districts that have completed the training show a 60 per cent decrease in 'local national casualties'.[40] By February 2009, 19 per cent of FDD-trained units were assessed as being capable of conducting primary operational missions, 25 per cent as capable of conducting operational missions with international support and 31 per cent as capable of partially conducting primary operational missions with international support.[41] At its current rate, the programme is expected to take up to five years to complete all districts. ANBP officials have considered adjusting the DIAG roll-out schedule to match that of FDD. This would allow the DIAG programme to build on the momentum of FDD in targeted districts, benefit from the level of security provided for it to take place and sensitise the police involved on the intricacies of weapons collection and control. As of early 2009, this was only a proposal and there was little to indicate that it would materialise. Nonetheless, it is a positive sign that DDR and SSR stakeholders are actively considering innovative ways to mesh their programming.

These nascent initiatives to align the DIAG programme with police reform activities, while late (more than six years after the launch of the two processes), could set a precedent for the construction of other bridges between the DDR and SSR spheres. There are a number of areas where joint programming could yield positive results for the wider state-building agenda.

Veterans' administration. There is a clear need in the Afghan administration for a body capable of providing assistance and support to DDR beneficiaries and retired military personnel, both disabled and able bodied. There were, in the initial phases of the ANBP, tentative plans to transition the ANBP gradually into such a structure, but these notions have largely faded from consideration. The Ministry of Defence, ANA and ANBP should come together to develop plans for such an institution, which would be vital to ensure that former fighters receive the appropriate care and do not fall back into patterns of violence. It is also possible that the institution could be expanded to provide support for former police and internal security forces, providing an entry point for the ANP and Ministry of Interior.

Demobilization of police. It has become clear over the past seven years that a large cross-section of the ANP, many of whom emanated from militia groups, is unsuitable for policing and should be phased out of the force. Some observers of the process have called for a specialised programme to purge unqualified police, providing incentives to facilitate their retirement from the force and reintegration into civilian society. Rather than follow this route, international and national stakeholders have sought to strengthen the training regimen as a means to overcome existing gaps in professionalism, although with marginal effect.

Vetting and management of informal security structures. As the security situation has deteriorated over the past seven years, there have been increasing calls for the mobilization of informal security structures, akin to militias or community watch structures, to supplement and complement the formal security architecture. Recent iterations of such thinking are the Afghan Public Protection Force – district-level militia units chosen by specialised district *shuras* and overseen by the Ministry of Interior – and the Afghan Guard Force – a centrally directed force of local security personnel responsible for static guarding and facility protection. One of the major problems encountered in establishing such structures is the vetting of personnel to militate against infiltration by spoiler groups and criminal entities. The ANBP with its database of armed groups could assist or even manage this process. It could also be involved in the registration of all weapons used by these informal personnel, providing another layer of accountability and oversight. To step into this role, the ANBP would have to update its existing database on armed groupings, which was assembled with questionable methodology and has not been appropriately updated. It is in the process of implementing a remapping exercise to address these gaps.

Weapons management. According to a report of the US Government Accountability Office, 'roughly 17 percent of small arms, mortars, and grenade launchers supplied to the Afghan security services since 2002 are unaccounted for'.[42] There are numerous reports of weapons provided to the Afghan security forces leaking on to the black market and even to spoiler groups.[43] To address this urgent problem, the CSTC-A is working to develop more stringent asset management procedures for both the ANA and the ANP. Nonetheless, as of early 2009 a senior ANBP official reported that there was still no way of fully verifying where weapons transferred by the demilitarization programme to the ANA go after they reach the main weapons depot. While the ANBP does have a peripheral role in the development of new weapons and ammunition management systems for the security forces in cooperation with the CSTC-A, that role should be expanded.

Demilitarization and judicial reform. After the fall of the Taliban, Afghanistan's laws regulating firearm possession were convoluted, poorly understood and rarely enforced. Consistent with the wider judicial reform process, efforts to rationalise legal statutes regarding small arms and light weapons were characterised by inertia during the first two years of the reconstruction process. In spite of the importance of endowing the demilitarization process with a solid legal foundation, little consideration was accorded to the reform of the existing weapons laws until 2004. In that year, President Karzai issued an important presidential decree endowing the demilitarization process with the political authority that it required. The decree, issued on 14 July 2004, recognised disarmament as 'one of the substantial conditions of the restoration of law, provision of a permanent peace, improvement of the economic situation, safeguarding of human rights and ruling on the basis of the people's will'.[44]

The strongly worded decree was a response to the slow early pace of the DDR process engendered by rampant commander obstructionism and Ministry of Defence obstinacy. The donor community, led by the Japanese government, had placed increasing pressure on Karzai to take a hard line on the issue. The decree went on to threaten 'the severest punishment for any actors who attempted to circumvent the process and maintain armed groups'.[45] The decree seemingly marked the emergence of a new level of political will among the Karzai government to advance the flagging process; however, it still lacked a coherent legal framework to draw upon or an effective security apparatus to enable implementation.

The development of a legal framework

Demilitarization activities have overlapped with the judicial reform process in the development of laws governing weapons ownership and possession. However, even in this area the judicial and demilitarization spheres have tended to act in parallel rather than in concert.

The Law on Fire Weapons, Ammunitions and Explosive Materials. The Law on Fire Weapons, Ammunitions and Explosive Materials, which came into force on 24 June 2005, provides the demilitarization process with the legal basis it was lacking. It firmly establishes that 'the government has sovereignty over those fire weapons, ammunitions and explosive materials which are existing in this country' and affirms that 'other persons and authorities without legal permission have no right to produce, import, export, gain, use and keep them'.[46] The law outlines a licensing and registration system for the acquisition, possession and sale of small arms, to be managed and overseen by the Ministry of Interior. It stipulates that a weapons licence must feature a photo of the licensee and list the weapon's serial number.

While the law places strict conditions on firearm ownership, it recognises that to protect their lives and property 'individuals and non-governmental bodies can gain non-hunting fire weapons and ammunitions', a concession to a significant constituency of disarmament sceptics. As such, it tacitly recognises the prevailing gun culture and the difficulty of completely removing the gun from Afghan society amid rising levels of insecurity. Failure to register a weapon will result in fines commensurate to the value of the weapon and associated ammunition, confiscation and legal prosecution. The weapons licensing programme will draw on citizen information collected under the auspices of the electoral registration process; the electoral registration cards represent the country's only reliable form of national identification.

The application of the weapons registration system will enable the collection of data on weapons possession in the country, developing a better understanding of the shifting patterns of weapons ownership and use. The government has proposed monitoring two indicators to gauge its progress in reducing the availability of guns: the proportion of firearms licensed and the statistical rates of gun crime as a share of overall reported crime.[47] However, it has not identified any specific benchmarks or milestones to be achieved in either of these areas. Despite being in operation for four years, the number of privately owned weapons registered by the state has been negligible (roughly 15,000). This can be attributed to both a lack of capacity to carry out registration and the adverse security climate. As the 2005 'Millennium Development Goals Country Report' states, 'encouraging those who currently own weapons to apply for licenses, and identifying and punishing those who fail to comply with the new law will be a resource-intensive process'.[48] As of early 2006 the Afghan National Police lacked the means to carry out basic policing functions, thus the enforcement of a countrywide registration system seemed beyond its capability.

The development of the DIAG unit in the Ministry of Interior should help address the capacity problems, but until security conditions improve there will be little desire among police and government officials to invest resources and political capital in weapons registration. Had the work of the ANBP, Ministry of Interior and Ministry of Justice been better coordinated in the development of the weapons law, needed implementation capacity could have been in place at the time of the law's launch rather than after a four- to five-year gap, a period sufficient to delegitimise the statute in the eyes of the population.

The Law on Private Security Companies. Another legal statute that seeks to regulate gun ownership in the private security industry was developed concurrently with the weapons law. Since 2001 the number of private security companies (PSCs), primarily international, operating in Afghanistan has risen exponentially. Both Afghan and international law lack mechanisms to regulate the activities and behaviour of these firms. PSCs both surreptitiously import weapons, circumventing Afghan customs duties and import regulations, and illegally purchase arms on the black market.[49]

In 2005 the government began to develop legislation that would curb such actions through the establishment of a comprehensive registration system. The Law on Private Security Organizations, produced in late 2005, requires PSCs, individual contractors and any associated armed personnel to acquire permits to operate and to carry firearms.

Annual fees are levied for registration, ranging from US$10,000 for a PSC to US$250 for an individual guard.[50] Contractors could also be required to submit fingerprints, photographs and detailed personal information upon application for a licence, including a *curriculum vitae* detailing the five previous years of employment experience.[51] Following background checks undertaken by the Ministry of Interior, the contractor is issued an identification card that includes the serial number of the duty weapon; contractors are required to carry the card at all times. If an individual is apprehended without an identification card, he or she could face monetary fines ranging from US$500 to US$2,500, have the firearm seized and possibly have registration revoked.

The law calls for the establishment of a commission to hear complaints about individual contractors or companies. In the event that complaints directed against a specific company or contractor are deemed valid, the commission has the authority to take a number of punitive measures, including the revocation of the individual's licence. In all cases, contractors are subject to Afghan law and would be prosecuted for any criminal offences arising out of their use of firearms in Afghanistan. As of early 2009, 39 companies had registered with the Ministry of Interior under the law; however, there have been widespread allegations of corruption in the application process.

Challenges and Lessons

Any effort to introduce integrated DDR and SSR programming in Afghanistan faces a number of distinct challenges, including the lack of a political settlement and insufficient political will; insecurity; the absence of a security strategy and deficits in coordination; poor monitoring and evaluation mechanisms; and deficits in local ownership. These, outlined in more detail below, account for the lack of operational linkages between the two programmes.

Lack of a political settlement

There was no classical peace agreement to anchor the DDR and SSR processes in Afghanistan and tie the main power brokers to them. The Bonn Agreement was a strategy for political transition, not a peace agreement signed by all parties to the conflict. In the case of DDR, the lack of a grand bargain for peace had two impacts. First, it meant that the process could not access spoiler groups such as the Taliban and Hizb-i Islami. With the process unable to access two of the main players in the conflict, others were unwilling to engage in it fully. Second, the lack of a peace agreement explicitly requiring its various signatories to disarm gave the government and the international community little leverage with which to compel compliance. It forced them to forge numerous spot contracts with individual commanders to disarm, which made the process more politically cumbersome by constantly shifting the parameters for negotiation.

For SSR the lack of a peace agreement deprived the process of a foundational document upon which to build a coherent system-wide strategy that recognised the intrinsic connection with demilitarization. The mention of SSR in a peace agreement could have endowed the process with greater legitimacy and authority and empowered a specific actor or actors to serve in a leadership role, two areas that have been problematic.

Strategy and coordination

The creation of the lead-nation donor support system for the SSR agenda created monumental challenges for coordination. The system fostered donor competition rather than collaboration and joint programming. A public, Afghan-owned national security policy and strategy could situate SSR and DDR within a wider policy framework, establish a coherent leadership structure and mandate lines of communication and collaboration for the DDR and SSR processes. While efforts have been undertaken under the auspices of the Office of the National Security Council to develop such a document, it has yet to be finalised or publicly released. The lack of an overarching strategy for the security sector has contributed to the 'siloed', compartmentalised approach to security policy and programming that has blocked the emergence of creative thinking on how to integrate reforms and activities in different areas.

Funding and support

DDR and SSR need durable supplies of funding and long-term support to succeed. Flexible funding mechanisms that encourage joint planning and project implementation are required. Funding modalities for DDR and SSR in Afghanistan reflect the compartmentalised nature of policy and programming. Particular tranches of funds, whether from individual donors or UN trust funds, have been established for specific areas of the process. The terms of reference or conditions set for the use of those funds have not emphasised cross-sectoral cooperation, particularly between DDR and SSR.

Local ownership

Chronic shortages in human and institutional capacity in Afghanistan coupled with weak domestic political will for reform have hindered the emergence of genuine Afghan ownership over the reform process. This partially accounts for the lack of a coherent SSR strategy. Organizations like the ONSC have been in a position to assert a leadership role in the process, but have not done so. This has left the security sector without an actor capable of coordinating and rationalizing the interests and agendas of a diverse set of stakeholders.

Understanding the context

One of the foremost challenges facing demilitarization and SSR activities from the onset of the state-building process in Afghanistan has been tailoring programmes to the socio-cultural environment. Effective contextualization of DDR and SSR programming requires good planning and preparation, something that did not occur in Afghanistan. Needs assessments that addressed the specific political and security conditions in Afghanistan were not undertaken for either the DDR programme or the SSR agenda. In fact, a comprehensive needs assessment was not undertaken for any of the five pillars of the SSR process.

The lack of solid data for planning purposes meant that reform programmes were often out of touch with local realities. For instance, the initial design of the DDR programme featured no elements to engage commanders, the lynchpin holding together militia networks, in the process. In the case of SSR, the process was overtly state-centric during its first five years of operation, ignoring the plethora of informal/traditional security and justice structures that dominate the rural periphery, enjoying wide popular legitimacy. A year would pass before the DDR programme established the Commander Incentive Programme, and it was only in 2006 that serious attention was given to reconciling formal and informal security and justice structures in the context of SSR. This was precious lost time that could have been used more effectively had proper preparatory work been undertaken prior to the launch of the programmes.

Political will

Perhaps the most profound challenge to the demilitarization process has been the tepid and variable political commitment displayed towards it by many of its stakeholders. For instance, the Afghan government, despite publicly supporting the demilitarization of armed groups, has tolerated the presence of numerous government officials with links to armed elements. According to some sources, up to half of the parliament has links to illegal armed groups, despite a clear provision in the electoral law barring such figures from candidacy in the legislative election.[52]

On the part of the international community, the US-led coalition through its patronage of subnational proxies in the south and east of the country has directly undermined demilitarization efforts. While NATO has made robust declarations supporting the DIAG, issuing directives to its provincial reconstruction teams mandating their support for the process, it has not translated into constructive engagement on the ground. Without the active support of either the indigenous government or international military forces, the demilitarization process will continue to face an uphill struggle to achieve its aims.

The security dimension

Perhaps the foremost challenge to the DDR and SSR processes is the adverse security environment in Afghanistan. As security conditions deteriorate, the prospect of successful demilitarization diminishes. In mid-2009 more than a third of the country was off limits to staff of the ANBP.

The continuation of the DIAG programme, as well as ammunition collection and destruction activities, in stable parts of the country (primarily the north and west) could in fact have adverse middle- to long-term consequences. Asymmetrical disarmament, demilitarizing some areas and groups but not others, can not only alter power relationships in a destructive manner but create sentiments of inequity and injustice that can stimulate new opposition to the state and reignite dormant cycles of violence. For instance, many groups in the north have begun to decry the lopsided nature of the disarmament process and hint at rearmament.

In the case of SSR, the concept is not designed to withstand the stresses and pressures of implementation during an ongoing conflict. It is a process of institutionalization that assumes a level of security, political stability and institutional capacity presently absent in the Afghan context. The current SSR process in Afghanistan can be likened, as US General David Petraeus has remarked in reference to its Iraqi counterpart, to 'repairing an aircraft while in flight – and while being shot at'.[53]

Adverse security conditions have made communities and groups reluctant to disband and submit their weapons. Demilitarization is seen as a distant priority in the context of an ongoing insurgency. In fact, a number of programmes are being advanced in the security sector with both tacit and overt support from the international community that could roll back some of the limited gains made by the DDR programme. For instance, international and domestic stakeholders supporting the Afghan Public Protection Force, piloted in Wardak province in 2009, have given little consideration to the impact of the initiative on demilitarization activities.

UN engagement

UN engagement in the security sector has been limited, a legacy of the light-footprint approach to Afghanistan's reconstruction launched under the leadership of SRSG Lakhdar Brahimi, who favoured the encouragement of Afghan initiative and ownership over the deployment of a robust UN presence. This has made it difficult to develop a holistic approach that would build on natural complementarities between the DDR and SSR programmes.

While the United Nations is working to expand its capacity in the security arena and continues to play an important political role as interlocutor between the Afghan government and the international community, its position within the security sector is likely to remain focused on encouraging shifts in policy or acting as a coordination agent.

One area where the United Nations has played a critical role is demilitarization, where the UNDP-operated ANBP has spearheaded every element of the process and provided indispensible technical assistance to the Afghan government. It was initially envisioned that the ANBP would be disbanded after the completion of the DDR process in the summer of 2006, but it was given an advisory and technical assistance mandate for the DIAG process. Plans to wrap up the ANBP after the completion of the DIAG in

2008 have again been delayed due to the slow pace and disappointing results of the programme.

Resources

In an environment where the needs are so great in every sector, there will always be claims that insufficient resources have been an impediment to change. In Afghanistan, the problem with the security sector relates more to where money is being spent rather than how much. There is a massive disparity between the amount of money being allocated to the security forces on the one hand and to justice and governance structures on the other. For instance, as of 2005 less than 3 per cent of donor funds sent to the Afghan security sector were going to justice institutions. While the Afghan DDR process is among the best funded in history, credible arguments can be made that the community-based incentives for the DIAG process have been similarly underfunded.

As of early 2009, only five community development projects had been implemented under the auspices of the DIAG programme, despite the fact that 42 districts were in a state of compliance with the programme.[54] The failure to provide promised incentives in a timely manner has had the effect of delegitimizing the process in some communities, threatening to roll back some of the gains that have been made. The delayed provision of the incentives can be attributed to bureaucratic mismanagement of projects by the DIAG programme's government implementing partner, the Ministry of Rural Rehabilitation and Development, and 'unrealistic expectations' of citizens over the pace of implementation. An argument can be made that the US$300,000 grant for compliant communities is insufficient in light of the major development needs of the recipients and the lack of corresponding individualised incentives for armed actors. The programme is heavily reliant on two assumptions: first, that commanders will view the localised prestige accrued from facilitating community development projects through their act of disarmament as outweighing the monetary benefits of maintaining arms; and second, that those same commanders will have the capability to compel their units to disarm and keep them in line despite a lack of material incentives. The limited returns of the DIAG programme has shown that neither assumption is valid. It is possible that a hybrid programme involving both more extensive community incentives capable of benefiting a larger cross-section of the community and specialised individual incentives for commanders and aggrieved former combatants would be more efficacious.

Monitoring and evaluation

Monitoring and evaluation of DDR and SSR programmes is crucial for their success. The scope and complexity of the Afghan case demand a wide range of analytical tools, both qualitative and quantitative, to assess continuously the impact of DDR and SSR initiatives and contribute to the adjustment of policy and programming where appropriate. Systemic cross-sectoral monitoring and evaluation can highlight the connective tissue between DDR and SSR, maximise scarce resources and identify problems where joint or individual programming can have a mutually beneficial effect. There is a conspicuous lack of robust monitoring and evaluation instruments in the SSR process. Donors have tended to rely on statistics to gauge progress, like the number of soldiers trained and the number of weapons delivered to the police. However, such statistics are notoriously unreliable and potentially deceptive in the Afghan case, as the number of confirmed ghost soldiers – soldiers on the payroll but not serving in the ranks – clearly attests. The existing measures and benchmarks tend to be more supply than results-oriented, focusing largely on the resource levels disbursed by donors rather than their actual impact on the ground. The lack of good qualitative measures assessing short-, medium- and long-term progress has undercut the ability of donors to plan effectively and adjust their programmes during implementation. More nuanced and textured metrics involving public surveys and focus groups, assessing evolving attitudes towards the security environment and the state, are needed.

The ANBP reflected this wider trend. While the process highlighted the number of soldiers demobilised and arms collected, DDR programme beneficiaries were not monitored after the completion of reintegration assistance. This obscured whether the programme had achieved the permanent breakdown of militia groupings and the commander patronage networks that sustain them. The ANBP did launch a series of client evaluation surveys by 2007 to assess beneficiary attitudes towards the programme that revealed positive attitudes. However, a more comprehensive process could have helped to identify long-term trends and future employment prospects for ex-combatants.

The monitoring and development component of the DIAG programme is also underdeveloped, reflecting wider information gaps. For example, given the absence of accurate and verifiable information regarding weapons holdings, it is difficult to determine whether particular groups are compliant. Afghanistan's armed groups were initially mapped in 2005 prior to the launch of the programme, but the database formed by the study was not adequately maintained or updated. For this reason a remapping study was commenced in 2008. Any attempt to assess the number of illegal weapons and militia groups in the country will invariably involve guesswork, due to the difficulty of counting concealed weapons and militia organizations that mobilise and demobilise on an *ad hoc* basis. Additional detail is nonetheless needed to provide a baseline from which to work.

A well-constructed mapping study that identifies and profiles all armed groups in the country, providing information on their structure, motivation, behaviour and links to the state and formal economy, could benefit the security sector as a whole. For instance, it could aid security sector institutions to vet current and future staff, provide intelligence for counterinsurgency and counternarcotics operations, and highlight the needs for rule-of-law capacity in particular areas.

Regional dimension

Conflict dynamics in Afghanistan are regional rather than national in character. For instance, you cannot understand the situation in Afghanistan without having an awareness of developments and currents in the Pakistani tribal areas. Although this reality is widely accepted, SSR and demilitarization initiatives tend to feature a narrow national focus. There are some limited cooperative programmes with Afghanistan's neighbours, particularly Pakistan and Iran on border policing, but they are small in scale and only scratch the surface of the wider problems that exist. There are tremendous scope and need for cooperative arrangements and joint reform programmes in areas such as counternarcotics, counterterrorism and customs.

Thousands of small arms continue to flow unimpeded into Afghanistan from neighbouring countries each month, mostly from Pakistan and Iran. While the ANBP and the Disarmament and Reintegration commission are aware of this, their programming does not seek to address the problem. This is a point of convergence between the SSR and DDR processes that has to be understood and developed. Programmes addressing weapons smuggling in the border areas, integrated into broader border policing programmes, could give a significant boost to wider demilitarization efforts, as they would stem the continuous flow of new arms into the country. Cracking down on unlicensed weapons development and distribution in the tribal areas on both sides of the Afghan-Pakistan border, something the Pakistani government has attempted to do in relation to the arms bazaars in the North West Frontier province, could be a good entry point for further action on more thorny issues of border management.

Sustainability

Surprisingly little attention is being provided to issues of reform sustainability in the implementation of SSR activities. The process is being driven by short-term imperatives of addressing the insurgency and creating security conditions conducive for international military disengagement, rather than fostering the creation of a self-sufficient security apparatus attuned to meeting domestic threats. Donor funding programmes have reinforced Afghanistan's historic position as a rentier client state, dependent on external revenue flows to maintain the integrity of central state structures. In 2007 security expenditures were equivalent to more than 300 per cent of domestic revenue, demonstrating the unsustainability of current security spending. Even with the most optimistic revenue projections over the next five years, Afghanistan will not be capable of financing even a significant portion of its security budget, a reality that has dangerous long-term consequences when you consider that the international commitment to Afghanistan will not be indefinite.

In the area of demilitarization there has been a similar failure to consider the long-term dimension of programming. For instance, it is widely accepted that Afghanistan's thousands of former combatants will require some form of continuing assistance: psycho-social support, assistance to the disabled and employment services. This is central to the overarching goal of keeping ex-combatants out of militia structures. Plans were raised during the early phases of the DDR programme to establish a veterans' administration within the Afghan government, perhaps as a part of the Ministry of Labour and Social Affairs. But by the beginning of 2009 all such plans had been discarded, leaving no framework for the government to provide long-term, ongoing support to its war veterans.

Conclusion and Policy Recommendations

Among the factors that have contributed to the setbacks and slow progress of the DDR and SSR processes in Afghanistan is the lack of integration between them. Whether it was the development of weapons management structures for the security forces or the demobilization of unqualified police personnel, significant opportunities were missed to develop mutually beneficial links between the programmes. A number of new initiatives emerged in 2009, particularly in the area of police reform, which held some promise for greater collaboration, but in many areas the window of opportunity for meaningful engagement has passed. The reasons for the compartmentalised approach to DDR and SSR are manifold – from adverse security conditions and an absence of political will to the lack of an overarching strategy and coordination framework in the security sector – but the argument can be made that more active intervention in the sector by key actors like the United Nations could have overcome some of these obstacles. Perhaps the biggest gap in the DDR and SSR process was a coordinator or connector, an actor capable of bridging the multiple agendas, approaches and interests of stakeholders. With the Afghan government unable to assume that role, the only other logical and capable alternative is the United Nations. However, with UN capacity in the security sector limited and the geopolitical interests in the area so high, the United Nations was reticent to fill this role. The Afghan experience with demilitarization and SSR clearly shows that more robust UN engagement in the DDR and SSR programmes of a post-conflict state, particularly in an advisory, oversight and coordinating capacity, could greatly enhance the effectiveness of programming.

Recommendations

Undertake comprehensive mapping. It is critical that the current remapping process is undertaken in a comprehensive and rigorous manner and forms the basis of a sophisticated database of armed groups. That database should inform the development of more targeted incentives for armed groups and assist in efforts to remove officials linked to illegally armed groups from security sector posts. To date, the process has not been sufficiently ambitious, relying largely on crude questionnaires delivered to provincial governors and district officials. There are few mechanisms to verify or cross-reference data obtained. A more comprehensive data collection process is needed that taps into resources across the security sector.

Consolidate political consensus. If the DIAG process is to remain in operation, it will require reinvigorated political will from both international and national stakeholders. The decision of the US and Canadian governments to withdraw funding from the process over the past year shows that confidence in the process has waned. It is not the shortfall in funds that is the most disturbing aspect of this development, but the implicit withdrawal of political capital from two key donors. The ambivalent position of the Afghan government and international military actors towards the process further demonstrates the need for the development of a new consensus on the utility of the DIAG programme. A conference in Kabul among key stakeholders to discuss not only technical elements of implementation but the necessity of the broader effort is needed.

Address the enforcement gap. The DIAG cannot be successful unless there is a credible threat of enforced compliance. The DIAG programme has three components of voluntary, negotiated and enforced compliance. As of January 2009, there was not a single case of enforced compliance despite rampant non-compliance by identified armed groups. Addressing the enforcement gap is dependent on the progression of police reform and the development of the DIAG unit in the Ministry of Interior. Recognizing that the success of the DIAG is intricately intertwined with the capacity of the police, the Japanese government, the main sponsor of demilitarization activities in Afghanistan, is considering a US$100 million commitment to the Law and Order Trust Fund for Afghanistan.[55]

Establish a veterans' administration. Ensuring that ex-combatants do not re-enter military life, a state structure is needed to monitor their status and provide assistance where required. While plans are in place to establish a police unit to oversee weapons collection, enforce the weapons law and administer the nascent PSC regulatory framework over the long term, no plans have been introduced to establish a body responsible for the welfare of ex-combatants.

Improve coordination. The SSR process is marred by coordination deficits. There is no one single strategic framework linking the various initiatives under the rubric of SSR. This has fostered imbalances in the process, with some pillars significantly outpacing others. Clear synergies between demilitarization activities and SSR have not been identified or leveraged.

The Afghan SSR process was advanced in a compartmentalised, 'siloed' fashion. Links were not adequately developed between pillars. This is partially attributable to the lead-donor system initially established to support the process, in which a lead donor was assigned to each of the five recognised SSR pillars. This framework was intended to ensure balanced donor support for the process, but in actuality it territorialised it. Rather than nurture synergies across the pillars, the lead donors treated them as national fiefs to be insulated from outside interference. The lack of coordination among key stakeholders coupled with weak Afghan ownership over the process inhibited the formation of an integrated strategic approach. Some national planning processes, such as the Afghan National Development Strategy, address security sector issues, but only in a general fashion, offering some broad, largely unrealistic, benchmarks.

The Afghan case shows the need to establish an SSR-specific strategy, addressing demilitarization activities, that clearly establishes joint coordination and decision-making structures at the political and technical levels. One such structure could be a coordination body at the ambassadorial level, under US (the largest SSR donor) and Afghan government leadership with significant input from UNAMA, which meets on a monthly basis to ensure policy coherence. It would have to be complemented by a working-level body that addresses operational issucs. This coordination framework is hardly new; it largely mirrors a structure that the ONSC proposed in 2005, which never materialised.

Empower the Office of the National Security Council. The ONSC is the only Afghan government body in a position to assert an Afghan leadership and coordination role in SSR. It is officially mandated to oversee the SSR process but lacks the resources or the inclination to do so. The national security adviser has instead positioned the institution as a personal advisory body to the president. The structure should be reframed and expanded to fulfil its more ambitious mandate.

Integrate demilitarization into the SSR agenda. The ANBP must seek to integrate its demilitarization activities more clearly into the SSR agenda. The new FDD programme which targets specific districts for police training and transformation in a phased countrywide process represents a tremendous opportunity for closer integration. The ANBP has recognised the need to synchronise its district roll-out with the FDD, to ensure that it can build upon FDD momentum. As a stand-alone programme, the DIAG has not been successful, but it can potentially deliver greater effect if it is mainstreamed and seeks to piggyback on such programmes.

Institutionalise the weapons and PSC laws. Weapons and PSC laws have been enacted, leading to the registration of roughly 15,000 weapons and 20,000 PSC staff. However, no transgressors of these statutes, of whom there are many, have been tried in the Afghan courts. There is a need to focus attention on enhancing the capacity of the Afghan Attorney General's Office to prosecute weapons cases. Mirroring the wider SSR process, judicial and governance structures have received inadequate attention relative to coercive security sector institutions. There is a distinct need to strengthen the regulatory framework for weapons possession.

Consider discontinuance of the DIAG. Serious thought has to be given to discontinuing the DIAG programme, which has achieved little. The inability of the ANBP to implement the programme on a countrywide level, the waning interest of key stakeholders and the lack of a credible enforcement tool, among other factors, seem to support the disbanding of the programme. ANBP officials would claim that despite the programme's lack of practical achievements it plays an important symbolic role in highlighting the importance of demilitarization. This does not justify the continuation of a failing programme. It also doesn't take into account the reality that a poorly designed programme can have the perverse effect of spurring violence. The perception of some Afghans that northern communities are being disarmed while southern communities are left untouched and even rearmed through militia mobilization programmes could serve to dampen support for the government and reignite conflict.

Include demilitarization in political settlement. The Bonn Agreement which launched the Afghan state-building process did not feature a provision on SSR and only a vague statement on demilitarization. This missed an important opportunity to institutionalise both processes and develop a broad-based consensus on their purpose and direction. References to SSR and demilitarization could also have laid the foundation for an integrated SSR and demilitarization strategy, something that has yet to materialise seven years into the post-Taliban era. Among other things, the agreement could have mandated the demobilization of all non-state armed groups within a reasonable timeframe, called for the development of weapons control legislation, made specific reference to the creation of oversight and accountability structures for the security sector and laid out the democratic principles upon which the ANA and ANP would be founded.

The Afghan case demonstrates the need for the United Nations not only to push for the SSR and DDR processes to be addressed in a peace settlement, but to foster a consensus on these issues among key stakeholders early in the post-conflict period. Despite the UN's limited capacity in the security areas, it could have leveraged its honest-broker status and good offices to foster greater cooperation among security stakeholders. As the United Nations was largely outside the lead-nation donor framework, despite its role as implementer for the ANBP, there was some scope for it to emerge as an impartial coordinator and observer of the process.

More attention to sequencing. SSR is a process of long-term institutional development and transformation, not a tool to address immediate security threats. However, in cases like Afghanistan and Iraq it has tended to be thrown into the latter role, a function it is ill-equipped to undertake. In countries facing high levels of insecurity the sequencing of the process becomes all the more important. There is a tendency among donors supporting SSR in insecure environments to dedicate the vast majority of their resources to building up the coercive capacity of the state, the 'hard' security elements of SSR, to the detriment of some of its 'soft' components such as justice and governance. While shoring up the security forces in order to provide a baseline of security for the population and state should be a priority of the process, it should not be done at the expense of efforts to rebuild justice and governance structures. This will only foster repressive tendencies and a culture of impunity in the security forces that could not only impede the country's democratic transition but threaten the peace.

Sequencing in a post-conflict SSR context like Afghanistan should be conceptualised as a continuum. In the early phases of the process the bulk of security assistance, although not all, should be dedicated to shoring up security and governance institutions. As security force development tends to be particularly cost intensive, it will invariably absorb a significant amount of resources. As time passes, the proportion of resources dedicated to the 'hard' and 'soft' security spheres should gradually converge. However, in Afghanistan the initial funding disparities favouring the security forces have remained constant, paralysing efforts to establish robust governance and oversight mechanisms and rebuild the legal system.

In terms of demilitarization efforts, more thought has to be given to the question of when would be an appropriate time to advance demilitarization. In 2002 the situation across the country was stable enough to launch a DDR programme, despite the problems with political will that the programme encountered. The process was seen as opening the way for the creation of a new professional army, the ANA. Although few formal links were established with the US-led military reform process, it did lay the groundwork for the formation of the ANA.

It is clear however, that the DIAG is being advanced in an environment that is unconducive for demilitarization. The national security forces are not capable or willing to support the programme and ANBP staff are restricted from implementing it on a countrywide level. Premature demilitarization programmes, particularly those that target some groups but not others, can have an adverse security impact, fostering security dilemmas among some actors and igniting cycles of violence.

Undertake more comprehensive needs assessments. Designing effective SSR and demilitarization programmes requires a comprehensive understanding of the historical, socio-cultural, economic, political and security dimensions of the local context. The Afghanistan case demonstrates the deleterious implications of failing to undertake an adequate needs assessment to inform programme design. In the case of SSR, programming failed to comprehend the dominance of informal security structures across much of the country, the depth of corruption and clientelism in the security forces and the challenges of establishing Afghan ownership of the process. In the case of demilitarization, programming failed to understand the central role played by commanders in militia networks, the challenges of gathering accurate data on militia numbers and weapons holdings, and the problem of weak political will for the process. The United Nations is well placed to spearhead such needs assessments, which must be carried out in a rigorous and methodical fashion. Quick-and-dirty assessments may be as bad as no assessment at all.

A good assessment could have better guided the shape and sequencing of reforms, imbuing the process with greater balance. It could have anticipated looming security problems which dramatically altered the political and security picture, and more effectively gauged the resource needs of the process. Perhaps most importantly, a competent assessment could have alerted stakeholders of the need to manage expectations and recognise the long-term nature of the process.

Ensure adequate staffing and support structures are in place. In Afghanistan the United Nations was unprepared to engage in SSR in a meaningful manner. The light-footprint approach to Afghanistan, which resulted in a much leaner UN mission than in contexts like Bosnia and East Timor, limited the resources which the United Nations could deploy to the security sector. Accordingly, it largely stayed within the confines of the political and development processes, leaving SSR to the bilateral donors. Had the United Nations possessed adequate human resources and expertise in the security field, it could have filled the coordination gap created by the G8 five-pillar SSR donor support framework. Moreover, the United Nations could have been involved more actively in developing Afghan ownership over the process. However, with little more than a handful of police, judicial, penal and military advisers, the United Nations was not able to assume this important role. The Afghan case shows that even in cases where bilateral donors are providing the bulk of the assistance to SSR programmes, the United Nations can serve in an important coordination and management role.

Ensure reforms are sustainable. Ensuring that reforms are viable and sustainable over the long term is a central principle of the SSR model. This means ensuring that the security structures being created can be sustained through the partner country's domestic revenue sources and are seen as politically viable in the absence of a third-party presence. Similar logic applies to a demilitarization process, which should not be undertaken unless measures are put in place to deter the mobilization of armed groups and curb the proliferation of weapons in non-state hands. This principle was not observed in Afghanistan. Accordingly, the gains made in both the demilitarization process and SSR are fragile and prone to reversal. It serves as a lesson for the need to consider issues of sustainability from the very onset of the SSR and DDR processes. The United Nations could act as a watchdog in this regard, warning against the curse of short-termism in the design and implementation of SSR and demilitarization programmes.

Empower local actors. It is almost a cliché of the development and peacebuilding fields that local ownership is the key to change. Despite the prevalence of this truism, it is rarely put into practice. Part of the trouble lies in the very definition of ownership. What constitutes ownership in the Afghan context? Is it the support of a government agency or department, the endorsement of the executive or the acquiescence of civil society actors? There is no one formula for strong local ownership, and all three forms are critical. Ownership will invariably be contested, particularly in conflict or post-conflict settings. What is easier to detect and define is when ownership is lacking, when a reform agenda is being driven by international actors either to serve an external agenda or informed by an external understanding of the best interests of the partner country. Often local ownership is overridden due to the lack of institutional and human capacity in the partner country to dictate the structure, pace and direction of reform and recovery programmes. Such an obstacle is not insurmountable but cumbersome enough to convince donors, fixed to short-term funding cycles and impatient political masters and electorates, to go it alone. Whatever the reason, bypassing ownership will surely undermine the popular legitimacy of reforms and could render them unviable over the long term.

In Afghanistan, donor efforts to impose a Western-modelled security apparatus and undercut informal security and justice mechanisms have unsurprisingly encountered major setbacks. Not only were the reform programmes insufficiently tailored to meet local conditions, but insufficient attention was given to identifying and cultivating credible and legitimate local champions for reform in the security sphere. Whereas a number of reform champions emerged within the development sphere and were seen as highly competent leaders representative of the Afghan population, acutely aware of the need for change and capable of working with donor states, the security sector did not see such a development. There is a tendency for donors to seek like-minded elites as domestic partners: actors who are not necessarily seen as legitimate by the local population but can speak English and possess an understanding of the aid industry. It is important for donor actors to resist this temptation for cronyism, and seek legitimate reform champions in partner countries even if their political/ideological positions differ from their own. The United Nations could play a role in the identification of such actors.

Ownership comes from many sources, thus it is crucial that stakeholders such as the United Nations cast a wide net in cultivating it. From individual leaders to civil society groups and state agencies, long-term sustainable change requires broad-based buy-in in post-conflict societies. External stakeholders should focus on providing an enabling environment for such actors to emerge, build their capacity and engage with each other. This could involve the provision of resources and support to non-governmental agencies, the sponsoring of talks between local actors and the strengthening of state capacity in key areas.

Monitoring and evaluation. The lack of effective monitoring and evaluation instruments for the demilitarization and SSR processes has made it difficult for donors to measure progress adequately and define a viable end state. Part of the problem lies in the fact that no baseline data were collected under the auspices of a needs assessment at the beginning of the process, leaving little to measure the current situation against. Nonetheless, tens of millions of dollars have been squandered on programmes that were ill-designed and achieved little but continued for months and even years due to the lack of monitoring and evaluation mechanisms to alert donors to their poor performance. Deep problems of corruption in Afghanistan make monitoring and evaluation infrastructure even more indispensible, as donor funds have been the victim of malfeasance by both Afghan actors and international contractors. The Afghan case demonstrates the need for the erection of robust monitoring and evaluation mechanisms at both programme and process levels at all stages of the programming cycle.

Work with informal structures. In any post-conflict or fragile state context it is critical to work with existing structures, actors, customs and traditions rather than around them. Some donors tend to bring a 'blank slate' mentality to fragile and failing states like Afghanistan, equating the destruction of infrastructure with the destruction or removal of societal norms and political traditions. In reality, while state authority and formal power may break down during conflict, informal and traditional security structures often come to the fore to fill the void. These structures cannot merely be dismissed or pushed aside during the post-conflict period, as they have acquired heightened legitimacy due to their role in maintaining a modicum of order and community integrity during conflict.

For instance, in Afghanistan it is now widely accepted that up to 80 per cent of disputes are resolved in informal justice and dispute resolution bodies like the village *shura* (council). However, up to 98 per cent of donor funding to the justice sector is channelled to the creation of formal state structures which many communities view as corrupt, expensive and out of touch with local realities. Many Western donors and civil society actors justify their unwillingness to work with traditional justice structures on the grounds that the majority of their decisions violate fundamental human rights, particularly women's rights. Again, this represents a flawed understanding of this structure, as the majority of disputes addressed in the informal system are not criminal, but rather civil in nature – such as land disputes. Decisions on such civil matters might not conform to Afghan legal codes, but do not violate citizen rights as outlined in the constitution.[56]

As damaging as donor failures to engage some traditional structures are their efforts to instrumentalize others. The manner in which some external actors have sought to mobilise militia structures in Afghanistan is ahistorical and inconsistent with existing norms. For instance, proposals have been made to establish *arbacki* units, a Pashtun structure akin to community self-defence forces, in targeted locations across the country. Although framed as an indigenous Afghan structure, the *arbacki* is only present in Pashtun communities of three eastern border provinces of Afghanistan. The concept would be completely alien to actors from other ethnic groups in other areas of the country.

What these examples show is that there is a need to work with traditional norms and structures, reconciling them with formal state structures and legal norms. Donors must base their interaction with these traditional social forces on a detailed understanding of their role in society.

The need for regional security solutions. Just as most contemporary conflicts have a regional character, so too must programmes intended to address them. Whether it is in the area of border security, weapons control and management or counterterrorism, there is a need for multilateral approaches to SSR and demilitarization initiatives. Afghanistan clearly shows the near futility of reforming security institutions or disarming armed groups without parallel developments in the lawless Pakistani tribal areas, from which weapons and militants flow. It is critical that the regional dimensions of SSR and demilitarization initiatives be considered in programme design and a consensus sought with regional actors.

Notes

1 After almost three decades of war, Afghanistan is littered with weaponry – from 500,000 to 1.5 million small arms and light weapons, according to the Small Arms Survey – and a significant proportion of the male population is affiliated to non-state armed groups.

2 The Bonn Agreement was a plan for governing and stabilizing Afghanistan agreed by prominent Afghans and international donor actors under UN auspices during December 2001 in Bonn, Germany.

3 Opening address by President Hamid Karzai to National Symposium on Security Sector Reform, 30 July 2003.

4 Mark Sedra, 'Security Sector Reform in Afghanistan: The Slide Toward Expediency', *International Peacekeeping* 13, no. 1 (2006).

5 See Emma Sky, 'The Lead Nation Approach: The Case of Afghanistan', *RUSI Journal* (December 2006).

6 The framework had been introduced at the January 2002 Tokyo donor conference, but took form in Geneva.

7 Hamid Karzai, statement at Tokyo conference, 'Consolidation of Peace in Afghanistan – Change of Order "From Guns to Plows"', 22 February 2003.

8 Quoted in Mark Sedra, 'Challenging the Warlord Culture: Security Sector Reform in Afghanistan', Paper 25, Bonn International Center for Conversion, (2002), 3.

9 Afghanistan New Beginnings Programme, 'Afghanistan New Beginnings Programme', brochure for second Tokyo conference on Consolidation of Peace in Afghanistan, 15 June 2006.

10 International Crisis Group, *Afghanistan: Getting Disarmament Back on Track* (Brussels: ICG, 2005), 3.

11 Weapons constructed locally or in the Pakistani weapons workshops that dot the border with Afghanistan were viewed as equivalent to unserviceable and rejected. Rossi and Giustozzi quote a UNAMA official as saying that 36 per cent of all weapons collected were constructed in workshops in Pakistan: Simonetta Rossi and Antonio Giustozzi, 'Disarmament, Demobilisation and Reintegration of Ex-Combatants in Afghanistan: Constraints and Limited Capabilities', Working Paper No. 2, Series 2, LSE Crisis States Research Centre (London, 2006), 4.

12 Mark Sedra, 'Securing Afghanistan's Future: Accomplishments and Strategic Pathway Forward – Disarmament, Demobilisation and Reintegration of Ex-Combatants Technical Annex', Islamic Transitional State of Afghanistan (Kabul, 2004), 3–7.

13 International Crisis Group, note 10 above: 6.

14 Political Parties Law, Art. 6, No. 5.

15 International Crisis Group, note 10 above: 6.

16 Christian Dennys (2005) *Disarmament, Demobilization and Rearmament? The Effects of Disarmament in Afghanistan*. Kabul: Japan Afghan NGO Network, p. 4; Rossi and Giustozzi, note 11 above: 4; interview with International Organisation for Migration consultant, Kabul, 5 May 2005.

17 Afghanistan New Beginnings Programme, note 9 above, p. 2.

18 The majority of ex-combatants chose the agricultural option (41.9 per cent), with small business support (24.6 per cent) and vocational training (15.5 per cent) the next most popular options. The reintegration programme cost approximately US$1,200 per ex-combatant, with US$700 being directly expended on reintegration packages and the remaining US$500 absorbed by overhead costs. Afghanistan New Beginnings Programme, note 9 above, p. 5.

19 UNDP, *Afghanistan National Human Development Report 2004* (Kabul: UNDP, 2004), 57.

20 It is important to note that this was a self-evaluation conducted by the ANBP rather than an external actor, making its results more vulnerable to criticism.

21 Michael Bhatia and Mark Sedra, *Afghanistan, Arms and Conflict: Armed Groups, Disarmament and Security in a Post-war Society* (London: Routledge, 2008).

22 Afghanistan New Beginnings Programme, note 9 above: 2.

23 Bhatia and Sedra, note 21 above.

24 International Crisis Group, note 10 above: 11–12.

25 Islamic Republic of Afghanistan, 'Strategy for Disbandment of Illegal Armed Groups in Afghanistan' (Kabul, January 2006), 1. Available at www.diag.gov.af/.

26 Ibid., 11.

27 The Afghan government defines an illegal armed group as 'a group of five or more armed individuals operating outside the law, drawing its cohesion from (a) loyalty to the commander, (b) receipt of material benefits, (c) impunity enjoyed by members, [and] (d) shared ethnic or social background'. Ibid., 2.

28 Bhatia and Sedra, note 21 above.

29 The members of the committee include the national security adviser, Ministry of Defence, Ministry of Interior, National Directorate of Security, Ministry of Rural Rehabilitation and Development, Ministry of Agriculture, Ministry of Labour and Social Affairs, Ministry of Finance, Ministry of Commerce and Industries, Ministry of Counter Narcotics, Japan, the United Kingdom, Canada, the United States, the Netherlands, Switzerland, Italy, the EU, UNAMA, the ANBP, the coalition and ISAF.

30 Islamic Republic of Afghanistan, note 25 above: 4–5.

31 Islamic Republic of Afghanistan, '11 Province Main Phase DIAG Proposal', 5 November 2005, unpublished.

32 Islamic Republic of Afghanistan, 'Guidelines for DIAG Development Activities', 2005, unpublished.

33 During the national assembly and provincial council election stage of the DIAG process, 124 candidates submitted 4,857 weapons and 34 candidates were disqualified for non-compliance.

34 Bhatia and Sedra, note 21 above.
35 Islamic Republic of Afghanistan, *Millennium Development Goals Islamic Republic of Afghanistan Country Report 2005: Vision 2020* (Kabul: Islamic Republic of Afghanistan and UNDP, 2005), 105.
36 Afghanistan New Beginnings Programme, note 9 above: 4.
37 Bhatia and Sedra, note 21 above: 166.
38 Ibid.
39 Centre for International Governance Innovation, *Security Sector Monitor: Afghanistan*, no. 1 (Waterloo, ON: CIGI, July 2009).
40 Combined Security Transition Command – Afghanistan, 'The Enduring Ledger' (January 2009), 12. Available at www.cstc-a.com/News/enduring%20ledgers/2009endledger/January2009EL.pdf.
41 US Government Accountability Office, 'Afghanistan Security: U.S. Programmes to Further Reform Ministry of Interior and National Police Challenged by Lack of Military Personnel and Afghan Cooperation' (Washington, DC: GAO, March 2009), 14–15. Available at: www.gao.gov/new.items/d09280.pdf.
42 Quoted in Centre for International Governance Innovation, note 42 above.
43 Bhatia and Sedra, note 21 above.
44 Presidential Decree 50, 14 July 2004.
45 Ibid.
46 Law on Fire Weapons, Ammunitions and Explosive Materials, Ch. 1, Art. 4.
47 Islamic Republic of Afghanistan, note 37 above: 106.
48 Ibid., 108.
49 Bhatia and Sedra, note 21 above.
50 Draft Law on Private Security Organizations, Ch. 2, Art. 6.
51 Ibid., Ch. 3, Arts 8–9.
52 International Crisis Group, *Afghanistan's New Legislature: Making Democracy Work* (Brussels: ICG, 2006), 6.
53 David Petraeus, 'Battling for Iraq', *Washington Post*, 26 September 2004, B07.
54 Interview with ANBP official, Kabul, 8 January 2009.
55 Interview with Japanese Embassy officials, Kabul, 15 January 2009.
56 Interview with USIP Rule of Law Project representative, 14 January 2009.

Chapter 3

Burundi

Serge Rumin

Introduction

The Defence and Security Corps (DFC), which was traditionally used by the Tutsi elite to assert its authority over the Hutu majority, played a central role in the Burundian conflict. Therefore, the reform of the DFC was one of the main requirements for peace of the various Hutu rebel groups involved in the conflict. This demand was translated into provisions for the disarmament, demobilization and reintegration (DDR) of ex-combatants within the August 2000 Arusha Peace and Reconciliation Agreement and other subsequent agreements. In this way, active members of the former Tutsi-led *Forces Armées Burundaises* (FAB), the Burundian gendarmerie and several former armed political parties and movements (APPMs) have been integrated into the restructured armed forces and police.

The history of the various armed and political movements in Burundi is characterised by their fracturing into numerous armed groups. Consequently, the lengthy peace process has generated a series of non-inclusive agreements, protocols, declarations and ceasefires. The first of these, the Arusha Agreement, was signed by the government and a number of APPMs, including three Hutu armed groups. A second set of agreements was signed in 2003 by the then transitional government and the *Conseil National pour la Défense et la Démocratie / Forces pour la Défense de la Démocratie* (CNDD/FDD), the most important Hutu rebel group. A final agreement was signed in December 2008 by the elected government (dominated by the CNDD/FDD) and the *Parti pour la libération du peuple Hutu – Forces nationales de libération* (Palipehutu-FNL), the oldest Hutu rebel group. Each set of agreements was negotiated independently, generating differing and contentious provisions on ethnic and APPM quotas for the integration of the APPMs into the DFC.

This chapter, placing emphasis on the specific historical context of Burundi, presents an overview of both the DDR and the security sector reform (SSR) processes and the roles of the various actors involved. It then explores the linkages between the DDR and SSR processes, including the impact of peace agreements on sequencing, pre-cantonment as a common DDR/SSR entry point, the reintegration and integration of former combatants, the separate mechanisms for DDR and SSR programme coordination, and other issues such as land disputes, the regional context and distinctions between war and political prisoners. The chapter concludes by identifying lessons learned and policy recommendations relating to the nexus between DDR and SSR.

Context for DDR and SSR

Political and security context

Burundi was a German protectorate before becoming part of a Belgian-controlled League of Nations mandate from 1923 until its independence in 1962. During this time, the Tutsi minority dominated national politics and maintained the privileged status they had gained in the nineteenth century under the rule of Tutsi kings. Some semblance of inter-ethnic power sharing existed under a UPRONA (*Union pour le Progrès National*) government after 1962, but this balance collapsed in 1965 when the king refused to appoint a Hutu prime minister after a Hutu election victory. In 1966, following a military coup, Prime Minister Michel Micombero replaced the monarchy with a presidential republic. After an abortive Hutu uprising in April 1972, he engaged in a savage campaign against the Hutu population. Micombero installed a Tutsi-controlled one-party state under UPRONA, but was overthrown in a 1976 coup by another Tutsi officer, Jean-Baptiste Bagaza, leading to a further decline in Hutu political representation and increased inter-clan intrigue among the Tutsi military class. Bagaza was removed in yet another coup by another Tutsi officer, Pierre Buyoya, in 1987.

August 1988 brought a new wave of violence between Hutus and Tutsis, after a call by the Hutu-led Palipehutu-FNL for Hutus to take up arms against Tutsi domination. Buyoya ultimately agreed to multiparty elections, which were held in June 1993. In July 1993 Melchior Ndadaye, leader of the Hutu-led *Front pour la démocratie au Burundi* (FRODEBU), was sworn in as Burundi's first democratically elected president. On 21 October 1993 Tutsi paratroopers assassinated Ndadaye, which led to a further outbreak of violence. The Hutu-led government remained in place and the parliament appointed Hutu Cyprien Ntaryamira as president. Ntaryamira died in April 1994, together with the Rwandan president Habarimana, in the plane crash which sparked the Rwandan genocide. The speaker of parliament, Sylvestre Ntibantuganya, was appointed president but was soon deposed in a 1996 coup staged once again by Pierre Buyoya.

In 1998 a transitional constitution was agreed, under which Buyoya was formally sworn in as president. In 1999 talks between the warring factions were held under the auspices of the former Tanzanian president, Julius Nyerere. The Arusha Peace and Reconciliation Agreement was signed in 2000 between the government and three armed groups: the CNDD, *Front Libération National* (Frolina) and Palipehutu. Significantly, it failed to include the main Hutu movements, the CNDD/FDD and Palipehutu-FNL. The non-inclusive nature of the Arusha Agreement became a key factor conditioning and shaping the development of the DDR and SSR processes. The signatories endorsed a provision preventing any ethnic group from representing more than 50 per cent of the defence and security services. As discussed below, in the absence of consensus among the main Hutu groups, these provisions have raised serious challenges to the integration of former combatants in the police and the army, and the subsequent rightsizing of these institutions.

In 2001 a three-year transitional power-sharing government was established. Renewed political tensions and armed violence were followed by an agreement in 2003 to form a multi-ethnic transitional government. This political settlement allowed the long and difficult peacebuilding process to move forward, although it also raised a second set of challenges in terms of integrating ex-combatants into the defence and security corps, given the requirement in the agreement that the CNDD/FDD should have 40 per cent of the positions in the army and 35 per cent in the police. This presented difficulties for the subsequent rightsizing of the two institutions.

A new constitution was adopted by referendum on 22 December 2004, reinforcing many of the agreements reached in Arusha in 2000, including the ethnic quotas. It was added that 'the defence and security forces must reflect the will of all Burundians and are obligated to function as instruments of protection for the entire population'. The referendum was followed by democratic parliamentary elections and the election of a new president, Pierre Nkurunziza, who took office at the end of 2005. Finally, in June 2008, following a joint declaration by the Palipehutu-FNL and the government concerning the cessation of hostilities,[1] Agathon Rwasa returned to Burundi after 20 years in exile to participate formally in the implementation of the two peace agreements signed in 2006.[2] After two years of stalled implementation and a short outbreak of violence in April 2008, the commitment of both parties to the 2006 agreements was renewed successively in the Magliesburg Declaration of June 2008, the Declaration of Ngozi in August 2008 and again in the Declaration of the Summit of Heads of State and Government of the Great Lakes Region on 4 December 2008.

Negotiations have remained blocked on issues such as the criteria for DDR eligibility, quotas for the integration of FNL fighters into the defence and security corps and the type and number of positions to be reserved for the FNL within the command structures of these security forces. The various texts signed so far have neglected to address these substantive issues. Instead, they focus more on the implementation processes to be adopted regarding issues such as immunity, the release of war prisoners, the cantonment of combatants and their participation in the various peace monitoring and implementation mechanisms, among others. However, following the 4 December 2008 declaration it was agreed that the Palipehutu-FNL would change the movement's name to FNL (in conformity with the constitution which prohibits reference to ethnic groups in the names of political parties) and that the FNL's political aspirations would be accommodated by offering it 33 posts within state institutions.[3] It was also agreed that the FNL would join the assembly areas as soon as possible, while the government agreed to release all war and political prisoners.

DDR overview[4]

The history of the various armed and political movements in Burundi is characterised by their fragmentation. The first faction to break away from Palipehutu in 1990 was Frolina, and it has split again twice since then. The CNDD, created in 1994, went through its first division in 1998, resulting in the creation of the dissident CNDD/FDD. The CNDD/FDD itself split in 2001, creating the CNDD/FDD-Nkurunziza. In total, the APPMs (without Palipehutu-FNL) were estimated to comprise 21,000 combatants when the DDR process was first initiated.[5] Palipehutu-FNL was generally believed to number 3,000 combatants,[6] although it claimed to have at least 21,000 including political and war prisoners.[7] These figures are a serious point of contention when it comes to defining the eligibility criteria, mechanisms and donor budget envelope for DDR. Concerns also include the criteria for deciding who is or is not a war or political prisoner.[8]

A DDR process involving all the parties to the conflict (except Palipehutu-FNL) took place from 2004 to 2008 based on:

- The agreement, subsequent ceasefire and forces technical agreement that were signed by the government and all APPMs (except the CNDD/FDD Nkurunziza and Palipehutu-FNL), founded on the Arusha Agreement.[9]
- The ceasefire agreements, joint declarations, Pretoria Protocol and forces technical agreement signed between the transitional government and the CNDD/FDD, negotiated between December 2002 and November 2003.

In order to implement the DDR process, as agreed in Arusha and in subsequent agreements, a set of structures were established according to the provisions outlined in these texts. These structures include the following:

- The Implementation Monitoring Committee (IMC): tasked through the Arusha Agreement to monitor the implementation of the Arusha provisions. The IMC is a mixed body composed of the Arusha signatories, international community representatives and civil society representatives.
- The Joint Ceasefire Commission (JCC): composed of FAB and APPM members (chaired by the UN Operation in Burundi). The JCC is mandated to oversee compliance with the ceasefire and the provisions for military reform.
- The National Commission on Demobilization, Reinsertion and Reintegration (NCDRR) and the National Programme on Demobilization, Reinsertion and Reintegration[10] (NPDRR) tasked to:

    - Demobilise an estimated 55,000 ex-combatants from the FAB, members of APPMs, and support their reintegration into civilian life.
    - Support the reinsertion of an estimated 20,000 members of the Gardiens de la Paix government militia and approximately 10,000 *combattants militants* from various APPMs.
    - Contribute to the reallocation of government expenditures from defence to social and economic sectors over a period of five years.[11]

In addition, the DDR process has been guided by a joint operations plan (JOP) for pre-disarmament operations, disarmament, combatant verification and demobilization.[12]

Finally, following lengthy and difficult negotiations, a number of ceasefires, agreements and declarations were signed between June 2006 and December 2008 leading to a second DDR programme to be focused mainly on FNL combatants. This programme began in 2009 and aims to integrate 3,500 combatants into the army and police, to formally demobilise 5,000 combatants, and to support the return and reinsertion of approximately 11,000 *'adultes associés'* linked to the FNL.[13] This chapter focuses mainly on the first DDR programme that took place between 2004 and 2008, although it touches upon some of the potential challenges associated with the second DDR programme.

DRR rather than DDR

The National Commission was named the NCDRR (for demobilization, reintegration and reinsertion). This is not to suggest there was no disarmament but to note that, in accordance with the provisions of the JOP, disarmament in Burundi has been dealt with outside the current programme, which starts at the demobilization stage.[14] Figure 3.1 describes the main steps of the entire process.

The APPMs had requested that the FAB be dissolved to give everyone an equal opportunity to join the new army. This request was dismissed by the government, and integration without disarmament was decided upon as a compromise.

Operational overview

In a first phase, the DRR process demobilised volunteers, child soldiers and those with disabilities. Other ex-combatants and soldiers were integrated into either the Force de Défense Nationale (FDN) or the newly established Police Nationale du Burundi (PNB). In a second phase, the process aimed to downsize the army and the police to comply with respective maximum strengths of 25,000 and 15,000 while also respecting quotas for ethnic and APPM affiliations. Lists based on criteria such as age and disciplinary records of those to be demobilised were transmitted by the general staff of the APPM and the FDN to the executive secretariat of the NCDRR. Ex-combatants and soldiers who agreed to demobilise (after verification of identity and HIV/AIDS screening), received training, an ID card, a reinsertion package equivalent to nine months' salary (approximately US$600 for a foot soldier and up to US$1,800 for a senior officer) and a

Figure 3.1: Demobilization and reintegration process

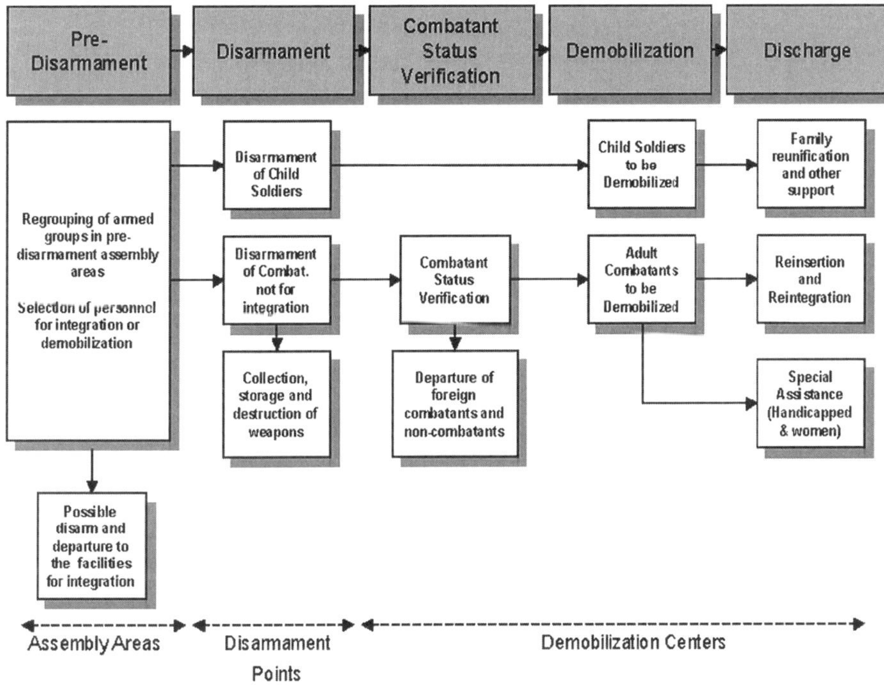

Source: Joint Operational Plan (2004).

lump sum for transport home. Demobilised combatants were also entitled to a reintegration package, equivalent in value to the package described above, but intended to allow ex-combatants to start or support income-generating activities. This reintegration package included various types of training (on self-employment and entrepreneurship), support for purchasing school books, supplies and agricultural kits etc.

As of September 2008, according to the NCDRR executive secretariat, 26,283 ex-combatants had been demobilised.[15] The FDN had reached a personnel strength of around 26,500, with around 16,500 police. These numbers are only estimates, as a census of the army and police has yet to be completed (or started, in the case of the army). In addition, the different militia groups have been listed by the Ministry of National Defence and leadership of CNDD/FDD. Gathering sites were identified in the communes and militias were requested via a sensitization radio programme to congregate at these sites, turn in their weapons and receive a demobilization lump sum equivalent to US$100. Returning arms was not a condition: 28,383 persons received payment but only 1,570 small arms and light weapons were collected.[16]

One of the major challenges of the DDR process in Burundi was the absence of a peace agreement and ceasefire framework that included all parties. Fortunately, military disarmament and demobilization have been largely successful by most accounts. Despite this, economic issues, regional instability and the pending full political settlement have hampered the long-term reinsertion and reintegration of ex-combatants. The delay in carrying out the reintegration process put many ex-combatants in debt resulting in their selling reintegration packages for cash.[17] There was also a very limited absorption capacity within the civilian economy – in practice, it would have been helpful to undertake enhanced market surveys to identify the few options available and to link reintegration programmes to longer-term economic recovery programmes. The dominant view is that reintegration contributed to security problems at the community level leading to some demobilised combatants joining the FNL, while other ex-combatants are reported to be contributing to the violence in North Kivu in neighbouring Democratic Republic of the Congo (DRC).

As the last group to join the peace process, the new DDR process for the FNL is particularly important. Negotiating alone with the legitimate government has given the group significantly more leverage than if it had signed earlier. The FNL has had the opportunity to learn from the first round of DDR and is in a position to bring new demands to the table, especially regarding the reinsertion and reintegration package. One important issue has been the need for equity, in particular to ensure that the packages offered at the later stages were of comparable value to those received by ex-combatants who had entered the DDR programme earlier. Additionally, the discrepancy between the number of ex-combatants claimed by the FNL and those estimated by the government of Burundi and the international community has impeded progress on important questions such as funding, mechanisms for the verification of former combatants and the acceptable ratio of arms to combatants. It is also reported that the FNL numbers may well have been inflated to influence the negotiations and attract support in the community through the DDR package. These newcomers, more supporters than combatants, are still integrated within their own communities and therefore it has been argued that they should not create significant problems of reintegration.

SSR overview

To date, there is no comprehensive strategic framework for SSR in Burundi.[18] SSR is approached in a piecemeal manner, often relegated to the armed forces, the police and the judicial sector.

The armed forces

The post-independence Burundian *Armée Nationale* was a Tutsi-dominated body that supported UPRONA. After the 1967 coup the army was renamed *Forces Armées Burundaises*. Ethnically and regionally unbalanced, the army's support for the Tutsi elite's domination of state institutions became one of the primary issues to spur the Hutu rebel movement.

Within the Arusha negotiations, the reform of the defence and security forces emerged as the most controversial issue. Before the DDR process, the FAB was estimated at around 43,400 soldiers.[19] Since 2004 the renamed FDN has integrated all APPMs, with the exception of the FNL which is set to integrate its ex-combatants into the army in accordance with recent agreements. Quotas governing the integration of the latter into the FDN are still a major element of the tensions between the government and the FNL. Because this last group is Hutu, it means that in order to comply with the 50 per cent ethnic group quota within the Arusha Agreement, the FNL will have to take over positions already occupied by Hutus from other APPMs, to fill its quota for representation in the army and police. This is likely to generate tensions among all parties.

The gendarmerie and other policing institutions

Since Burundi's independence policing has been largely conducted by the gendarmerie, a component of the FAB. Several other institutions with specific policing mandates were created and put under the control of the Ministry of Public Security (MoPS) and the Ministry of Justice (MoJ), dominated by the Tutsi elite. The main institutions were:

- *Police de la Sécurité Publique* – under MoPS;
- *Police de l'Air, des Frontières et des Etrangers* – under MoPS;
- *Police Judiciaire* – under MoJ;
- *Police Pénitentiaire* – under MoJ.

Police reform was at the centre of the Arusha discussions. As a result, various institutions, including the gendarmerie, were dissolved and their members integrated, together with former fighters from the APPM, into a single new police institution, the *Police Nationale Burundaise*. The PNB is a composite institution of around 16,500 police officers (the census is still under way),[20] an overwhelming number of whom have no police background or training. Its composition is a challenge to the day-to-day management of activities. The PNB leadership is conscious of the poor performance of the institution,[21] mainly manifested through inappropriate behaviour towards the public. In addition, the PNB is subject to political interference.

Other key institutions – justice and intelligence

Justice and intelligence institutions have always been under the control of the Tutsi elite. In the judiciary, only the lowest-ranking judges were from the Hutu majority. The cycle of violence following the Ndadaye assassination in 1993 resulted in the imprisonment of hundreds of alleged Hutu perpetrators who were not given fair trials because of the mono-ethnic composition of the judiciary. In 2005 a process to balance the ethnic quotas in the judiciary system was initiated by training the lower-court judges, mostly Hutus, to take positions in the higher-level courts.

The intelligence service, on the other hand, has always functioned as an oppressive arm of the state. The sovereign prerogative attached to this type of institution, as well as the large scope of constitutional powers it is granted to investigate outside of government control, is, in the context of a government largely dominated by one political party, certainly not conducive to enhancing the level of accountability and transparency within the institution.

SSR approach

The SSR approach in Burundi can be considered a combination of heterogeneous building blocks drawn from provisions in the various peace agreements. The first elements of a framework for SSR can be found in the 2000 Arusha Agreement, in the two sets of ceasefire agreements and in their respective technical agreements. Though the Arusha Agreement defines the mission of the security and defence forces and the 50 per cent ethnic quota, it falls short of defining maximum strength or other management issues and was not signed by the most important APPM, the CNDD/FDD. The 2003 Pretoria Protocol, signed by the CNDD/FDD and the transitional government of Burundi established that out of the 50 per cent of positions accorded to Hutus, 40 per cent of the senior officer posts in the new army and 35 per cent of the positions in the new police should be filled by CNDD/FDD members. In the context of the future integration of the FNL, these two clauses (ethnic ratio and CNDD/FDD ratio) become highly contentious. Constraints on the state budget represent another contentious structural parameter for the integration process.

In Burundi, SSR focused narrowly on the DFC until early 2004. In January 2004 a roundtable was held in Brussels between donors and the transitional government to support an emergency programme for the state budget, mechanisms of governance and DFC reform. From an SSR perspective, this resulted in provisions to support the integration and restructuring of the police and, less extensively, the army. The SSR vision at that time did not include the intelligence and corrections services, civil society or questions of oversight and accountability.

Following this roundtable, representatives from Belgium, France, the Netherlands and the United Kingdom undertook a joint mission to Burundi, aiming to develop an integrated and coordinated approach to SSR in cooperation with the transitional government. Beyond a commitment to coordinate their actions, the main output of this joint effort was the proposal to organise an SSR workshop which would include the relevant ministries and develop a strategic plan for SSR. Although the proposal was officially welcomed, the initiative was subsequently quashed by the president. The struggle to integrate the APPMs into the army and police, the implementation of the separate agreement with the CNDD/FNL and the forthcoming elections (which were preceded by a constitutional referendum) were not deemed conducive to such a strategic exercise.

Despite the magnitude of the logistical challenges and the management problems raised by addressing sensitive issues such as rank harmonization, grades, numbers, ratios, etc., integration had to be completed before the 2005 elections, starting with the referendum in February. The most significant step to be taken in building the policy framework was the plan for the Burundi National Police, created in February 2005.

The 2005 elections and establishment of a legitimate government occurred in a context where the government was still engaged in fighting against the Palipehutu-FNL. This environment was not politically conducive to developing a comprehensive and strategic SSR policy, despite renewed attempts by various international actors, including efforts to link SSR with the poverty reduction strategy paper. In the absence of such a policy framework, the process consisted of bilateral assistance mostly driven by *ad hoc* demands from the government. Finally, the Ministry of Defence and Former Combatants adopted a sector-specific policy for 2006–2016 and the PNB adopted a strategic plan (2007–2017).[22] In addition, development of a subsectoral plan for the National Intelligence Service (*Service National de Renseignement*) is under way.

A survey published in August 2007 showed that of the four main sources of insecurity identified by the population, the three greatest areas of concern after criminality are the rebel groups, the armed forces and the police.[23] Reform efforts have focused on the professionalization and rationalization of the police and the army through the physical reconstruction or rehabilitation of buildings, logistical and IT support, census and identification, audits and training of personnel. Committees to harmonise and reduce the rank structure have also been established. However, no recent research has been undertaken to measure the impact of these efforts on public perceptions of security.

Both parliament and the senate have Defence and Security Commissions, established after the 2005 elections. However, despite the prerogatives that legally fall under its mandate, the Parliamentary Commission faces difficulties in exercizing its oversight role over the police, army, intelligence and prison services. Beyond internal political obstacles, this weakness is due to a lack of capacity of the commission.[24] In addition, both the internal challenge of the integration of former combatants in the DFC and the external challenge posed by the security situation in the country create institutional tensions. The Senate Commission for Defence and Security is responsible for the nomination of the heads of the Defence and Security Corps and guaranteeing ethnic quotas within the DFC.[25] However, this will only be possible once the data collected through census and identification in the police and army become available.[26] A notable development in August 2008 was the passage of a law creating a national security council. This advisory body to the president and the government will define policy, coordinate the various security institutions, monitor the national security situation and allocate resources to defence and security institutions. The council is also mandated to coordinate a threat assessment and establish a national security plan to serve as the foundation for the missing comprehensive SSR strategy.

Ongoing political struggles between different parties as well as related security challenges have not created a favourable environment in which to establish an integrated SSR policy framework. A number of interlocutors have suggested that a window of opportunity will not exist before the 2010 elections or before the DDR and integration of FNL elements into the DFC.

Key actors in DDR and SSR

The DDR process has mobilised a large range of actors, including the Burundian government and, more specifically, the first vice-president (in charge of security matters), the Ministry of National Defence, the MoPS,[27] the NCDRR and the Ministry of Health (especially on the issue of HIV/AIDS). The main international actors are the World Bank – notably through the Multi-Country Demobilization and Reintegration Programme (MDRP) and its international donors – a succession of peacekeeping operations starting with the African Mission in Burundi (AMIB), which was replaced by the UN Operation in Burundi (ONUB) and then by the UN Integrated Office in Burundi (BINUB), as well as the UN Peacebuilding Fund.[28] Other UN agencies such as UNDP and UNICEF played a key role in dealing with child soldiers. The magnitude of the World Bank's involvement in Burundi is demonstrated through its support for 11 governmental programmes with a total amount of US$347 million, in various sectors such as agriculture, education, HIV/AIDS, roads, etc., including US$33 million for DDR channelled through the MDRP Trust Fund.[29]

Several bilateral actors have been strongly engaged in SSR and DDR, even before the Arusha Agreement. Belgium, France and later the Netherlands and South Africa are among the main bilateral donors involved in police and military reform. Assistance has focused on providing advice, training personnel and supplying material for the reconstruction of buildings. In addition, South Africa has played an important and specific role, having taken over the facilitation process in 1999 after the death of Julius Nyerere. South Africa also currently contributes the troops for the African Union Special Task Force, which secures the assembly areas for DDR and supports disarmament operations, while also providing security to the FNL leadership in Bujumbura. This guarantee has been significant in encouraging the return of exiled leaders who did not trust the government security forces, but for obvious reasons could not be allowed to maintain their own security services.

The African Union undertook the first in-country operation to provide security to leaders returning from exile. Importantly, only South Africa contributed in 2001 to what is now known as the South African Protection Service Detachment (SAPSD). In April 2003 AMIB was deployed, absorbing the SAPSD. AMIB's aim was to monitor the ceasefire agreements and provide for a stable defence and security situation in Burundi. Within this broad framework, AMIB provided operational support to the DDR process and the MDRP until replaced by ONUB in May 2004.[30]

The United Nations has been involved in the efforts to resolve the conflict since the establishment of the UN office in Burundi in 1993 under the supervision of the UN Department of Political Affairs. In addition, the United Nations participated in the peace process through experts appointed to assist with the facilitation of the peace talks, which started in 1998. In May 2004, after Burundian parties reached key agreements, the UN Security Council decided to dispatch a peacekeeping operation, ONUB, to assist the Burundians in managing the political transition. Under Resolution 1545 (2004), ONUB was given a broad mandate by the Security Council under Chapter VII as well as DDR and SSR-related responsibilities.[31]

On the DDR side, ONUB was mandated to provide security at the pre-disarmament assembly sites, collect and secure weapons and military material, contribute to the dismantling of militias, carry out the disarmament and demobilization portions of the national DDR programme and monitor the quartering of the armed forces and their heavy weapons. On SSR, a broad mandate included providing assistance to the transitional government in carrying out institutional reforms to constitute integrated national defence and internal security forces that are democratically governed and fully respect human rights and fundamental freedoms. In addition, ONUB was requested to assist with judicial reform and support the extension of state and police authority across the country.

A four-person DDR-SSR section was created in ONUB to implement this mandate and assist in the double challenge of demobilization and reintegration/restructuring of the FDC. In terms of division of labour, there was no specific assignment to deal with DDR or SSR – the section worked simultaneously on both processes. ONUB was also provided with a civilian police (CivPol) component specifically to support police restructuring through advice, training and mentoring. The CivPol component then became UNPOL, tasked to support police reform and staffed by up to 120 international police officers. UNPOL was separate from the DDR-SSR section, generating an uncomfortable situation regarding division of police reform responsibilities. To simplify this, the DDR-SSR section became more involved in the strategic dimension, assisting the police in its relationship with donors, etc., while UNPOL supported practical training.

With the conclusion of the political transition, exemplified by the election of Pierre Nkurunziza as president at the end of 2005, the UN mandate in Burundi had to be reviewed. In October 2006 the Security Council established BINUB. BINUB's mandate, through Resolution 1719, includes support for the implementation of the Dar-es-Salaam Comprehensive Ceasefire Agreement; the development of a national plan for reform of the security sector; the completion of the national programme for the demobilization and reintegration of former combatants; and efforts to combat the proliferation of small arms and light weapons. The mandate also has a provision on rule of law, with the purpose of 'strengthening the justice and corrections system, including independence and capacity of the judiciary'.

At the same time, in 2006, the newly established UN Peacebuilding Commission (PBC) formally recommended that Burundi receive support from the UN Peacebuilding Fund (PBF). In its decision to recommend Burundi as a PBF recipient, the PBC highlighted a number of key priorities, including DDR and SSR, where a lack of progress could hamper the further consolidation of peace. In January 2007 the PBF allocated US$35 million to peacebuilding efforts in Burundi. One of four priority areas of intervention identified by the government was strengthening the rule of law within the security forces.[32]

The integration of the UN agencies has bridged UNDP and DPKO efforts on SSR, small arms and DDR. The DDR-SSR section was replaced by an SSR-Small Arms section comprising 30 staff, including UNDP representatives. Support to DDR remains in the BINUB mandate. A programme of action, endorsed in March 2008 by both the government and Palipehutu-FNL, envisaged two phases: first DDR and second the integration of the FNL within the national institutions. Negotiations on the modalities of these processes have been slow, complicated by a lack of political will on both sides.

The most significant evolution in the mandate was the integration of the police adviser and military adviser components within the new SSR-Small Arms section, creating a more consistent and broader approach to SSR. This shift acknowledges the linkages between SSR, civilian disarmament and the police and military sector. The facilitation and hosting of an OECD-DAC event on the SSR handbook[33] by the SSR-Small Arms unit is an example of the broader approach to SSR that prevails within BINUB.

A capacity-building programme through the PBF supports both police (IT network, uniforms, vehicles, training, etc.) and defence forces (training, rehabilitation of barracks, etc.). But both the DDR and the SSR framework suffer from political blockages. BINUB is strongly involved at the political level, offering continued support in the effort to create the necessary conditions for the emergence of an SSR strategic framework. As an example, BINUB has been instrumental in the creation of the National Security Council, in promoting concepts and facilitating contacts and debate among stakeholders. BINUB also assists the ongoing peace negotiations through its continued support to the political directorate and joint verification and monitoring mechanism.

The DDR/SSR Nexus in Burundi

This section analyses the DDR/SSR nexus in Burundi, identifying key opportunities to link DDR and SSR and highlighting areas where there have been gaps or missed opportunities. In particular it examines opportunities to link DDR and SSR through peace and ceasefire agreements, and through common activities at the pre-disarmament assembly points. Challenges are also discussed throughout the reintegration and integration phases.

The political and legal framework: peace agreements and ceasefires

Even though the various agreements provided the necessary building blocks to undertake DDR, they failed to provide an integrated vision and a comprehensive and strategic framework for SSR. At a sectoral level, there was no coherent framework for the integration of former combatants into the army and police (recall the contentious provisions on ethnic and APPM quotas), which in turn hampered opportunities to link DDR and SSR in policy and programming. The sequence of agreements and the successive split of parties over each political settlement have not allowed for the emergence of a comprehensive political solution. It is clear that the lack of a universally accepted political agreement has delayed the implementation of a comprehensive SSR programme. This can be explained by a number of factors. First, the transitional government did not enjoy the necessary legitimacy to engage in such a process. Second, once a legitimate authority was elected, the new CNDD/FDD-dominated government was more interested in establishing and consolidating its power over other Hutu rebel APPMs than engaging in a global, comprehensive and open process of SSR. However, although this situation made conditions difficult, it did allow for the successful disarmament and demobilization of the signatories.

Primary needs of combatants: a security issue for the community and potential risk for stability

When the DDR process is under way, combatants' primary needs (food and water, shelter and basic healthcare) must be covered. In 2003 the

CNDD/FDD were known to loot communities to cover these needs. In 2008 Palipehutu-FNL also reportedly created a security problem in the community as a result of pillaging.[34] This was a source of tension since, in both cases, preserving a safe and secure environment for the community is the responsibility of state security services, which have also been accused of targeting the civilian population through theft and extortion. This situation generated clashes between the conflicting parties over an issue that was basically a consequence of the peace agreement.

Pre-disarmament assembly: a common operational entry point

The preliminary phase of DDR that brings together all the APPMs (excluding the militias) in the assembly area constitutes a common operational entry point for ex-combatants entering the DDR and SSR processes. However, the decisions made by ex-combatants to integrate within the DFC or to undergo disarmament and demobilization at this stage are mutually exclusive. Despite the fact that this preliminary DDR step was crucial in shaping the nature of the future Burundian army and police, in the absence of an SSR framework and mechanism to coordinate reform of the DFC, it was entirely driven by the JCC, ONUB and the executive secretariat of the NCDRR.

The pre-disarmament assembly areas provided a unique opportunity to collect and compile information on ex-combatants. This information could then help create a consolidated database of former combatants, dividing them into those returning to civilian life, those joining the army and those joining the police. Unfortunately, the opportunity to create such a database was missed, almost certainly because the process was seen uniquely under the lens of DDR. This approach prevented a broad perspective on data collection for the integration process and the management of incoming army and police personnel. As a result, in 2008 the police increased almost tenfold through integration, but there is still no reliable personnel database. The same is true for the army. If the identification of former combatants had already been effected at the pre-assembly site, the recipient institutions would only have had to run a complementary and limited census during the pre-disarmament stage before integration in order to identify those personnel already part of the institutions. Moreover, this would have ensured compatibility across both databases, making it possible to cross-check information and prevent individuals from being on both army and police payrolls. It would also make it much more difficult for former combatants who received the DDR reinsertion and/or reintegration package(s) to join these institutions at a later stage.[35]

Demobilization and rightsizing

The demobilization of APPMs included a number of detainees defined as either war or political prisoners by the APPM leadership. This study was not able to collect reliable information on the number of detainees freed to join the first DDR process. However, it was reported by different interviewees that some detainees, under arrest for criminal acts unrelated to the civil war and awaiting trial, claimed to be war or political prisoners and succeeded in getting released to join the DDR programme.[36]

Representatives of the Palipehutu-FNL claimed in an interview that there are around 3,500 war and political prisoners who should be released to participate in the DDR process. However, using a list submitted by the Palipehutu-FNL, a joint liaison team composed of BINUB, FNL and government officials identified only 687 war and political prisoners[37] who should be released under the 4 December 2008 declaration, which stipulates that war prisoners will enter the DDR process and political prisoners will return home. The distinction between the two groups is to be made by a commission under the leadership of the Ministry of Justice. However, the criteria to be applied are unclear. Functioning justice and law enforcement systems should be able to differentiate between these categories of prisoners. The inability to do so has had a direct impact on the public's confidence in the justice system, creating a sense of impunity and resentment from victims.

After the integration of the APPMs into the armed forces, a significant number of ex-gendarmes were demobilised. This occurred during the creation of the new Burundi National Police while other police forces were dissolved – including the gendarmerie that was part of the former FAB. These gendarmes counted toward the ex-FAB quota so, in order to balance the quotas, many reportedly professional and well-trained gendarmes were demobilised. The DDR and integration processes have thus directly affected the functioning of the army and the police. While the police increased tenfold, absorbing an overwhelming majority of untrained and unqualified former combatants (SSR), many qualified officers had to leave the force (DDR). In particular, the police force has been deeply disrupted, resulting in an increase of human rights violations.[38]

Integration versus reintegration

Failing to ensure that ex-combatants faced with the choice between reintegration into society or integration into the security institutions were subject to equal conditions regarding their future was a lost opportunity to develop synergies between DDR and SSR. A former combatant with the opportunity to demobilise voluntarily has two options: join the police or the army (through the SSR process of integration) or return to civilian life (through the DDR process of reintegration). This has different implications, depending on the option taken.

When a former combatant integrates into the defence or security corps, several steps are taken:

- His or her past and current membership in an APPM is assessed. This is the only reason why the former combatant obtains a job in the state institutions. Former combatant status becomes a formal status.
- He or she will enter an intensive socializing and identifying environment. Most of the time is spent in uniform socializing with colleagues, providing a sense of identity and possibly elevated social status within the community.
- He or she will secure a package of long-term economic resources.

When returning to civilian life, the combatant must:

- Abandon his/her former status in exchange for civilian status.
- Be prepared for the challenges posed by reintegration into the civilian community (former combatants often have a bad reputation since they are viewed as having violated social rules and been rewarded with a reintegration package).
- Recognise that his/her economic future is only assured in the short term.[39]

Individuals must choose between these two options, without being fully aware of the consequences of options which offer them unequal chances for their future.

Further compounding the problem, after some former combatants had voluntarily demobilised and entered the DDR process, salaries for the police and army were considerably increased in order to create an incentive and guarantee allegiance to the newly integrated institutions.[40] When interviewed, the former combatants who had voluntarily demobilised felt tricked and unfairly treated. They observed that if they had known salaries for the police and army were going to increase, they would never have demobilised. It seems that the decision to increase salaries was completely disconnected from the DDR process, although pay scales are an important factor when it comes to encouraging voluntary demobilization.

A rushed and complex integration

In Burundi, a unique and deliberate approach was taken to first integrate ex-combatants into the army before downsizing in a subsequent phase. The imperative to organise elections in 2005 in a secure and peaceful environment required the creation of an integrated police force and army ahead of the polls. This was a major rallying point used by government and international stakeholders to instil public confidence in the run up to elections. The starting point was the presidential decree of January 2004 which required the appointment of integrated chiefs of staff in the police and army. In reality, the integration process was crammed into the last few months before the elections.[41] Furthermore, integration of the CNDD/FDD was dictated by the necessity to enlarge the capacity of the army to fight the Palipehutu-FNL more effectively.

The result of the integration process is a paradox. The existence of an integrated army and police force prior to elections raised public confidence due to the representation of various groups. It also made the police less effective[42] as the majority of the police officers were untrained. Integration was a symbolic demonstration of peace consolidation. In an ideal world, it should allow for the training of former combatants integrated into the army and (most importantly) the police before the next elections. However, with their inherently political nature, subsequent elections will impose considerable strains on both SSR and DDR processes.

Integration involves the mixing of ethnic groups and various APPM groups according to ratios, with the aim of distributing influence and thereby preventing any single group from dominating the state security institutions. But the integration challenge goes beyond the ethnicity or membership of a particular APPM group; it is also about social background, education and family situation. For example, a young ex-combatant who is appointed to a high-ranking position in the police or army may have limited education, few family assets and be married to a poorly educated wife. He will mix with officers from the former Tutsi-dominated elite of the police or army, who used to be socially privileged, well educated, wealthy and with educated families.[43] The conditions for sharing social space between the two groups are far from optimum and create an obstacle to a unified and integrated institution. Acknowledging the social history of the various groups is therefore part of the equation for successful integration.

The rightsizing of the police and army is a process governed by budget constraints since the Burundian state cannot afford to maintain large security forces. After being integrated, many thousands of police and army personnel were subsequently demobilised in order to reach the acceptable maximum strength of 15,000 police and 25,000 soldiers agreed upon by the government and the international community. The two-step process was guided by the national political transition agenda, requiring both DDR and the integration of the defence and security corps to move forward. It can be argued that this allowed the 2005 elections to proceed peacefully and that integration was a success since no major clashes occurred between groups inside the two integrated institutions, despite many internal challenges. On the other hand, this double-trigger mechanism has generated uncertainty, frustration and disappointment among those who were demobilised through the rightsizing. The process lacked transparency and the criteria used, as well as the way in which these criteria were assessed, was questioned (for example, disciplinary records). Consequently, at the beginning of 2008, 900 soldiers refused compulsory demobilization, demanding a review of the reintegration strategy. It may therefore be too early to assess the security impact of this process.

A second rightsizing process will be triggered by the integration of the FNL. Room will have to be made among the Hutu-dominated APPMs to allow the newcomers to join the police and the army, while complying with the stipulated maximum strength. This process will take place under less than favourable circumstances as the predominant perception of the reintegration process is negative. In addition, previously integrated combatants will have already spent a few years in the newly integrated institutions, generating legitimate expectations about their future. Finally, renewed fighting in the eastern DRC (primarily North Kivu) could attract disillusioned demobilised combatants. The establishment of a relevant, coherent and acceptable set of criteria is thus a tricky exercise. If the tension between integrating former FNL fighters and maintaining the agreed maximum strength poses a risk for stability, it is likely that the threshold of maximum strength will be temporally raised to ease the integration process.

The DDR process in Burundi was understood and designed from a purely military standpoint.[44] As a result, with regard to the rightsizing of the police, it must be noted that the mechanisms in place did not provide a procedure that allows the Ministry of Public Security to send names of police officers to be demobilised directly to the NCDRR. At present, the PNB and the Ministry of Interior have had to transmit the list to the Ministry of Defence, which then forwards them to the executive secretariat of the NCDRR. When political stability relies on a power-sharing arrangement that ensures the distribution of powers within the security sector, this type of procedural loophole creates unnecessary tension between the army and police leadership.

The reform of security institutions through rushed integration creates a large-scale management problem. Essentially, all management layers are disrupted. This was more pronounced with the integration of the police.[45] In this case, a dysfunctional police institution lacking the necessary management capacity implemented its own reform. The reform of these institutions was hampered by the unconditional integration which occurred prior to defining the institutional framework and roadmap for the reform process. This is a consequence of the 'DDR before the elections' paradigm taking precedence over the establishment of efficient security institutions.

Reintegration of former combatants

There are important distinctions between the reintegration of the FAB and the APPMs as well as between rural and urban reintegration. It is reported that the demobilization of former APPM combatants in rural areas created some problems within communities although the challenges of reintegration in urban areas were often greater.[46] In the absence of a comprehensive study to determine the magnitude of the problems and their underlying sources, the most recurrent reasons given for reintegration challenges in rural areas put forward during interviews were the following:

- Demobilised ex-combatants are perceived as negative social elements, having taken part in criminal and violent activities.
- They are perceived as being financially rewarded for past criminal activity.
- They have a tendency to resolve conflict with force.
- Ex-combatants refuse to take part in projects like building roads or wells and planting trees, etc., because they believe these activities are undignified.

- As with other returnees, some former combatants are involved in land and housing disputes (houses have been destroyed or occupied, etc.). Those who do not have a house are obliged to rent and therefore spend a large part of their reinsertion and reintegration package on housing rather than on an income-generating activity.
- They have difficulties initiating a sustainable income-generating activity, since the local economy is not a favourable environment;
- They had their basic needs covered while in the bush, and felt more like civil servants than peasants. On their return to their community they resent the perceived loss of social prestige that comes with relying on their own ability to cover basic needs.
- Many rebels left while they were very young and therefore have no experience in running a family economy in a rural environment.
- Local community leaders and officials have not been involved in planning the demobilization process; as a result the community was not prepared to deal with the returnees.
- The package received was not sufficient for reintegration or was not distributed at all.
- There is a lack of flexibility in addressing the different needs of the demobilised and an absence of follow-up to assist them within the community.

In urban areas, the difficulties of reintegration of the former APPMs were reported to be even more significant:

- Many former APPM members had faced social problems prior to joining the movements and were already engaged in criminal activities.
- The social network and peer pressure of the community are less powerful in urban than in rural areas.
- Although urban areas may potentially offer more job opportunities, the overall cost of living, especially housing, is much higher.

In addition, it should be noted that the reintegration process of ex-combatants took place at the same time as a massive return of refugees from Tanzania, increasing the strain on the extremely weak local economy and potentially contributing to land disputes. The office of the UN High Commissioner for Refugees has reported that 389,000 refugees have returned to Burundi since 2002.[47] This return of refugees put further pressure on the unstable economy and compounded an already difficult reintegration process, creating further housing and land disputes.[48]

Former FAB personnel in urban areas were usually well established, with a social network allowing them to start, or continue, small businesses. In rural areas, people from wealthy backgrounds who have spent most of their lives in the police or army as civil servants are at a severe disadvantage because they have no knowledge of rural activities and are unable to run a smallholding. On the positive side, security problems directly related to demobilised combatants may be marginal. While empirical evidence is lacking, it seems that for the most part, it is the overall lack of economic opportunities combined with reintegration dynamics that has played a role in exacerbating insecurity.

An overwhelming focus on the combatant emerges as a recurrent critique to the reintegration process. Importantly, to reintegrate former combatants into the community, the target is not the combatant *per se* but the restoration of social and economic links with the community. Establishing these links requires action on both sides, from the community and from the former combatant. But the reintegration process in Burundi focuses on the combatant exclusively, relying on her/him to establish these sustainable links.[49] It must also be noted that this process does not take into account the fact that, in many cases, it is not only combatants but also their families who have to reintegrate. Indeed, the families of many combatants follow them during their movements around the country, but the package does not take into account the family reinsertion factor.

In addition, the NCDRR mechanism was essentially composed of military staff and former combatants, with no significant role given to community leaders, officials and relevant ministries beyond the Ministry of Defence. Failed reintegration presents security threats for the community and should be envisaged as such. The local authorities of the Ministry of the Interior dealing with these issues in the community are actors within the security system. They represent a clear linkage between SSR and DDR and should be strongly implicated in both processes.[50]

Disabled former APPM members are not receiving the same treatment and attention as the ex-FAB because the former APPM did not contribute to the state welfare systems, rendering them ineligible for social and medical benefits. One former combatant reported that he had witnessed a seriously injured former colleague simply being given his reinsertion package and told to go home, despite the fact he was on a drip.[51] Even those ex-combatants entitled to welfare benefits have a hard time living off their benefits. This undifferentiated approach to the treatment of disabled fighters within the

DDR process is not conducive to establishing a new police and army that serves the state and respects its citizens.

DDR and land disputes

Like refugees, ex-APPM combatants have been away from home for many years, generating tension when they return to reclaim possession of their house and/or land. The *Commission Nationale des Terres et autres Biens* was a specific mechanism established to find consensual solutions to the huge number of cases generated by refugees from Tanzania, representing 90 per cent of the courts' caseload (approximately 43,000 cases).[52] At least 90 per cent of the Burundese population rely on agricultural income. Agriculture is more than an economic consideration: it is a question of social identity. The former combatants do not have a special mechanism and their cases are treated like those of other returnees. Former combatants, however, are more likely to use intimidation or force to try to resolve their disputes and therefore should arguably be considered a 'special case'.

Physical reconstruction

Beyond the question of personnel, quality of infrastructure is also an important issue. The Peacebuilding Fund and other bilateral donors have provided funding to rehabilitate barracks. One of the visible consequences of DDR is the disappearance of former fighters and the appearance of structures covered in plastic sheeting (meant for the provisional cantonment of government army personnel) within the community. The integration of armed elements into barracks sends a visible and positive signal to the population. In addition, it increases the level of control and limits their interaction with the population. Linking the reconstruction and rehabilitation process of security sector institutions and the DDR process is beneficial in terms of stability. The visible establishment of security sector institutions should be initiated to provide tangible evidence of positive change.

The economy as a structural determinant

The impact a country's economic context has on both DDR and SSR processes cannot be overstated. The challenges associated with reintegrating former combatants are directly related to the poor performance of the Burundian economy. Specifically, there is no explicit link between the reintegration process and broader economic recovery programmes.

Moreover, the number of personnel to be integrated into the police and the army that the state can afford in the long term depends on its budget.

Two conflicting remarks can be made:

- First, because an ailing economy is a disincentive for reintegration, integration into new security sector institutions seems to provide an ever more appealing future for former combatants.
- Second, successful reintegration of former combatants does not rely uniquely on the economy. It is also related to the restoration of social links and the reduction of future uncertainty.

Even though the economy is an undeniable structural determinant of both integration and reintegration, explaining the success of DDR/SSR processes solely from this perspective would oversimplify the complex dynamics at work.

Regional dimensions

Although it is difficult to assess the concrete influence of regional conflict on DDR and SSR in Burundi, it appears that persisting tensions in the neighbouring Kivu provinces of the DRC contributes to the continued proliferation of small arms and light weapons in the region. Moreover, renewed armed clashes offer the potential to attract demobilised combatants from both APPMs and FAB into the conflict zones. The former Tutsi-led government, the FDD and the FNL have been involved in the last two conflicts in Eastern Congo. It is believed that all sides have maintained linkages with various parties involved in the conflict. Another important element is the evolution of the Burundi stabilization process through integration and elections. Violent clashes during the election process between the FDD and the FNL and a worsening of the current Kivu conflict are the main risks threatening stability in Burundi.[53] However, beyond the small-scale movement of demobilised combatants (ex-FAB, FNL and FDD) joining armed groups in the Kivu area, it remains unclear how the current regional situation concretely affects Burundian DDR and SSR processes.

DDR/SSR and civilian disarmament

Burundi has a long history of arms proliferation.[54] This started with escalating distrust between the Tutsi elite and the Hutu population, followed by the arming of the Tutsi population by the government and the progressive self-arming of the Hutu population either to build a rebellion or to ensure security in a declining economic environment that saw the growth of criminal gangs. This phenomenon was exacerbated by the government distributing arms to local militias (*Gardiens de la Paix*). The proliferation of arms has been worsened by the crumbling security situation in neighbouring DRC.

The main reason for civilians to carry arms is to protect themselves, their families and their personal property in the absence of an effective and trusted security system. In addition, a frail economy and readily available small arms favour the rise of criminality, reinforcing the impression among the population that possessing a weapon increases personal security. These factors result in the sustained proliferation of small arms. Importantly, small arms are involved in the vast majority of violent incidents across the country.

There have been many attempts to tackle civilian disarmament. After the Arusha Peace Agreement, which included a provision for civilian disarmament (Protocol III), the government undertook a legislative process leading to the ratification in 2004 of the Nairobi Protocol for the prevention, control and reduction of small arms and light weapons in the Great Lakes region and the Horn of Africa. Civil society organizations have been active since 2005 in sensitization campaigns and the collection of weapons. [55] They have been largely unsuccessful in the absence of strong governmental support. In addition, it appeared that the population was expecting equal compensation for turning in their weapons as was given in the DDR process. In 2006, the new president launched a campaign of voluntary civilian disarmament supported by a technical committee. The campaign did not meet expectations: only some 4,000 arms were collected,[56] while a conservative estimate of weapons retained by the population is 100,000 small arms (guns and grenades).[57] More recently, the PBF has decided to allocate US$500,000 to support the implementation of the civil disarmament strategy and the fight against the proliferation of small arms. In addition, a sub-unit has been established in BINUB to coordinate related UNDP support programmes.

The ratio of arms returned through disarmament is very low for both former combatants and militias, leaving substantial stocks available within the civilian population. The combination of arms retention and a failed reintegration process may easily lead to increased criminality. The small arms issue is clearly at the core of the DDR-SSR nexus and cannot be resolved without a successful strategy that links both sets of activities. The weak capacity of the defence and security forces to deliver security encourages the population to retain small arms for self-protection. Weak control over PNB personnel, but also to a lesser extent the FDN, following integration has increased the level of insecurity. Inadequate capacity of the DFC to control its own stock of arms has facilitated proliferation, while weak capacity in border control has enabled the widespread circulation of small arms in the region.

DDR/SSR and transitional justice[58]

Transitional justice should be understood as a response to systematic and massive human rights violations. It encompasses a set of measures which enable societies in transition to pursue accountability, serve justice and achieve reconciliation. Measures include truth-seeking mechanisms, prosecution of perpetrators, the reform of abusive institutions to prevent repeated violations and the provision of reparations to victims. The 2000 Arusha Peace and Reconciliation Agreement for Burundi provides for the establishment of two transitional justice mechanisms, a Truth and Reconciliation Commission (TRC) and an 'international judicial commission of inquiry on genocide, war crimes and other crimes against humanity'. These provisions, following the Kalomoh Report in 2005,[59] were translated into UN Security Council Resolution 1606 urging the establishment of a TRC and a special court. No major steps have been taken thus far to implement these measures, but following the visit of the High Commissioner for Human Rights in May 2007[60] a commitment has been made by the government of Burundi to undertake a national consultation on transitional justice mechanisms.

If institutional reform is addressed through the requested reforms of the DFC, the various peace agreements have failed to address the issue of reparations for victims. The DDR package of reintegration, the release of war and political prisoners, and the integration of former combatants in the army or police are often perceived by communities as rewarding ex-combatants. However, many individuals among the population were victims of violent abuses during the conflict, and the national consultation may actually help to clarify the numbers of these victims. The absence of a mechanism to address reparations creates resentment and does not favour the emergence of a climate conducive to confidence building within communities.

From the perspective of institutional reform, conditions are not in place to design and implement measures such as the vetting of current police and army personnel to address past behaviour. Such processes are highly sensitive and require political will and effective authority[61] over personnel, both of which are missing. After conflict all parties are likely to have perpetrators among their senior officials. Engaging in a transparent vetting process thus implies that the party in power is strong enough to dismiss some of its own leaders without endangering stability. This would need to be balanced by some efforts by the PNB and the FDN. For example, initiatives have been undertaken to strengthen internal oversight of the police through capacity building for the inspector general as well as the development of an ethics code (*Code de Déontologie*) for the police. In addition, the military justice system – while weak – is functional, and there are a number of committed individuals within this system trying to increase its capacity to function as an effective internal oversight institution.

DDR/SSR and HIV/AIDS

Burundi has struggled with internal conflict since 1993 and, despite regular programming, has been late in responding to the HIV/AIDS epidemic.[62] Recently, Burundi started an ambitious programme to address HIV/AIDS but is challenged by resource deficits. The defence ministry and the former gendarmerie have been among the leaders implementing the national policy to prevent and fight HIV/AIDS. The national plan is centralised and does not specifically target special groups like former combatants. In theory, a person who has been diagnosed as HIV positive has free access to therapy through a dense and decentralised service system.

HIV/AIDS is a cross-cutting issue for SSR and DDR, thus it could be argued that former combatants who have integrated into the army or police are more likely to be reached by HIV/AIDS prevention efforts. The prevalence of infection in Burundi is much higher in urban than in rural areas; consequently, former APPMs are potentially less likely to be exposed. If integrated former combatants do indeed have better access to the HIV/AIDS prevention and care mechanism, this issue should receive consideration in designing the DDR package to ensure a balance of medical care between former combatants integrated into the security sector and those reintegrated into civilian life.

DDR/SSR and gender

Despite the fact that the DDR plan mentions gender sensitivity, when it comes to demobilization and reinsertion the actual consideration of gender issues is limited. On the SSR side, the gender approach in the army and police consists of trying to increase the very small number of female personnel, the exact number of whom is unavailable due to the absence of reliable census and identification data. It can be said, however, that none of the senior-ranking positions in the army or the police is occupied by a female. To the credit of the police, it must be noted that the institution has created a special unit to combat sexual violence. Additionally, another special unit, led by a female officer, was set up within the police to address moral misconduct by police officers.

The United Nations has played a leading role in gender mainstreaming, conducting sensitization training for the police and the army on gender issues. In addition, all PBF programmes include gender indicators. One strong critique of this cross-cutting approach is that it obliges programme designers systematically to identify indicators for gender activities rather than to provide a substantial and relevant gender dimension in programming. As a result, in some programmes the so-called gender activities lack relevance. In addition, this transversal approach has almost eradicated the design of a specific gender programme. It must also be noted that Burundi has yet to elaborate a national gender policy framework.

Challenges and Lessons

The opportunities and gaps identified earlier provide some insights into the numerous challenges of developing synergies between DDR and SSR. Lack of capacity, coordination dilemmas and planning difficulties are some of the challenges explored in this section.

Coherence, planning and programming within the United Nations

By establishing a DDR-SSR unit in ONUB, the United Nations was innovative in formally introducing the terminology of SSR, dedicating human resources to the issue and partly acknowledging the link between DDR and SSR. This link appears to be a consequence of the UN's long-term involvement in a lengthy peace process that has generated two main sets of provisions, side by side, on DDR and integration of combatants in the DFC. It also reflects the rationale of the Implementation Monitoring Committee, established based on Protocol V of the Arusha Agreement, which includes provisions for two subcommittees on DDR and SSR. It has generated a natural linkage, at both conceptual and operational levels, between these two sets of central and critical measures. However, the SSR concept was in its early stages and not formally used within the United Nations. The dynamic on the ground regarding SSR focused on the creation of political space for SSR on the one hand, and on army and police components of the security sector on the other. In contrast, the DDR process was moving forward, heavily operational and generating its own political dynamic. The challenges for ONUB were significant:

- There was no political settlement that would allow it to move forward with SSR.
- There was a lack of a single definition and guidance within the UN system on SSR, hampering translation from mandate to concrete strategic directions.
- The new institutional establishment of a DDR-SSR section in Burundi did not match the classical HQ reporting line, and caused challenges for reporting and guidance.
- A link had to be established between a broad and undefined theme that was to be addressed conceptually and politically (SSR) with a concrete and operational, and also very political, concept of DDR. Creating a nexus between DDR and SSR within the DDR/SSR unit in 2004 thus involved linking two distinct cultural mindsets.
- In addition, the UNPOL operational component, mandated to work on one key SSR sector (police reform) was outside the DDR-SSR reporting line.
- ONUB was not the leading actor in the DDR process, since the MDRP and the World Bank had the primary responsibility over the funding mechanism, coordination and support activities.

Unfortunately, during the ONUB period the overall context of the DDR-SSR unit was largely absorbed by the DRR operational dynamic. The absence of political space for SSR was unconducive to exploring and working on broader linkages. The context was politically volatile and tense. It must be recalled that the transitional government was still engaged in armed combat with the Palipehutu-FNL. The DDR-SSR section was not in a position to design a programme. Opportunities were shaped by the difficult political climate, and so the section was compelled to exploit emerging windows of opportunity on both DDR and SSR.

The engagement of the PBC, the establishment of the PBF and a more stable security and political situation have enabled BINUB to engage in more systematic programme design and planning. In addition, financial support provided by the PBF offered a single mechanism encompassing all elements of the security sector. It includes provision for police, army, intelligence, small arms and justice, although it fails to include parliamentary oversight. The integration of UNDP within the UN mission – mainly responsible for PBF activities, including SSR-related PBF projects – has allowed the SSR-Small Arms section to become more programme oriented. However, the political dynamics surrounding DDR and integration of the FNL still involve the section in *ad hoc* policy advisory, facilitation and coordination activities with various stakeholders.

Communication and coordination

Despite the absence of a comprehensive policy framework, a large number of activities have taken place in the SSR field. A survey by the International Center for Transitional Justice conducted during the summer of 2008 documents more than 60 active projects within the security sector: 37 for the Burundi National Police, 18 for the FDN, five for the National Intelligence Service, two for parliament and one for the National Security Council.[63] In the absence of an overall SSR framework, these programmes are identified, designed and implemented without reference to each other. In contrast, the PBF support programme to the police, which provides, among other things, uniforms for police personnel, was designed in conjunction with the census and identification programme. Supporting activities include a large array of services ranging from physical rehabilitation and IT support to various types of training, sensitization and the provision of hardware.

The first significant attempt to coordinate bilateral SSR programmes was the joint mission of OECD-DAC member states which resulted from the 2004 roundtable. In 2005, in response to donor interest (see below) and to further concerns about a disconnect between DDR and SSR, ONUB created and chaired an international coordination group on DDR/SSR to facilitate discussion and the exchange of information. Repeated efforts encountered substantial obstacles. In the absence of a domestic political framework, there was, in fact, very little to coordinate.

After the 2007 donors' roundtable, the government of Burundi was encouraged to establish the Coordination Group of Partners (GCP), a political body meant to facilitate dialogue and coordination to assist Burundi in consolidating peace and reducing poverty. The GCP, which published its terms of reference in 2008, is assisted by the National Council for Aid Coordination, a domestic coordination body established following signature of the Paris Declaration to coordinate international assistance. With two levels (political and strategic), the GCP is divided into groups responsible for monitoring and evaluating the strategic framework for peacebuilding, and for monitoring and evaluating the strategic framework for poverty reduction. Both groups have a security cluster, and the majority of the actors are the same in both clusters, raising questions about the relevance of splitting the GCP into two groups.[64]

On the policy level, apparent progress has been made. Since 2003 the World Bank has identified the need to integrate DDR and SSR within the MDRP programme. This link has been noted in policy documents: 'The Government has adopted the following guiding principles (…) the DRRP would form an integral part of a defence and security sector reform program that would begin with the integration of the FAB and different armed movements to form the NDF [FDN] and a new national police force.'[65] At the 2004 roundtable, the donors involved in the DDR process also highlighted the necessity for concrete intervention in linking DDR and SSR. However, the coordination and funding mechanisms in place have never led to a concrete intervention or the establishment of a mechanism integrating both processes. Two main reasons may be put forward for this phenomenon: the absence of internal political momentum on the SSR agenda; and the fact that the operational framework for donor assistance in the field of SSR, as outlined in the OECD-DAC handbook, was still under development. The donor community had no clear reference point from which to mobilise official development assistance in such a sensitive field.

Sequencing of DDR and SSR programmes

It must be said that bilateral support activities to the DFC never totally stopped during the conflict. This is characteristic of the Burundian conflict; institutions have been disrupted but have never collapsed or stopped functioning. However, in terms of sequencing, the DDR process has been the conditioning process to start security sector programmes. Given the complexity of the issues involved, determining the right sequence has proved beyond any stakeholder's power. The political climate was not conducive to building a strategic framework for SSR. It takes time to instil the necessary climate of trust between the integrating parties to promote change within the new police and army, especially if there is still conflict. In addition, the very radical change foreseen in terms of numbers and diversity of personnel to be integrated in the police challenged any reasonable effort to undertake other important security sector programmes before it was completed. Once the integration of former APPMs was terminated, the second phase of the DRR plan, the rightsizing of the army and the police, could start. From this point onwards, DDR and security sector programming could evolve in parallel.

It is important to recognise a conjunction of political opportunities that favoured DDR over SSR. First of all, an accumulation of various texts contained the necessary provisions for a DDR framework; secondly, the necessity to organise and secure the elections required the process of integration in the DFC to move forward; and thirdly, the new government led and dominated by the CNDD/FDD had a strong interest in an integration process which would provide them with an effective army to fight the last rebel group, the Palipehutu-FNL, their main political rival in the Hutu community.

Local ownership and sustainability

The DDR process was under Burundian authority through the NCDRR. However, actors have divergent views on the level of ownership of the process. From the donors' perspective the Burundian authorities have full control of the mechanism and the implementation of activities. When asking some Burundian counterparts, however, they stated that the level of autonomy to design and implement the DDR process was very low, and that they were bound by very prescriptive World Bank procedures. Ownership by the Burundian population is nonexistent, given that they are not consulted or involved in this process. When it comes to the sustainability of the process, the provision for long-term support to the reintegration of the former combatants is beyond the current state budget capacity.

The ownership of the SSR programme by the Burundian population is no stronger than that for the DDR process, since civil society has little capacity to influence this area.[66] On the PBF projects, although the government decides on priorities, the co-management of the programmes and the funding by the international community reduce the level of ownership. However, this should be nuanced by indicating that the poverty reduction strategy paper process, which has an SSR dimension, has included civil society consultation. According to some reports this has included civil society involvement in the overall PBF process of programme design.

Another challenge has been that in order for the Burundi government to access the Poverty Reduction and Growth Facility (the IMF's low-interest lending facility for low-income countries), it has negotiated limitations on state spending with the IMF. This state budget reduction commitment, monitored through the IMF bi-yearly review, imposed a maximum number of personnel who could be registered in the army and the police at any given time. This was a key factor in the decision to set the maximum strength of 25,000 for the army and 15,000 for the police. Also at stake is the cancellation of Burundi's external debt.[67] In defining the maximum strength of these two security institutions to comply with the IMF indicators, the government *de facto* defined the number of combatants to be demobilised. Therefore, the criteria for downsizing do not rationally define the qualifications required but are *ad hoc*, allowing for the demobilization of a fixed number of people, thus raising questions about ownership and sustainability.

Capacities of the United Nations

Human resources. During the ONUB period, the DDR-SSR section was a small structure. Given the lack of political momentum (and the need to operate as a team) it appears to have been adequately staffed. However, the effectiveness of a separate police component is doubtful given the disruptive training conditions for the Burundian police and the lack of specific supporting funds allocated for the 120 staff.[68] It was suggested during interviews that a reduced number of senior officers with competences to assist the police in managing its integration may have been more appropriate.

The head of the current SSR-Small Arms section has been involved since the peace process, thus providing continuity and institutional memory through the various UN interventions. However, this is an isolated case and is not a result of UN policy, which raises important questions concerning the grounding of such expertise in the mission rather than with a key individual.

Financial resources. From a UN SSR perspective, one of the most important developments was the provision of a US$35 million grant from the PBF in early 2007. In February 2007 the government of Burundi followed up with the PBC to develop an integrated strategic framework for peacebuilding and launched consultations with various stakeholders. This resulted in the adoption of a document in June 2007 which identified six priorities, of which one was SSR and civilian disarmament. Around US$13 million is dedicated to supporting security sector programmes.[69] The fund, combined with the integration of the UN agencies, has brought additional leverage to BINUB.

From a UN DDR perspective, financial resources have been outside UN control. The US$78.84 million of the trust fund for the MDRP's Burundi programme included US$3 million from the government of Burundi, US$33 million from the World Bank International Development Agency and

US$42.84 million from donor countries, UN agencies, multi-donor trust funds, etc.[70] The MDRP Trust Fund ended on 31 December 2008 with little over half the grant spent. An envisaged funding and coordination mechanism for DRR of the FNL will be national rather than regional in focus.

Insecurity and reintegration gaps. The persons interviewed and the documents considered for this study offer contrasting views of the link between reintegration and increasing insecurity. Nevertheless, the dominant perception is that the reintegration of former combatants has been highly challenging and produced limited results. Beyond the fact that the impact of reintegration varies from commune to commune, there are also urban/rural and class divides (different reintegration dynamics exist between wealthy, educated ex-FAB and former APPM members of poorer, more rural origins). The contrast between views has multiple explanations:

- At the time when the assessment took place, the impact of the flawed reintegration programme, which was initiated in 2005, may just have started to become visible.
- No comprehensive national assessment of the reintegration process has been undertaken. Only very partial assessments, including this study, have been conducted.[71]
- Assessing reintegration implies looking for failed reintegration cases. Most of these cases, *de facto*, would not be found within the community but along roads and in towns.[72]
- The criteria chosen against which to assess the failure or success of reintegration may vary. If Burundi enjoys a lasting peace ten years from now, one could argue that the main objective of reintegration will have been reached. Others may argue that hundreds or thousands of former combatants are fighting in other countries, involved in criminal activities or weighing down the corrections system.

Conclusion and Policy Recommendations

The Burundi experience requires us to clarify what the DDR-SSR nexus entails. There is a semantic, phonetic and visual effect of similarities between the 'DDR' and the 'SSR' acronyms that may lead some to consider them as two comparable activities. DDR is operational, clearly defined and conducted in the short to medium term (although it could be argued that reintegration is long term). It has an identifiable sequence of implementation phases (relying on *ad hoc* mechanisms), a clearly defined and limited scope and focuses on individuals. The SSR process reflects an emerging concept defining a long-term approach based on a set of principles, some of them common to the various international SSR policy frameworks and others more specific. SSR is not an operational concept, but a strategic framework and a process that encompasses a large array of different operational programmes. It is characterised by its holistic, integrated and coordinated approach and it relies on structural mechanisms (such as a state institution). It aims to deliver security services effectively to the public while respecting standards of good governance, and its primary target is state institutions and main social structures.

The DDR process links with some security sector-related programmes, but does not link with a holistic SSR process given that a comprehensive SSR strategy does not yet exist in Burundi. In the absence of an SSR framework, it is more appropriate in this context to discuss linkages between DDR and security sector programmes.

Recommendations

On the basis of this case study, it is possible to identify some recommendations for enhancing the UN's support to DDR and SSR.

Consider prison reform as an entry point for DDR. DDR is usually seen, from the sequential point of view, as the first part of a peacebuilding process. Addressing detention issues represents one type of project that could be classified as an SSR measure and could be implemented even before the signature of the peace agreements. This could have potential benefits for the DDR process. APPMs claim that combatants in detention are either political or war prisoners. The lack of clarity around the criteria used to define the real status of detainees is partially rooted in the lack of capacity of the corrections system to generate and maintain reliable records. Engaging technical support and capacity-building efforts during the early stages of negotiations could help prevent a potentially massive release of common-law criminals. This is a possible entry point for UNDP and other donors in anticipation of a peace agreement and subsequent DDR.

Optimise the usefulness of peace negotiations. Peace negotiations offer an opportunity to define a bridging mechanism between the early security system programmes, DDR, civilian disarmament and reparations for victims.

A provision establishing such a mechanism would be justified by the need to coordinate these important and interdependent issues.

Establish an integrated general staff. The establishment of an integrated general staff was dictated by the technical forces agreement. Its implementation is an early SSR measure linked to the DDR process. This integrated group of senior staff, or a similarly integrated mechanism, is likely to be on the front line of managing the massive merging of former combatants and government security forces. Peace negotiations thus provide an opportunity to bridge the DDR coordination mechanism and the establishment of an integrated senior staff, if this is supported by the peace settlement.

Define clear and balanced options for integration and demobilization. Cantonment is a starting point for the integration of personnel and DRR. It represents two options for future social and economic life for a large number of individuals and their families. There is a need to ensure that the integration and reintegration options are balanced, and viewed as such by the beneficiaries. Neither package should be developed or reviewed independently during implementation so as to make one more attractive than the other.

Balance DDR and integration provisions with reparations for victims. The overall challenge for a lasting peace is to restore a safe and secure environment which allows for social and economic development. Reintegrating former combatants into society without addressing the claims of the victims of combatants is unlikely to be successful. This is another strong argument for including local community leaders and representatives in the design and implementation of the DDR process.

Link disarmament and arms control efforts. Disarmament and integration are directly connected to the question of disarmament and arms control in newly integrated security forces. It makes sense that both are approached simultaneously. The Burundi experience demonstrates that the criteria set for the disarmament of former combatants are perceived by the civilian population as the standard for their own disarmament. All these issues should be analysed and addressed in conjunction with one another. This would facilitate the formulation of clear policies and their dissemination through an information campaign explaining the various set of measures decided.

Broaden the approach to former combatants. The DDR process is currently geared towards dealing with able-bodied former combatants. Considering the fate of disabled former fighters from armed groups is a confidence-building measure that is intended to promote unity. If disabled ex-combatants expect to be integrated, providing access to the same social package as disabled police officers or soldiers wounded on duty should be considered.

Dissolve temporary and wartime cantonment structures and rehabilitate barracks. The dissolving of wartime cantonment structures and the primary rehabilitation of barracks should precede more structural rehabilitation and building in the long term. The proper cantonment of integrated security forces, in addition to the two tasks mentioned above, serves as both a confidence- and stability-building measure for the parties themselves and also for the public. Furthermore, it makes sense that these operations are designed and presented as unique transitional processes towards restoring a sense of normality. Dissolving precarious cantonment facilities (DDR), while (re)building functional solid ones (SSR) is a visible physical marker of moving from insecurity to peace.

Encourage linkages at the implementation level. In the absence of political momentum to engage in a full SSR process, there are still opportunities to advance capacities to provide security services to the public, while simultaneously improving compliance with parameters of good governance. Opportunities include performing a census and subsequently identifying security personnel and providing them with ID cards. In addition, the production of reliable management data, as well as increased control over the payroll system, could be important improvements. But most of all, in a period where boundaries are uncertain as result of informal recruitment during the conflict, quick integration of former combatants into security institutions represents a strong confidence-building measure: it clearly allows the public to distinguish between who is officially part or not part of security institutions.

Consider the community as both security beneficiary and security actor. As the end user of security services, a failed reintegration process may create security problems within communities. The community should therefore play a role in reintegrating former combatants and providing solutions to maintain social cohesion. Community leaders and local officials should be involved in the design and implementation of the DDR process. Moreover, the reintegration of former combatants in the community generates social dynamics that provide a unique opportunity to redefine the dialogue between the police and the community, and to reshape their relationship by discussing local security plans.

Optimize the use of the management information system (MIS). The UN Integrated Disarmament, Demobilization and Reintegration Standards (IDDRS) mention the important role of the management information system. The system should be designed to allow the establishment of a central database in a standardised but flexible format that can then be evolved to serve both the follow-up management of former combatants and personnel management for integration at the level of each security institution. Beyond the database itself, the registration of former combatants is also a capacity-building opportunity for the census and identification of security personnel that should always be undertaken after the end of a conflict.

Plan for elections in relation to both DDR and SSR. Elections impose a unique dynamic on other processes, dominating both the political space and available resources. In the case of Burundi, elections have driven both DDR and the integration process. Since it seems to be a recurrent pattern, elections should be anticipated and taken into the planning processes for DDR and SSR whenever the political conditions allow it. The election security plan offers a critical, concrete entry point. This should lead all parties to establish an integrated command and address issues such as disarmament, relations between former APPM leaders running for elections and security forces, etc. The division of roles between the police and the army should be considered a priority.

Mitigate reinsertion risks through community-based security and reintegration programmes. A characteristic trait of former combatants is that they more easily use intimidation or force to resolve their disputes. This is a risk factor in an environment where small arms are abundantly available. When designing a DDR process, relevant actors should be able to obtain information in advance on the housing situation for former combatants and their economic prospects. Preliminary findings would help to mitigate DDR risks through more adequate community-based reintegration programmes and efficient sensitization. This reaffirms the need to involve local officials in DDR mechanisms, and to differentiate between the specific needs of youth, men and women.

Notes

1 The Joint Declaration by the Palipehutu-FNL and the Government concerning the Cessation of Hostilities was issued on 25 May 2008.

2 These agreements are the Dar es Saalam Agreement of Principles toward Lasting Peace, Security and Stability in Burundi (18 June 2006) and the Comprehensive Ceasefire Agreement between the Government of the Republic of Burundi and the Palipehutu-FNL (7 September 2006).

3 The posts offered by the presidency were subsequently rejected by the FNL.

4 For a comprehensive description of the DDR process in Burundi until the beginning of 2006, see Henri Boshoff and Waldemar Very, 'A Case Study for Burundi – Disarmament, Demobilisation and Reintegration during the Transition in Burundi: A Technical Analysis' (Pretoria: Institute for Security Studies, 2006)

5 See 'Réalisation du PNDRR dans le domaine de la Démobilisation, du Désarmement et du Démantèlement des milices', September 2008.

6 This is the official number reported by the Multi-Country Demobilization and Reintegration Programme (MDRP) funding the DDR (see section on DDR and SSR actors).

7 Interview with FNL leaders, 21 September 2008.

8 In addition to these APPMs, the FAB created paramilitary groups to support its operations. Called the *Gardiens de la Paix*, these militias were not part of the formal FAB structure. Composed of about 20,000 young men, they provided intelligence and logistical support to the FAB. The CNDD/FDD-Nkurunziza created a militia called the *Militants Combattants*, which was also composed of young people. However, besides providing intelligence and logistical support, members were also responsible for relaying political messages to local populations and ensuring their support for the CNDD/FDD cause. The *Militants Combattants* is reported to comprise about 10,000 individuals. Both groups qualified for reintegration benefits under earlier DDR programmes, although they were not deemed eligible for the full DDR package.

9 This set of agreements and the subsequent October 2002 ceasefire include a ceasefire agreement between the transitional government and two small dissident factions of the CNDD/FDD (the CNDD-FDD-Jean Bosco Ndayikengurukiye) and Palipehutu/FNL (Palipehutu/FNL-Alain Mugabarabona).

10 Dated 2 December 2004.

11 See 'Technical annex for a proposed grant of SDR 22.2 million (US$33 million equivalent) to Republic of Burundi for an Emergency Demobilization, Reintegration and Reinsertion Program' (MDRP Burundi, 24 February 2004).

12 Dated 9 November 2004, the JOP outlines a comprehensive set of procedures and mechanisms for the disarmament, screening for military integration and demobilization of members of APPMs. It also defines the roles and responsibilities of the actors involved in this process. The JOP was elaborated by a technical working group comprising the ES/NCDRR, MDRP secretariat, AMIB, UNICEF and ONUB.

13 UN Peacebuilding Fund, 'Annual Report on Burundi' (2009).

14 Part of the reason why disarmament was not included in the programme is because the World Bank/MDRP did not have the mandate to tackle this issue. The government was responsible for the disarmament of the *Gardiens de la Paix* and the *combattants militants*, with AMIB serving as observers. The disarmament of FDN personnel in stage I of the

programme was undertaken by the FDN itself, prior to transport to the demobilisation centres.

15 Split into 12,916 ex-FAB, 6,457 ex-CNDD/FDD and 3,152 from other APPMs. This includes 2,161 child soldiers (49 girls) and 516 women. For additional information see Executive Summary of NCDRR report, 'Réalisation du PNDRR dans le domaine de la Démobilisation, du Désarmement et du Démantèlement des milices', September 2008.

16 Comprising 1,255 weapons, 245 grenades, two mines and 68 self-made guns, called *mugobore*. The FDN was tasked with retrieving the weapons of the *Guardiens de la Paix*, while ONUB was involved in collecting the weapons of the *combattants militants*. Source: Interim report from the executive secretariat of the National Commission for Demobilisation, Reinsertion and Reintegration of former combatants, September 2008.

17 Pyt Douma, Jean Marie Gasana and Leontine Specker, eds., 'Reintegration in Burundi: between happy cows and lost investment' (Clingendael, 2009).

18 See also Willy Nindorera and Kristiana Powell, 'Security Sector Reform in Burundi: Issues and Challenges for Improving Civilian Protection', CENAP/NSI Working Paper (Ottawa: Centre d'Alerte et de Prévention des Conflits, Bujumbura, and North-South Institute, 2007).

19 Executive Summary of NCDRR report, note 15 above.

20 On 16 December the census had reached 94 per cent of its plan, and 16,038 persons had been registered. Source: International Center for Transitional Justice.

21 See Nindorera and Powell, note 18 above.

22 'Plan Quinquennal du Ministère de la Défense et des Anciens Combattants', 2006, and the 'Plan National Stratégique, 2007-2017, Police Nationale du Burundi', 4 April 2008.

23 Stéphanie Pézard and Nicolas Florquin, 'Small Arms in Burundi: Disarming the Civilian Population in Peacetime' (Bujumbera: Ligue Iteka, 2007).

24 Interview with member of Parliamentary Defence and Security Commission, 22 September 2008.

25 See Article 171/5 of the Constitution.

26 The presidents of both the Parliamentary and the Senate Defence and Security Commissions are members of the steering committee for the police census and identification programme.

27 The Ministry of Public Security used to be the Ministry of Interior and Public Security, which was split into the Ministry of Interior and the Ministry of Public Security in 2007.

28 PBF funds have been used more to support SSR than DDR to date.

29 See World Bank offical website, www.worldbank.org.

30 AMIB was assigned the following tasks: to ensure the liaison between the belligerents; to verify the implementation of the agreement provisions; to facilitate the activities of the JCC; to facilitate the movements of the combatants to the assembly areas; and to support DDR activities (primarily disarmament) and the verification process.

31 The Security Council, with Resolution 1545 of 21 May 2004, decided to establish ONUB in order to support and help implement the efforts undertaken by Burundians to restore lasting peace and bring about national reconciliation, as provided under the Arusha Agreement. See www.un.org.

32 See Peacebuilding Fund official website: www.unpbf.org.

33 The SSR workshop was held on 5–7 December 2008 and included more than 30 representatives from various local institutions and the donor community. See report on the OECD official website: www.oecd.org.

34 Interviews with PNB officers and communal administrators, 21–28 September 2008.

35 The International Center for Transitional Justice census and identification of police personnel programme has tried to access the DDR database to check for potential presence of demobilised combatants in the police database, but the incompatibility of data formats did not allow the verification.

36 Interviews with a PBF programme officer, 18 September 2008, and a bilateral donor programme officer, 21 September 2008.

37 See Fourth UN Report of the Secretary-General on the UN Integrated Office in Burundi, 28 November 2008, S/2008/745.

38 The high number of combatants integrated in a short period of time did not allow the management to maintain proper control over the entire personnel (no reliable personnel database). As a result, many individuals who report crimes implicate 'men in uniform', who could be either police officers or bandits dressing as police officers, with little risk of being identified by other police officers.

39 'Malgré la sensibilisation et les explications à l'endroit des candidats à la démobilisation, les démobilisés partent avec beaucoup d'angoisse et d'amertume causées par l'incertitude dans leur avenir.' See MDRP (2007) 'Ex-combatant in Burundi: Why They Joined, Why They Left, How They Fared', Working Paper No. 3, October , MDRP.

40 Numbers reported during interviews varied between four to six times the previous salary.

41 This included three sets of elections: communal, legislative/senatorial and presidential.

42 See Nindorera and Powell, note 18 above.

43 Interviews with senior PNB officer, 17 September 2008, and local analyst, 25 September 2008.

44 In Burundi, the World Bank was under considerable pressure from donors to have the DDR process targeted only at ex-combatants and therefore with a short-term security focus.

45 Interviews with former combatants and communal administrators, 19–24 December 2008.

46 See Douma, Gasana and Specker, eds., note 17 above.

47 In 2007 the government of Tanzania decided to put an end to the long-standing issue of an estimated 218,000 Burundian refugees who had been there since 1972; 46,000 of these refugees chose to return to Burundi, while the remaining opted to settle definitively in Tanzania. See report on the UNHCR official website: www.UNHCR.org.

48 Interview at the Commission Nationale de Terres et autres Biens.

49 As mentioned before, this approach reflects World Bank policy in the Burundian context.

50 It should also be noted that as of mid-2008 the NCDRR was actually under investigation for alleged fraud and corruption, resulting in the subsequent dismissal of the NCDRR leadership.

51 Interview with a former combatant, 17 December 2008.

52 Interview with a member of the commission, 22 September 2008.

53 Interview with a representative of Crisisgroup, 11 December 2008.

54 For a comprehensive description of small arms proliferation in Burundi see Stéphanie Pézard and Nicolas Florquin, 'Small Arms in Burundi: Disarming the Civilian Population in Peacetime', study by the Small Arms Survey and the Ligue Iteka, Special Report No.7 (Geneva: Small Arms Survey 2007).

55 Such as Iteka and the Centre d'Encadrement et de Développement de Anciens Combattants.

56 Projet de contrôle des armes légères et de désarmement civil (2007–2008), UNDP.

57 Small Arms Survey, note 54 above.

58 For a more detailed overview of DDR and transitional justice linkages in general, see Ana Cutter Patel, 'Transitional Justice and DDR', in *Security and Post-Conflict Reconstruction, Dealing with Fighters in the Aftermath of War*, ed. Robert Muggah, (London: Routledge, 2008).

59 See 'Report of the UN Assessment Mission on the Establishment of an International Judicial Commission of Inquiry for Burundi' (Kalomoh Report), 11 March 2005.

60 During her visit to Burundi in May 2007, Louise Arbour, HCHR, negotiated with the government the need to conduct a national consultation on transitional justice mechanisms.

61 Effective authority means that the vetting process can be applied to all personnel, in the knowledge that in a conflict no side can claim clean records for all its members. For more information on vetting see Alexander Mayer-Rieckh and Pablo De Greiff, 'Justice as Prevention: Vetting Public Employees in Societies in Transition', Social Science Research Council, 2007; available at www.ssrc.org.

62 In 2004 Burundi was ranked the sixteenth most affected country in the world, and the second most affected in Africa. ONUSIDA, 'Country Progress Report – Burundi', *Le point sur l'épidémie de SIDA* (Geneva: ONUSIDA, 2006).

63 See Stephane Mora, 'La Réforme du Secteur de la Sécurité au Burundi: Coordination des acteurs internationaux, prise en compte des besoins et des préoccupations des communautés au sein de leurs programmes et liens avec d'autres processus clés associés à la réforme du secteur de la sécurité', (European Union Initiative for Peacebuilding, November 2008). Available at www.initiativeforpeacebuilding.eu.

64 In addition, at least three other coordination mechanisms within the security sector must be noted. The Ministry of Public Security set up the *Cellule Mixte de Coordination de la Coopération Internationale du Secteur de la Sécurité Publique* in June 2008, a mixed body to coordinate international assistance primarily to the police. Another coordination body was created by establishing a department inside the Burundi National Police to coordinate training within the police, mainly provided through international assistance. On its side, the EU organised two informal information meetings with its member states, dedicated to security issues.

65 'Technical Annex for a Proposed Grant of SDR22.2 Million (US$33 Million Equivalent) to Republic of Burundi for a Demobilization, Reinsertion and Reintegration Program', Report T7616-BU, February 2004.

66 See Stephane Mora, note 63 above.

67 Interview with IMF official, 18 September 2008.

68 See Ženja Bašagic, 'UN Integration in Burundi in the Context of the Peacebuilding Office BINUB' (New York: Best Practices Section/UNDPKO, February 2008).

69 See www.unpbf.org/burundi/burundi-projects.shtml.

70 For more information see World Bank, 'Burundi – Burundi Emergency Demobilization, Reinsertion and Reintegration Program', Report AB403, updated project information document (Washington, DC: World Bank, 18 March, 2004).

71 See MDRP, note 39 above; Small Arms Survey, note 54 above; interview with Clingendael Institute team of consultants doing research on DDR, 28 September 2008.

72 Interview with communal administrators, 26 September 2008.

Chapter 4

The Central African Republic

Boubacar N'Diaye

Introduction

After many years of uncertainty pervaded by the threat of armed violence, the political and armed opposition groups, the sitting government and the partners of the Central African Republic (CAR) finally signed an agreement to launch a comprehensive reconciliation process in December 2008. This Political Inclusive Dialogue (PID) was made possible, in large part, by the heavy investment of the CAR's international partners. The agreement sustains the hope that the country will turn the page on violent conflict and debilitating political instability. For all parties involved in the process, this means concluding the stalled efforts surrounding disarmament, demobilization and reintegration (DDR) and security sector reform (SSR), critical processes both for security and longer term development.

The CAR is uniquely qualified as a case study of both the necessity of DDR and SSR and the linkages between them. Recurrent security crises fuelled by poor governance, military coups, ethnicization of the armed forces, rebellions, attendant widespread proliferation of small arms and light weapons, and dysfunctional institutions are all elements of the CAR's unstable security situation. This need has been explicitly and solemnly expressed in a national seminar on SSR held in April 2008. The necessity of such a seminar was impressed on national actors by their international partners. Arguably, the first expression of the need for SSR and DDR was indigenous and can be found in the recommendations contained in '*Les États généraux de la Défense Nationale en République Centrafricaine*' (national conversations on defence) held in Bangui from August to September 1996 following the April and May mutinies of the same year.[1] One of the recommendations specifically referred to the disarmament of militias and armed groups and the recovery of small arms that were already circulating among the population. This was just one of the measures aimed at addressing what was understood to be an utterly dysfunctional security apparatus.

Instability became a permanent feature of the CAR throughout the 1990s and early 2000s. Following the mutinies, looting of arms depots, rampages of armed groups coming from neighbouring countries and coup attempts, general disarmament and reform of the FACA (*Forces Armées de Centrafrique*) became a recurrent theme and an important objective of the political discourse. This was most clearly expressed by the 2003 letter of general political orientation, defence matters and DDR issued by the government shortly after General Bozizé came to power, and more generally during the 2003 national dialogue meeting. Subsequent measures included the creation of the *Commission Nationale de Désarmement, Démobilisation, et Réinsertion* (CNDDR) and the adoption in February 2004 of PRAC (*Projet de Réinsertion des ex-combattants et d'Appui aux Communautés*), a national programme aimed at reinserting former combatants and providing assistance to the communities affected by conflict. The international community supported these efforts with US$13.3 million, of which nearly three-quarters came from the Multi-Country Demobilization and Reintegration Program (MDRP).

A study conducted in 2006 noted the absence of a linkage between DDR and SSR, and recommended that this connection be acknowledged and acted on.[2] Since then, awareness of their interconnections has risen sharply; indeed, the various agreements, and especially the 2008 national seminar on SSR, have explicitly posited the linkage. One of the objectives of this study is to examine more closely the DDR experiment in the CAR and extract lessons learned, specifically concerning the nexus with SSR. The roles of key stakeholders will be addressed with a special focus on the UN system. At the heart of the case study is an examination of the challenges faced in the CAR and the question of whether lessons can be learned and translated into action. Lastly, this study will examine whether the accepted principles for designing and implementing DDR/SSR programmes have been integrated into the ongoing efforts in the CAR.

Context for DDR and SSR

Political and security context

The CAR gained international sovereignty on 13 August 1960, under the leadership of President David Dacko, the nephew of the nationalist pre-independence leader Barthelemy Boganda who died in a plane crash. From the start of his presidency, Dacko's power was contested by a vocal political opposition both within and outside the dominant political party, MESAN (*Mouvement pour l'Evolution Sociale de l'Afrique Noire*).[3] In response to this opposition, President Dacko resorted to violent repression to consolidate his power. It can be argued that this fateful set of circumstances set the scene for the political landscape in the CAR for the next five decades. Beginning with a coup d'état on 1 January 1966, carried out by then army chief of staff Colonel Jean-Bedel Bokassa, the CAR entered a period of political turmoil that persists to this day. Social and economic development, durable peace and stability have continued to elude this 623,000 km^2 resource-rich country of only 4 million people, despite the continued involvement of the international community, particularly in recent years.

The post-colonial history of the CAR has been marked by exceedingly poor leadership. Violence and arms have been the preferred means of gaining political power among a narrowly based political and military elite marked by regional and ethnic divisions with ideological overtones. Since March 2003, General François Bozizé appears to have gained the upper hand after a successful externally backed rebellion. His power was legitimised by the relatively free and fair elections organised in 2005. However, repeated efforts to bring lasting stability to the CAR by means of a national dialogue with a heteroclite armed and political opposition have been futile. The years of political violence, mass repressions and zero-sum politics resulting from coups, mutinies, rebellions and the political and ethnic manipulation of the armed forces have left lasting scars. It has proven extremely difficult for the CAR's elite to overcome the innumerable obstacles facing the country.

The CAR's chronic security crises have stemmed from a combination of factors, including dysfunctional and politicised armed forces and a neglect of the population's needs by the fractious and irresponsive civilian and military elites in power. Across successive regimes, the state has not met the needs of the average citizen. Thus, one of the most critical challenges has been how to overcome the severe crisis of confidence that has developed between the population, the state (represented by frequently changing fractions of the elite) and the security forces. DDR and SSR initiatives are likely to be met with cynicism and deep mistrust. Attempts at 'normalizing' the situation in the CAR are seen by the public simply as creating opportunity for national elites to misuse their power. The cynicism and lack of trust of the population in the national authorities are deeply felt.

The resolution of political disputes, the easing of social and economic frustrations and the nurturing of security sector institutions which will reduce the possibility of a resumption of violent conflict are all still merely objectives. Thus the sense of *éternel recommencement* by which many interlocutors characterise any attempts at change in the CAR constitutes an important challenge to successful DDR and SSR. Another critical challenge is the CAR's strong dependence on the international community and the difficulty that seems to exist for national actors to take matters into their own hands. While it is true that years of instability and poor management of national resources have put great financial strain on the government, this pervasive dependency complex is truly debilitating. The reality is that the CAR is in dire financial straits and cannot be expected to contribute financially to DDR and SSR efforts at this time. Unrealistic expectations regarding the available possibilities can prove problematic and undermine the collective efforts to carry on the process, especially in its early stages.

The post-2005 election environment was complicated by poverty, regional instability and unsettled political disputes with a partially armed opposition. Other challenges to DDR and SSR stem directly from this predicament. DDR was initially perceived as an opportunity for a large number of impoverished young urban dwellers to address their poor conditions, whether or not they qualified as combatants. It was also seized by some as an opportunity to make money, thus placing further strains on the DDR of genuine combatants and their dependants. The availability and ubiquity of small arms constitute another major problem in a region dominated by armed conflict; already plentiful within the national territory, weapons can circulate and be recycled region-wide and remain available for the next conflict. Finally, notwithstanding the thrust of the November 2003 general political orientation letter, with the armed forces fractional and without a national identity in a country marked by various mutinies, any attempt to design a new security equilibrium (DDR and SSR aims) was seen as threatening to the fledgling Bozizé regime. The national police was not as critical in keeping the regime in power, but the neglect and mismanagement it suffers from is such that it requires substantial rebuilding. Other practical challenges include the need to address the Zaraguinas phenomenon, which has resulted in the proliferation of independent armed groups unwilling to engage with the state under peaceful circumstances. The Zaraguinas, also called *coupeurs de route*, are bands of cattle thieves who occasionally abduct the children of wealthy cattle herders for ransom.

One of the most important developments since Bozizé's election in 2005 has been the PID, its resulting agreement and the Libreville agreement as apolitical statements of the political class (armed or not) on how to resolve the instability and insecurity that have gripped the country for so long. Both agreements explicitly link DDR and SSR and include a timetable to pursue both, with parties committing to specific activities. For example, the agreements include clauses that commit the FACA to integrating elements of demobilised former combatants who qualify. Similarly, various armed opposition groups committed themselves to making lists of their combatants and disarming and assembling them in designated areas. The language of both agreements seems to acknowledge the mistakes committed in the previous major DDR project (PRAC) and from the lack of progress in SSR.

DDR overview

The efforts made in DDR are a reflection of the rapidly evolving political context. Soon after securing control of the capital, General Bozizé set out to garner support among various actors, particularly the international community, to foster stability. The November 2003 general political orientation letter captures that intention, emphasizing the necessity of DDR *and* SSR. This letter was an attempt by the newly installed Bozizé regime to reach out to the international community, particularly development partners such as the World Bank and the IMF, and establish its *bona fides* as a regime genuinely committed to reforms and tackling the numerous challenges facing the country. The Bozizé government therefore moved quickly to implement DDR. A number of activities aimed at achieving this objective and improving the chances of sustaining a secure and stable environment were carried out. Chief among these was the establishment of the inter-ministerial CNDDR. Closer to the ground and aimed at implementing DDR activities was the externally funded PRAC programme. These were the main national DDR mechanisms.

DDR in the CAR has achieved mixed results, although without the support of the UN system the outcome would certainly have been much less remarkable. This is not to discount the notable achievement of the PRAC. According to the executive secretary of the *Commission Nationale pour le Désarmement et le Réinsertion* (which is the successor to the CNDDR), as of late February 2007 the programme had demobilised 7,565 former combatants (the number targeted), implemented 40 community micro-projects and collected 297 weapons and related items.[4] According to some estimates there were 50,000 small arms and light weapons (SALW) in circulation in the CAR in the mid-2000s.[5]

SSR overview

When the Bozizé government included SSR in its programme, the concept and its implications may not have been thoroughly understood. While the 2008 national seminar – and to a lesser extent the 2006 seminar – explored, explained and vulgarised the concept, in 2005 it may have been understood mainly as a limited opportunity to revamp the capabilities of the various components of the armed forces, reduce the number of troops and instil in them greater professionalism and discipline. It certainly did not imply more democratic control and genuine democratic governance. Since then, SSR and its implications are most certainly better understood, in particular its comprehensive nature (for example, the need to reform all the branches of the security sector) and the need for democratic oversight and control. Of course, carrying it out has been another matter and, given the particularly challenging environment, it is not surprising that to date there has been no real reform of the security sector. At best, with the strong backing and mentorship of its international partners, the country has been preparing itself for this arduous process. After the overthrow of the Patassé regime, restructuring activities were carried out within the gendarmerie with the assistance of France, and a few other activities regarding the FACA and the police by other external partners such as BONUCA (*Bureau de l'Organization des Nations Unies en Centrafrique*) and FOMUC (*Force Multinationale en Centrafrique*). However, these actions did not amount to SSR. What these initiatives and other awareness-raising activities did achieve was to impress upon national actors the critical importance of furthering and embracing SSR.

Since the national seminar on SSR and the Political Inclusive Dialogue, the CNDDR has become the anchor of DDR and SSR activities. It was headed by General Antoine Gambi, who was also the 'global defence'[6] special adviser to the head of state and national coordinator of the newly established Secretariat Technique Permanent (STP).[7] In this triple capacity, General Gambi became the embodiment of this integrated approach to DDR and SSR as well as providing the interface with the international community. The STP interfaces permanently with an eight-member international group of experts set up by the CAR's international partners and tasked with steering SSR (and DDR as its logical first step) following the security-related decisions in the PID and Libreville agreements, and the solemn commitment to carrying out the recommendations of the April 2008 national seminar on SSR. The socio-economic implications of these programmes are gradually being recognised, and SSR is now a central component of the strategic document for poverty reduction.

Key actors

As the post-conflict framework took shape in 2003, the main national stakeholders involved in DDR and SSR were essentially General François Bozizé, head of state; the remnants of the armed forces of the CAR; rebel opposition groups; and militias and armed groups with no political agenda. In addition to the UN system and other international institutions whose role became central (the IMF, World Bank, European Union), France, as the former colonial power, can be considered a major actor given its long-standing role in security issues in the CAR. Indeed, France was the main partner in the restructuring of the armed forces, gendarmerie and national police. There is a French advisory presence at all levels of the security apparatus, in addition to regular troops stationed in the country. More recently, South Africa has also become an actor. Given the role each played in previous crises, neighbouring countries (Chad and Sudan in particular, and to lesser extent the DRC and the Republic of Congo) are considered significant. The Economic and Monetary Community of Central Africa (CEMAC) has deployed troops, been active in DDR and been a facilitator of national dialogue.

The severity of the CAR's security situation prompted a heavy, sustained and multiform involvement of its international partners. The most visible form of international involvement in the quest for stability in the CAR has been the establishment of numerous peace operations. MISAB[8] (*Mission Interafricaine de Surveillance des Accords de Bangui*) was set up by the former Organization of African Unity with the financial support of France following the 1996 mutiny. MISAB was soon followed by a UN peacekeeping operation, MINURCA (*Mission des Nations Unies en République Centrafricaine*, 1998–2000),[9] subsequently replaced by a peacebuilding mission, BONUCA (2000–present)[10] and finally the CEMAC-sponsored FOMUC.[11] All the operations involved the dispatch of soldiers and/or considerable logistical means to monitor agreements and help stabilise the volatile security situation. In 2008 MINURCAT (*Mission des Nations Unies en République Centrafricaine et Tchad*) was mandated by the UN Security Council to monitor and stabilise the volatile area along the borders between the CAR and Chad. Concomitantly, the CAR's Central African neighbouring states have been attempting to set up a security-focused organization (MICOPAX) to shoulder their part of stabilization efforts, including joint border patrols and similar security-enhancing activities. The CAR's other development partners, such as the World Bank (through the MDRP), also became involved in stabilization efforts, most of which rightly focus on a broadly construed concept of security including DDR and SSR, but also macroeconomic growth and poverty alleviation.

Until the release of the Secretary-General's report on security sector reform[12] in January 2008, the United Nations lacked a definition of SSR and an overarching framework for a common UN approach. It is not surprising, therefore, that the security-related activities of the UN system in the CAR did not until very recently reflect SSR concerns and specific concepts, much less their linkage with DDR.

Since the army mutinies, coup attempts and multiplication of armed militias in the mid-1990s, the CAR has employed various weapons collection programmes in which the UN system played a major role. In 1997 UNDP, a major development partner present since 1976, attempted to support the downsizing of the country's armed forces. There has always been a relationship between the number of people under arms, whether under the control of the state or in more or less organised armed groups, and the widespread availability and circulation of SALW. As evidenced in the PID discussions, armed groups justify their existence and their right to use arms as a response to the repressive behaviour of the state security sector. The various mutinies and looting of arms stocks by members of the FACA – who, because they were poorly paid, if at all, sold weapons to anyone who could pay for them – also contributed to the widespread availability of SALW among the populace. It was therefore evident that any programme to collect these weapons must include a dimension that focuses on the FACA. In 1998 MINURCA continued the SALW collection activities begun by MISAB. UNDP also started a weapons collection campaign in 2002. However, the most comprehensive DDR project in which the UN system participated was the three-year PRAC programme. UNDP funded and supervised the programme. The security crises also led to the creation of a UN office in the CAR, BONUCA. Set up in 2000, BONUCA was involved in a variety of activities contributing to DDR and the overall fostering of political stability and security (including police training, human rights and good governance promotion and political and technical advice). Overall, the UN system played an important part in engaging the country on the path of DDR and SSR. The United Nations pushed for the national seminar on SSR, in addition to helping to create a political environment conducive to the implementation of DDR In particular, UNDP played a critical role in building capacity to support the national seminar. A number of measures are pending, including the establishment of coordination and monitoring bodies in the political sector and at the technical level to play their part in the realization of DDR/SSR commitments. However, the explicit linkage between DDR and SSR in the activities of the UN system is a recent development. As discussed below in further detail, the initial lack of a comprehensive approach to SSR made DDR the main focus of UN action.

As its supervising role within PRAC indicates, UNDP has been the lead agency on DDR and (to some extent) also SSR issues in the CAR. Within UNDP, the Governance and Crisis Prevention unit is the structure typically charged with the management and implementation of relevant programmes and projects. The unit manages a portfolio of projects that are executed in a variety of areas in support of the CAR government's socio-economic development efforts. These programmes are carried out on the ground, sometimes in conflict-affected communities, through NGOs. Programmes focus on rule of law, human rights and security, activities aimed at rehabilitating court buildings in the provinces as well as helping citizens, especially women, gain access to justice. Other projects seek to improve prison conditions and rehabilitate women convicts. These programmes contribute to the overall improvement of the most disadvantaged and also help lessen the likelihood of conflict. They would certainly be more effective if they were part of an integrated approach to DDR and SSR. There is no doubt that there is awareness of the relationship between DDR and SSR, and that the experience of PRAC in this regard and the lessons it holds are not lost on the unit.

BONUCA supports DDR/SSR-related activities as a facilitator and enabler, thanks to the high profile of the special representative of the UN Secretary-General and his access to the highest authorities of the country. BONUCA's involvement in fostering good governance and better policing in the CAR (with insistence on human rights), as well as advising stakeholders in the various crises, gave it a crucial role in complementing the more project-oriented activities of UNDP.

The DDR/SSR Nexus in the CAR

It is now accepted that many DDR programmes have failed in part because those who conceptualised them did not take into account that in order to reduce the probability of former combatants taking up arms again, their harmonious integration into the regular armed forces may be the best option. Similarly, some civil conflicts' origins can be found in the mistreatment of entire segments of a population by unprofessional armed and security forces. Decommissioning combatants must be accompanied by efforts to correct certain behaviours likely to trigger conflict. DDR is therefore intimately linked to SSR in that both must be conceived as part of an overall post-conflict stabilization and long-term recovery programme. In examining the relationship between DDR and SSR in the CAR it is necessary to analyse aspects of the main DDR programme, i.e. PRAC, to determine the extent to which it took into consideration the precepts and prescriptions of SSR. As a new phase of the efforts to extricate the CAR from its security predicament gets under way, it is also necessary to examine the extent to which the emerging DDR/SSR framework integrates these two concepts and implements lessons from past experience. The 'new phase' refers to the political environment created after the SSR national seminar, the adoption of bold statements and resolutions to implement SSR and the recent decisions of the PID emphasizing the linkage between DDR and SSR. In the national seminar, the Libreville accord and the PID agreement, the government and its counterparts in the armed and political opposition agreed to specific activities that explicitly link DDR and SSR. The CAR decision-makers have committed themselves to carrying out these decisions according to a clear timetable with short and long-term objectives and deadline actions.

In order to put this analysis into perspective, it is important to recall that PRAC was implemented without a formal ceasefire, with belligerents unwilling to move toward peace and with particularly ill-prepared national partners. More importantly, 90% of the programme was funded through MDRP. This funding reflected the dominant thinking at the time that only strictly 'DDR' operations were to be carried out with the nearly express exclusion of 'SSR.' The concept of SSR was still emerging and was somewhat misunderstood and controversial. Therefore although most theoreticians and practitioners of SSR had already posited as self-evident the necessary linkage with DDR, it was not clearly articulated. The role of the UN system, particularly the UNDP in the most prominent DDR programme must therefore be analysed in this light.

Although PRAC is now severely criticised because of its poor financial management, in many ways it was an innovative DDR programme in its support to conflict-affected communities. It was intended to carry out important post-conflict operations, while ensuring that communities affected by conflict were also beneficiaries of disarmament and demobilization. In other words, PRAC was intended to link DDR to community-centred development. Indeed, 40 community projects resulted from PRAC.[13] The programme's main activities deemed mutually sustaining are listed below:

- Disarmament of civilians holding weapons;
- Demobilization of combatants and their return to their communities;
- Strengthening the capabilities of communities to reintegrate ex-combatants harmoniously;
- Support to most-affected communities to alleviate the effects of insecurity;
- Strengthening security sector governance locally.

While all these objectives can be considered part and parcel of any comprehensive post-conflict SSR programme, they were not approached as such. It has been argued that PRAC was a 'cut and paste' of DDR practice that might have worked elsewhere but was not necessarily adapted to the realities of the CAR situation. A close look at many of PRAC's activities would suggest that these did not reflect SSR imperatives, nor, for that matter, sound DDR practices. To emphasise this point, while the November 2003 general political orientation letter to the newly installed regime did mention SSR as a necessity, the DDR programme it subscribed to was designed without any reference to it. This was the first lost opportunity to link the two concepts in practice. DDR, though clearly necessary, was pursued as a free-standing cure to the country's ills. However, whether or not the authors of the general political orientation letter were being disingenuous when they mentioned the need for SSR (assuming its implications were clearly understood), the context in which the document was issued was certainly not propitious. There was no democratically elected government, and though the need for SSR was not debatable, given the utter dysfunction of the security sector, the necessary steps to launch a comprehensive SSR process (building buy-in from the ground up, for example, and involving other domestic actors) were not taken. Finally, it was doubtful that the conception of security implied in the SSR concept was compatible with the political calculations and objectives of a newly installed power. The implementation of DDR through PRAC was conducted almost in abstraction of the institutional dynamics of the CAR state and some of its most pressing needs.

Another aspect of PRAC that contributed to the delinking of DDR and SSR was that the national team in charge of steering the programme was not sufficiently trained to carry out all aspects of DDR. There appears to have been no deliberate plan to transfer competence and expertise to CAR nationals involved in the programme. They had even less understanding of SSR, since this was also the case for the non-nationals responsible for supervising them and guiding their actions. The linkage could not even be established as a by-product of actions and suggestions that might have been influenced by 'SSR thinking' among international experts involved in PRAC.

Critical dimensions of SSR clearly had an impact on other dimensions of PRAC operations, but they were often not taken into account due to lack of thinking in terms of this relationship. The following sections look at some of the issue areas related to DDR and SSR in the CAR.

DDR and the FACA

As per MDRP guiding principles, PRAC demobilization was limited to ex-combatants who did not belong to state-controlled armed forces (a very relative term in the context of the time). While some of these disarmed ex-combatants were supposed to join the regular armed forces, many aspired to leave them. The guidelines and their outcome were clearly a disservice to well-rounded post-conflict DDR, not to mention SSR. As noted earlier, an inter-ministerial body, the CNDDR, was tasked with overseeing the activities of PRAC. To carry out its oversight duties, the CNDDR was divided into two subcommittees in charge of disarmament and demobilization activities and reinsertion activities respectively. SSR was once again noticeably absent from the agenda. Consequently, the limited mandate of PRAC and the 'red line' preventing it from dealing with 'regular' forces – although these most definitely needed DDR as much as any militia or rebel group troops – meant that the FACA and the national police were left almost entirely unchanged throughout the life of PRAC. In the case of the gendarmerie, France did manage to alter the status quo, although it did not change the security framework as a whole.

PRAC and the national police

Of all the 'regular' security bodies, it is arguably the police force that has been most affected by the absence of SSR. With aged, ill-equipped, unprofessional and demoralised personnel, it has still not recovered from the neglect, looting and destruction of its equipment and offices. Since there was no parallel process concerning the main security bodies, their dysfunctions persisted, when some of them could have been addressed through the exposure that PRAC enjoyed as the main, if not only, post-conflict security game in town. This also goes for the intelligence services, which will have to be reformed if the security sector is to be managed democratically.

DDR/SSR and gender

Because men, women, boys and girls are differently affected by violence and its consequences, in the CAR, as in other post-conflict countries, no DDR and SSR can succeed if the gender dimension is ignored. The central role of women in rebuilding communities is widely acknowledged. During the recurring violent conflict and on numerous occasions, women were targeted by rape and brutality, particularly in 2002 and 2003. The UN Office for the Coordination of Humanitarian Affairs reported in 2007 that 'sexual and gender-based violence strikes well over 15 percent of women and girls' in northern CAR. Some women also took part in armed conflict as combatants. The various programmes, particularly those targeting communities that UNDP has supported, include an important gender-focused dimension. During the April 2008 seminar, gender was addressed as a part of the discussion on 'the role of the media, civil society and gender dimensions'. The issue presents, of course, specific challenges for DDR and SSR, if only because, according to the national SSR seminar final report, over 10 per cent of demobilised combatants were women. UNDP supported these DDR efforts both financially and technically through its special programme in support of PRAC. While PRAC is credited for taking into account the needs of women, either former combatants, dependants of combatants or victims of insecurity, the financial difficulties that besieged it forced a drastic cut in efforts to address the special needs of affected women. The complaints raised against this aspect of the PRAC experiment have been renewed as a new round of DDR is set to start. UNDP has carried out programmes targeting women as part of its assistance to the CAR government in its four priority areas. BONUCA also has a human rights and gender-specific issues officer on its staff. The extent to which these efforts have contributed to enhancing the gender dimension of DDR/SSR remains to be seen. A scheme that earmarks funds for integrating female ex-combatants associated with armed groups into restructured and reformed state security bodies could help establish and strengthen the linkage between DDR and SSR through gender. While the national seminar discussed the issue of gender extensively, there did not seem to be much emphasis put on the gender dimension in the PID and Libreville agreements. Many women's rights advocates within civil society continue to maintain that women are still excluded from significant decision-making frameworks and bodies that deal with security issues.

DDR/SSR and SALW

By 2003, a massive number of small arms and light weapons was in circulation in the CAR. In PRAC, the second 'D' indicated disarmament of combatants, with the explicit exclusion of non-combatants. The assumption was that the some 7,500 individuals targeted for demobilization had one weapon. As mentioned above, the number of weapons recovered was very low even as a function of PRAC's own expectations. The issue of small arms and its impact on (political and criminal) insecurity was largely ignored because there was no wider SSR framework. In its post-PRAC activities, UNDP funded the Security for Development project, limited to the eight Bangui precincts, which came to an end in 2008. The Small Arms and Light Weapons project is currently continuing these activities. In both the SSR seminar and agreements to stabilise the country, the issue of small arms was considered critical to post-conflict stabilization and the re-establishment of security.

DDR and security sector oversight bodies

The parliament was kept out of any supervisory role in the DDR activities conducted by PRAC. While some civil society organizations followed these activities and were occasionally consulted, post-2003 DDR was mainly the responsibility of (some) state entities. As a result, yet another SSR principle was not taken into consideration. However, this major flaw seems to have been addressed in the SSR seminar process and its decisions, as well as in the PID agreement. The roles of both the parliament and non-statutory actors in civil society were discussed and recognised as critical to both DDR and SSR.

DDR/SSR and transitional justice

The pre-trial hearings in January 2009 for Jean-Pierre Bemba[14] and his continued detention in The Hague brought to the fore a critical aspect of the nexus between DDR, SSR and other post-conflict peacebuilding activities. Should those who committed crimes including rape and murder be forgiven, or should they be held accountable for their actions? The rampaging troops of the accused Bemba coming to the rescue of the besieged President Patassé in 2002 certainly resulted in egregious war crimes. While more recently a consensus was reached granting amnesty from national prosecution, when DDR was first implemented there was no attention paid to these sensitive issues and no process for the compensation of victims or retribution for atrocities. For many, the issues of justice, impunity and compensation to victims will continue to be silent but contentious, particularly for the victims of war crimes. However, for transitional justice to be possible, the judicial system needed to be functional, which wasn't and still isn't the case in the CAR. Transitional justice requires adequate human and financial resources. It also requires a penal system capable of absorbing – and rehabilitating – those found guilty of crimes. Only more recently has tackling this situation been acknowledged as a formal part of the SSR process.

Challenges and Lessons

By the end of 2008 the CAR had entered a new phase with the signature of a number of agreements between armed opposition groups and the CAR government. These agreements were very much informed by SSR commitments made during the national seminar. Indeed, considerable efforts were made by the CAR's international partners, particularly the United Nations, to ensure a high degree of coordination between the various documents signed between the parties and monitoring the implementation of decisions. Central Africans have also increased their awareness of the need to fulfil their commitments and make the SSR/DDR process their own. It can be said that with these activities, the CAR has entered a critical juncture in its efforts to turn the page on conflict and instability. This makes it even more important for CAR actors themselves, first and foremost, but also their partners, to ensure that this is not just another attempt that will end in frustration, disillusionment and further instability. Undoubtedly, one of the most critical challenges is to get the process, particularly DDR, right. What is particularly unsettling is that many of the candidates for DDR were already involved with the PRAC DDR process, while others, unable to see the effect of the commitments made in previous peace agreements, simply returned to the bush. Hopefully, the dire consequences of failure will ensure that past mistakes are not repeated and that DDR is closely tied to a long-term SSR process.

This section highlights some of the challenges and lessons learned in supporting the DDR/SSR nexus and sets the tone for the recommendations listed in the conclusion.

Coherence

On paper, DDR has been linked to SSR measures such as restructuring the FACA and national police and resurrecting the judicial system. The challenge now is to ensure that in carrying out the various activities, a high degree of coherence is maintained, particularly when it comes to integrating ex-combatants into the FACA and other state security bodies such as the national police. The *Commission Nationale pour le Désarmement et le Réinsertion*, the *Secretariat Technique Permanent*, the international partners' *comité pluridisciplinaire* and the regular meetings between them seem to indicate a keen awareness of the need to ensure cohesion. The international community's acknowledgement of this challenge and its efforts to meet it are reflected in the specific measures called for in the timetable emerging from the national seminar. One example is the insistence that recruitment in the FACA should be multi-ethnic, multi-provincial and include about 10 per cent of former combatants. In practice, however, there does not seem to have been any specific national commitment to this figure. Another linkage can be found in the joint planning of DDR/SSR activities through the various agreements for the multi-year defence programme legislation.

While there is still not much to show for the efforts of various stakeholders, there was a high degree of interface between various national actors and the CAR's international development partners in an attempt to support coherent processes. A lesson here is to persevere in systematically instituting multi-stakeholder consultation and decision-making structures and not to expect positive results overnight in building coherence.

Planning for DDR and SSR

While awareness of the need for coordination seems to exist, it is hampered by the lack of adequate planning. First, the lack of foresight in resource mobilization, as well as in anticipating the approximate financial needs to cover at least part of the DDR process, was surprising. A challenge for the planning of DDR and SSR activities is the necessity to have financial resources at hand to initiate a DDR process and ensure its continuance through adequate longer-term funding. The Front for the Central African People, one of the armed groups that agreed to disarm and demobilise, had its troops in cantonments for months while waiting for the DDR process to move forward. Not surprisingly, they were increasingly showing signs of restlessness because expected demobilization benefits had not materialised by the beginning of 2009 as the international partners were still garnering sufficient financial resources. Subsequently, some limited attacks against the FACA were carried out in early 2009, threatening to unravel the entire DDR/SSR process.

An obvious lesson is that if the required funds to initiate and sustain early and time-sensitive DDR activities cannot be made available rapidly, there is great risk that frustrations will mount and jeopardise a still fragile peace process. This in turn can drastically reduce the willingness of a government to pursue SSR. Thus, international partners (and the national government) should take care to anticipate the financial consequences of DDR/SSR agreements and be ready to deliver on them in a timely manner.

Communication, sensitization and coordination

With regard to communication, a critical dimension of the entire process, the consensus is that the process has not adequately served the individuals and communities in the north who were most affected by the conflict. Many believe that information on the various DDR activities remained confined to the level of the participants in the PID and national elites, and that those who should have been targeted by a sustained campaign of information, sensitization and education were left out. Of course, in this communication vacuum, rumours and misinformation have free rein and cynicism can rapidly take hold.

There appears to be a keen awareness of the need to improve coordination, reflected in the decision to structure SSR into seven pillars, or sectors, each with a committee and focal point. Mixed working groups and structures involving national and international partners have been established at various levels. A three-level coordination support structure for the SSR process developed by the international community seems to reflect lessons from the failures of the PRAC experience. At the political level is the *Cellule de Concertation* (CC), which is co-chaired by the representative of UNDP and the EU delegation chief and made up of the ambassadors of France and Belgium, the UN peace consolidation office chief and a CEMAC representative. The CC addresses politically sensitive questions that arise from the SSR process by undertaking efforts at the highest level of the state. At the intermediary technical level there is a multidisciplinary team chaired by a mission chief and made up of seven specialists in SSR issue areas such as defence, police, justice, etc. These members are placed as international experts in each of the seven sectors involved in SSR. Their task is to ensure the coordination of SSR assistance from international partners and to advise sector committees. The multidisciplinary team also interfaces with and supports the national structure in charge of SSR coordination (the STP) and its national coordinator. Finally, at the technical level, *Comités de Pilotage Technique* have been created. They are made up of technical assistants from donor countries and are assigned to SSR sectors with the mission of making sure that the assistance by donor countries is appropriate and complementary. While these structures do address the failings identified with earlier processes and activities, they raise other challenges, in particular whether or not it is practical for these various committees to be chaired by a single individual (then General Antoine Gambi) on behalf of the government.

Sequencing

There is widespread recognition in the case of the CAR that it is most urgent to carry out DDR in order to bolster reconciliation and peace consolidation. However, while the PID decided that it was essential to carry out DDR 'immediately', it also highlighted that SSR needed to be carried out according to the timetable agreed during the national seminar. While DDR remains contingent on funding mobilization and availability, a number of targets for SSR have been missed. Among these was the setting up of an *ad hoc* committee to update security-related legislation and executive acts (*arrêtés* and *décrets*) to create the appropriate legislative and regulatory framework. For the police, the initiation of a process to create a code of conduct was envisaged. These activities have not yet taken place. This is partly because they involve long-term objectives and quick results are unlikely, which is problematic in an environment where visible results are much needed to meet high expectations. This does not mean, however, that SSR should be left aside until DDR is completed. On the contrary, many SSR activities can, and indeed must, be undertaken even as the DDR process unfolds. In the CAR, even fairly resource-neutral SSR measures could not be carried out successfully without first following up on the cantonment of former combatants with visible reinsertion activities.

The challenge of sequencing was exacerbated by the need to demonstrate tangible results to sceptical and impatient former combatants and their leaders. This points to a clear lesson in dealing with armed groups who are (potential) spoilers. Taking care of ex-combatants during their cantonment and making available tangible benefits which improve their immediate living conditions should be a priority. Only when there is clear evidence of decreased tension around the issue of the immediate fate of the demobilised former combatants should SSR measures such as restructuring the FACA or downsizing the police be initiated. However, it should also be kept in mind that some DDR/SSR linkages remain critical to the process and are not dependent on any sequencing calculation. For example, the rehabilitation of infrastructure and communication capabilities for the police in some of the provinces affected by conflict is important for the DDR process, as there will be a need for capable police/law and order to accompany DDR operations. UNDP's Rule of Law Programme supported such rehabilitation.

Local ownership and sustainability

There seems to be a high level of awareness of the need for local ownership. The SSR process was well publicised and generated a good deal of interest. In addition, there is an understanding of why SSR is crucial in the CAR. The national authorities at the highest level publicly adhered to SSR objectives and processes, including the involvement of traditionally excluded stakeholders. In addition, shortly after the national seminar, a decree was enacted by the prime minister to set up a sector committee on SSR that is backed up by a permanent technical secretariat. The secretariat is made up of representatives of several ministries, including justice, defence and interior, as well as civil society groups and expert civil servants from a variety of technical and financial state agencies. It also includes representatives of external development partners. This decree certainly denotes a level of commitment to local ownership.

In a country characterised by very weak capabilities, heavy dependence on external partners, a lack of inclusiveness and the legacy of poor leadership, there are bound to be serious challenges to the principle of ownership. Some of these challenges have to do not only with the need to include all stakeholders, but with the question of whether this will serve the objectives of SSR/DDR. This is not an easy issue, since the principle may clash with the reality that some stakeholders may act as spoilers at a particular juncture.

The parliament is conspicuously absent from the SSR process. True local ownership will be impossible to achieve until the parliament, (even if still dominated by the president's party and allies) is made a full partner, if only because many of the measures will take the form of laws, or involve the disbursement of funds from the national budget.

For local ownership to be meaningful, an attitude of self-reliance as opposed to dependence on external partners must be adopted and pursued. This is particularly important for the sustainability of the processes. Other stakeholders who have not been fully included in the process, particularly women's groups, must also be given a more prominent role and should be involved in decision-making and monitoring in the PID and to no lesser extent in the follow-up to the national seminar on SSR. Part of operationalizing ownership is the involvement of national actors in the decision-making process, and there is no doubt that the established structures allow for this. However, capacities are missing to make those decisions competently. Finally, given the less-than-optimum management of the PRAC programme by its national administrators, there is some tentativeness about the application of national ownership if it implies the management of programmes by nationals. This is not to say that programmes cannot be managed professionally and with integrity by CAR nationals. However, given the experience of PRAC and the apparently massive misuse of funds that occurred, a critical challenge is to ensure that those tasked with making decisions and carrying out DDR/SSR activities have integrity and resources are used optimally.

There is no reason why the CAR should continue to depend so heavily on its development partners for processes so vital to its future as a state and the well-being of its people. A lesson to be derived from the experience of the externally driven DDR/SSR project so far is the necessity of the CAR to be able to mobilise and rely on its own resources. No national DDR/SSR programme can be successful in the long run when it depends almost entirely on development partners, however well intentioned. A related lesson is to ensure that there is a constant transfer of competencies. For example, UNDP and other programmes systematically match international experts with CAR nationals in order to ensure that local expertise is created through the transfer of expertise. One of the reasons for the chequered progress in DDR and SSR is the near exclusion of the parliament as a major player. It must be systematically included, and should take a leading role in the process.

Political will

Perhaps the most critical challenge to the linkage between DDR and SSR in the CAR context, is the use of the rhetoric of DDR and SSR without a real intention of carrying them out; in other words, using these processes as a means of obtaining foreign support and pacifying opponents, particularly armed groups. This is true in the pursuit of each activity, but is even more significant when linking them is so central to success. This challenge is underscored by the fact that among the various activities that the CAR authorities committed themselves to at the close of the national seminar on

SSR, very few were actually carried out by the agreed deadline, despite the fact that some of them neither entailed nor depended on a financial commitment on the part of the national government. Efforts to mitigate this risk need to be taken by ensuring that the short-term measures the CAR government committed to, both symbolic and substantive, are pursued in a timely manner.

One lesson may be that, from the outset, governments be made to commit to clear benchmarks. Activities that clearly highlight and strengthen DDR/SSR linkages should be undertaken within a defined period of time. This will enable other stakeholders and external partners to gauge early on the degree to which political will exists on the part of the executive branch.

Financial and human resources

It is well known that the CAR is severely resource-deficient and cannot, on its own, mobilise resources to finance either DDR or SSR. The CAR relies entirely on its international partners to provide funds to make these processes possible. Only a few million CFA francs remaining of DDR funds were still available in early 2009. The UN Peace Consolidation Fund, estimated at US$4 million, is also available for DDR. These funds are not enough to finance DDR, SSR or the indemnification of victims of violence. In fact, this has been a major challenge, as many activities in the various SSR pillars are in limbo awaiting the mobilization of DDR funding.

An obvious lesson for all involved is that significant funding for DDR and SSR must be mobilised and secured before the process of carrying them out in conjunction is started. The risk of exacerbating tensions and increasing the likelihood of conflict resumption is serious when expectations are raised but are not met. The reservations expressed by the European Union about funding certain DDR activities *after* the Libreville and PID agreements were signed are a case in point. Such reservations should have been voiced before there was expectation that EU funds would be forthcoming to support the process.

Among the human resource challenges is that the residue of expertise from the past DDR experiment does not equate to a vast reservoir of national DDR experts with proven hands-on DDR experience. There will be a need to tap into foreign expertise in DDR and most definitely SSR, despite a significant increase of SSR literacy and awareness. Nevertheless, the latter concept is still very alien to how the security sector has been managed, even in the recent years since its introduction in the national discourse. It will take time to entrench a new mindset and approaches.

Monitoring and evaluation

The international community has organised itself to exert monitoring and evaluation at various levels. The most critical mechanism is at the politico-strategic level with the *Cellule de Concertation*, intended to anticipate hurdles and have them addressed at the highest level of the state. At the operational and technical levels there are other monitoring structures that serve to keep their CAR counterparts in SSR on track. In all these organs, UNDP and other components of the UN system play an active and prominent role. One of the innovative aspects of the CAR experience is that multilevel structures were integrated in such a way as to be able to monitor and evaluate both DDR and SSR activities. Periodic stocktaking at the political and operational levels could assess progress accomplished as well as identifying hurdles encountered.

What may be missing is a mechanism outside the bilateral structures between the CAR and its development partners to carry out independent monitoring and evaluation. This could focus on whether or not the various activities carried out sustain linkages between DDR and SSR. A formal evaluation body would be able to provide periodic reports of its own on the progress accomplished in maintaining these linkages on the ground.

Conclusion and Policy Recommendations

This study examines the CAR's experience in addressing linkages between DDR and SSR during the post-conflict period, which began with the rise of General Bozizé after an armed rebellion. This concluded a period of conflict which had left the country with a highly dysfunctional security sector and rampant political instability. Following the relative stabilization of the political situation after the 2005 elections, which confirmed General Bozizé as the head of state, the international community supported various efforts to carry out DDR. The most prominent of these efforts was PRAC, a programme funded by the MDRP and UNDP. This programme, though innovative and credited with noteworthy accomplishments for future programmes to build on, was conducted without taking into account potential DDR-SSR synergies. Indeed, many of its features and operations precluded a comprehensive approach to the post-conflict transformation of the security sector. Several factors can account for the absence of a linkage between DDR and SSR, including the political context at its inception, the policy choices of its main funders, its aims and the lack of knowledge or acceptance of the SSR concept at the time.

While UNDP took the lead role in supervising certain aspects of the programme on behalf of the donor community, the conduct of DDR operations was managed under the auspices of the CNDDR, a CAR state organ. Subsequently UNDP did carry out a number of projects that went beyond the 'narrow' DDR embodied by PRAC, but these were not part of a coordinated, comprehensive approach based on SSR as the guiding concept. A coherent framework now seems to be emerging that will enable these projects to be part of a comprehensive SSR process as a post-conflict stabilization and rebuilding strategy.

A new phase is evident with the agreements that followed the Political Inclusive Dialogue and the national seminar on SSR. A fresh opportunity to learn from past experiences thus presents itself. Several lessons can be drawn from the PRAC experience to inform recommendations for the UN system on the integration of DDR and SSR in future post-conflict situations. So far, the way that the CAR stakeholders and their partners in the international community have prioritised SSR in their strategic approach and in the operationalization and implementation of agreements on DDR, seems to indicate that the lessons of the past were not lost. The task ahead is no less daunting for that. It is necessary in particular to focus on all critical dimensions of DDR/SSR integration, i.e. coherence, effective communication strategies, sequencing of activities, ensuring sustainable and genuine local ownership and finally establishing effective monitoring and evaluation mechanisms.

Recommendations

The CAR needs to put an end to its vicious cycle of rebellions, multiple peace agreements and successive DDR programmes by supporting comprehensive and well-rounded DDR and SSR processes. The following recommendations aim to shed light on what can and should be done. Recommendations for the CAR's international partners should make their commitment to post-conflict peacebuilding more reflective of the lessons learned from past experience.

Maintain political will. There should be no mistake that DDR and SSR are eminently *political* processes, not just technical undertakings. Therefore the political leadership of the CAR at the highest levels must remain fully engaged. Symbolic as well as substantive actions to convey the right messages at the right time must be given as much weight as advances at the operational level. For example, at this juncture high-profile action by the head of state, e.g. visiting a cantonment of former combatants who have been waiting for demobilization for at least two months, should be undertaken. Care must be given to conveying unequivocally and consistently through the appropriate media the notion that the political leadership is focused on the issue and working hard to resolve it. To this end, an extensive campaign of information, sensitization and education of the population directly affected by DDR/SSR should be initiated and involve the highest levels of political authority, in particular the head of state and prime minister. They should insist on the linkages between DDR and SSR and on a long-term commitment to seeing through a genuine and lasting transformation of how security is conceived and managed.

Encourage a quick start and sustainability in funding. The international community, and the UN system in particular, should better anticipate the financial implications of conflict-ending agreements. As signs point to a likely agreement inclusive of DDR clauses, a proactive fund-raising process should be initiated to make funds available to facilitate a speedy DDR operation and enable key SSR activities that are closely linked to the DDR process to take place. As the UN system typically plays a role in the agreement-reaching process, it should use its influence to make DDR part of an overall SSR provision. In the case of the CAR it did, and to that extent this country may be a good model. Again, better anticipation and mobilization of necessary funding are indispensable complements to efforts of the UN system and its international partners. DDR, which the PID recommends be initiated 'immediately', must be done without delay.

International and locally generated financial resources should be mobilised at once to carry out the census operation for combatants already in cantonment, in accordance with the Libreville agreement. Any delay to a quick start of DDR is likely to have an adverse effect on the overall process. It is one of the hopeful aspects in this context that there may not be a need to create huge cantonments of former combatants. Many of them can, without prohibitive cost, be relatively easy to demobilise, identify, vet and track for further reinsertion purposes. However, this reinsertion should not take a disproportionate amount of time to initiate after the demobilization phase. Simultaneously, the international community must strive to mobilise additional funds to enable the continuation of the DDR operations. These resources will become indispensable when DDR reaches a 'cruising speed', when the most difficult and contentious aspects must be tackled. It will be a tragedy if funding difficulties jeopardise critical DDR operations after so much energy and effort have been invested or if a lack of funding for SSR means that this progress may be lost.

Acknowledge the former combatant-community nexus. The dual approach that PRAC initially pursued, i.e. the focus on micro-programmes that help sustain peaceful communities and support the reinsertion of ex-combatants in these communities should inspire the upcoming DDR process. However, one of the main mistakes associated with PRAC – the very loose conceptualization of who is a combatant and how to ascertain that status – must be avoided. Care must be taken to ensure that only genuine former combatants and not 'complaisance' combatants are beneficiaries of DDR operations.

Address the DDR-army reform linkage. While DDR is a key focus, this does not mean that SSR in the FACA pillar can wait. There must be a demonstration that the regular armed forces will be 'rightsized' and reformed, and that this is as much a part of the conflict resolution process as DDR for non-state-controlled armed groups. Consequently, an initial list of retiring senior and junior officers should be made available to illustrate that SSR has also started within the FACA and the army in particular. Without delay, a broadly representative committee should be established to create a draft code of conduct for armed and security forces, adapting elements of existing codes elsewhere. The ECOWAS (Economic Community of West African States) code of conduct could be a good model. A draft should be quickly circulated for input and introduced as a joint opposition/government, executive/legislative bill for rapid adoption as a law. The window of opportunity for the restructuring of the FACA and enacting this critical element of SSR should not be missed. A delay will make it far more difficult to accomplish this later. Other measures, such as organised 'open day' visits of parliamentarians, ordinary citizens and civil society organizations to various military installations and lodging facilities to see the conditions armed combatants live in and the challenges they face, will, at minimal financial cost, go a long way towards starting the reconciliation process and much-needed confidence building.

Address the DDR-police reform nexus. So far the police has proven a difficult case for reform because of its high level of dysfunction. The UNDP-managed Rule of Law programme was, in early 2009, carrying out a project aimed at rehabilitating police offices in a number of prefectures and helping equip remote areas with communication equipment. This programme must be expanded and additional funding sought to focus on the needs of the police, which has received less attention than other areas of the security sector. A concerted effort should be made to ensure that a reasonable percentage of ex-combatants are recruited into the paramilitary bodies and police. This entails a transparent and concerted process of identifying and vetting qualified ex-combatants for integration in the police and other bodies to be reconfigured and reconstituted. While the guidelines for vetting ex-combatants to be absorbed into the law enforcement forces will be the subject of technical negotiations between the parties (without the possibility of veto, as often requested by the government side), a certain level of education and ethical and psychological fitness to serve will necessarily be part of the requirements.

Establish an appropriate division of labour. It is critical that the restructuring of the FACA is not perceived as the 'reserved domain' of any of the CAR's external partners. SSR must be seen as being carried out for the sole benefit of the CAR. Even the suspicion of ulterior motives will be bitterly resented and adversely affect the integrity and success of SSR. In this regard, the offer from South Africa to train and equip three battalions should be encouraged and pursued, and its example followed by the other partners of the country. In other words, for the SSR/DDR linkages to be sustained there shouldn't be even the appearance that some partners, particularly historically interested powers, are involved only to pursue their own security agendas under the guise of helping to implement these programmes.

Avoid victor's justice. Although the involvement of the FACA in demobilization and disarmament operations could be interpreted as a 'victorious' FACA ensuring its enemy is out of commission, there may be objective reasons to involve it to some degree. Indeed, the FACA will be undergoing demobilization of certain of its members. Their retirement will free up not only spots in the army but also financial resources that can be used to recruit troops who are lower ranked compared to those who retire. There is therefore the opportunity for increased engagement between those responsible for DDR and for army reform in two ways. First, by pre-identifying possible future recruits for the FACA and gendarmerie, a percentage of whom should come from the ranks of demobilised ex-combatants. And second, by extracting from the 'regular' DDR process lessons learned relating to the reinsertion of ex-combatants into civilian life that could be applied to the FACA retirees. Due to the aforementioned need for credibility, there should be a way to involve, even symbolically, the leadership of the armed groups to be demobilised in specific SSR activities concerning the FACA. For example, leaders of the armed groups should be invited to be part of state commissions charged with deciding the priorities for the multi-year military budget and overall strategic orientation agreed in the Libreville and PID agreements. In addition, for confidence-building purposes, the same leaders can be invited to participate, along with members of civil society groups, in the drafting and adoption of the draft code of conduct. In short, if done intelligently, there is no reason why the FACA and more prominently the gendarmerie cannot be included in certain DDR activities, provided that there is some reciprocity (leadership of armed opposition associated with SSR activities concerning the FACA), and these cross-cutting activities are construed as confidence-building measures.

Notes

1 See Dominique Bangoura, 'Réformes ou… refondation des armées africaines?', paper presented at Interactive Workshop on Francophone Defence Committees Needs Assessment, Lomé, 23–24 August 2008.

2 Boubacar N'Diaye, 'Beyond Demobilization: The Challenges and Opportunities for Security Sector Reform in the CAR', MDRP Working Paper Series No. 2 (Washington, DC: MDRP, May 2007), 37.

3 A moderate, anti-colonial, pan-African political party created by Boganda.

4 Ndjaye Sakanok, 'Situation du DDR', paper presented to National Seminar on SSR, Bangui, April 2008, 10.

5 Eric Berman, 'Une Étude de Cas sur les Armes légères et les Conflit', Small Arms Survey report (Geneva: Institut Universitaire des Hautes Etudes Internationales, 2004).

6 A new concept of an integrated and all-encompassing construction of defence and security concerns of the Central African state.

7 The STP is the steering committee for SSR implementation, organised along seven 'pillars' that are directly concerned with the SSR process.

8 Led by former army general Amadou Toumani Touré, its aim was to monitor the agreement that was arrived at to resolve the 1996 mutiny against President Patassé.

9 A UN peacekeeping mission starting in 1998, with the mandate of stabilizing the situation in Bangui and creating the conditions for a sustainable peace, including conducting disarmament, training operations and capacity building.

10 It took over from MINURCA with the mission of consolidating peace and promoting national reconciliation.

11 FOMUC is the 350-man standing force set up in 2002 by the Economic and Monetary Community of Central Africa to secure Bangui in order to create a space for the peaceful resolution of tensions between then President Patassé and his opposition.

12 United Nations, 'Securing peace and development: The role of the United Nations in supporting security sector reform', report of the UN Secretary-General, UN Doc. A/62/659–S/2008/39.

13 Sakanoko, note 4 above.

14 Jean-Pierre Bemba, former vice-president of the DRC, is currently held in The Hague facing three counts of crimes against humanity and five counts of war crimes in relation to alleged activities in the CAR.

Chapter 5

The Democratic Republic of the Congo

Vincenza Scherrer

Introduction

The disarmament, demobilization and reintegration (DDR) of ex-combatants and security sector reform (SSR) lie at the heart of peacebuilding in the Democratic Republic of the Congo (DRC). DDR and SSR figure prominently in both the Global and All-Inclusive Peace Agreement and the Security Council resolutions that provide the UN Mission in the DRC (MONUC – now MONUSCO) with its mandate.[1] The mission has been present at every stage of the peace process since 1999, from the disengagement of foreign and Congolese troops to the preparation and holding of elections and the post-election period. MONUC has played a key role in supporting DDR and SSR in the DRC, including through the peacekeeping mission's unprecedented engagement in defence sector reform. To be properly contextualised, this role must be understood in relation to other international actors and, fundamentally, national DDR and SSR stakeholders.

Efforts to support DDR and SSR in the DRC have been hampered by evolving political dynamics, prevailing insecurity and limited access to different regions within the DRC. Such challenges have affected the ability to foster linkages between DDR and SSR. In particular, the need to deal with a plethora of urgent priorities has meant that strategic analysis of the longer-term consequences that DDR may have on SSR and vice versa has been lacking. The absence of a UN system-wide approach to DDR/SSR has also impacted on the ability to link, sequence and prioritise activities.

This case study seeks to assess the relationship between DDR and SSR in the DRC, while recognizing that they are distinct processes with different stakeholder groups, objectives and timelines. The chapter argues that strengthening the nexus between certain components of DDR and SSR could contribute to the overall effectiveness of these processes. It highlights how despite the non-enabling environment, opportunities to support mutually reinforcing DDR and SSR activities do exist. The chapter first provides an overview of DDR, SSR and the mandate and role of the United Nations. It then sets out a number of potential entry points for linking DDR and SSR in the DRC, as well as identifying lessons and challenges. The chapter ends by developing a set of recommendations aimed at recognizing and operationalizing the nexus between DDR and SSR.[2]

Context for DDR and SSR

Political and security context

The Democratic Republic of the Congo has experienced political instability and social turmoil since its independence in 1960. Following decades of dictatorship, President Mobutu Sese Seko was overthrown in May 1997 by the *Alliance des Forces Démocratiques pour la Libération du Congo*, a Rwandan and Ugandan-backed coalition that installed Laurent-Désiré Kabila as president. Attempts by Laurent Kabila to free himself from dependence on his former allies led to the dismissal of the Rwandan elements in the Congolese army in July 1998. Rwanda and Uganda subsequently backed new rebel groups in an attempt to overthrow the president, sending troops into the DRC to support the rebel movements.[3]

The signing of the Lusaka Ceasefire Agreement in July 1999 by Angola, the DRC, Namibia, Rwanda, Uganda, Zimbabwe, the Congolese Rally for Democracy and the Movement for the Liberation of the Congo provided a framework for the disengagement and withdrawal of foreign troops. This was conducted under the auspices of MONUC. Following the assassination of Kabila in January 2001, his son Joseph Kabila assumed power. This provided a new impetus to the peace process, leading to the Inter-Congolese Dialogue resulting in the signature of the Global and All-Inclusive Agreement by the Kabila government and main rebel groups in December 2002. The agreement, which formally ended the civil war in the DRC, outlined power-sharing principles and established some key parameters for future SSR, including the formation of a restructured and integrated national army and the disarmament of ex-combatants. The government of national unity and transition, established in June 2003, organised a referendum on a constitution and nationwide elections, which culminated in the victory of Joseph Kabila in 2006. Elections did not signal a return to normalcy: the conflict has contributed to the breakdown of the economy,[4] damaged government institutions and caused great suffering to the civilian population.[5]

The success of reconstruction efforts depends heavily on events in the Kivu provinces, where the root causes of the conflict – including uneven access to land and unfair distribution of profits from natural resources – have yet to be addressed. In recognition of the importance of the problems in the east to the stability of the DRC and the Great Lakes region, the governments of the DRC and Rwanda signed a joint communiqué on 9 November 2007 (known as the Nairobi communiqué). This called for stricter border controls, humanitarian and public information activities and the voluntary disarmament and repatriation of ex-Rwandan Armed Forces (ex-FAR) and Interahamwe[6] away from the DRC/Rwanda border.

Increased fighting in North Kivu at the end of 2007 between the *Forces Armées de la République Démocratique du Congo* (FARDC) and the *Congrès national pour la défense du peuple* (CNDP), commanded by Laurent Nkunda,[7] led the DRC government to organise a conference on peace, security and development in the Kivus held in Goma on 6–25 January 2008. On 23 January two statements of commitment for North and South Kivu were signed by the Congolese government, Laurent Nkunda and the Mayi Mayi,[8] among others. The Goma Agreement required all signatories to accept a MONUC-monitored ceasefire, subject all militias to DDR or *brassage*[9] and facilitate the return of refugees and internally displaced persons. Based on the Goma Agreement, the government launched the Amani programme to support the pacification of the east.[10] Renewed fighting starting in August 2008 signalled the breakdown of the agreement,[11] and the fast turn of events since early 2009 has once again escalated tensions in the east.[12]

Insecurity has significantly constrained the international community's ability to support DDR and SSR in the DRC. These limitations must be understood in the context of the geographical, political and security environment, including the operational difficulties of deploying in Africa's second-largest country without functioning communication or infrastructure systems. The rapid developments in the past few years have resulted in shifting priorities for both national stakeholders and the international community. During the months prior to the 2006 elections, election security was the key priority so efforts were channelled into supporting the capacity of the police. Subsequently, given the threat of renewed fighting among rebel groups, DDR and DDR-RR (DDR plus repatriation and resettlement) became a first priority. The political and security context has therefore played an important role in setting the tone for DDR and SSR support in the country, and can partly account for a perceived bias in favour of short-term security measures at the detriment of longer-term security sector governance.

DDR overview

DDR in the DRC has been composed of three separate processes which are detailed below. While DDR is challenging in any context, the task in the DRC has been particularly difficult. DDR has been hampered by the limited infrastructure which has affected efforts to organise the processing and payment of ex-combatants seeking reintegration. The large caseload of combatants as well as the lack of accurate figures on their numbers has proved difficult to manage.

The first process, DDR-RR (disarmament, demobilization, repatriation, reintegration and resettlement)[13] targeted mainly Rwandan armed groups present in the DRC. The second, national DDR process, addresses the forces of the signatories of the Global and All-Inclusive Agreement. This process is closely linked to SSR through the *tronc commun* (see below). The third has involved the demobilization and community reinsertion (DCR) of armed groups in the Ituri region.

Disarmament, Demobilization, Repatriation, Reintegration and Resettlement programme. The DDR-RR process in the DRC was established to address the disarmament and repatriation of foreign combatants. These are mainly former FAR, Interahamwe and *Forces Démocratiques de la Libération du Rwanda* (FDLR), but in the past MONUC also disarmed, demobilised and repatriated members of Burundian, Rwandan and Ugandan armed groups. MONUC's DDR-RR team has played a key role in supporting this process. Between 2002 and 2008 the repatriation of approximately 16,000 ex-combatants, plus their families, was supported. Efforts were further intensified when the joint military operation was launched in North Kivu in 2009, resulting in increased repatriations as a result of this 'push and pull' strategy.[14]

National DDR programme. The National DDR Programme (PNDDR) is intended to disarm, demobilise and reintegrate the forces of the signatories of the Global and All-Inclusive Agreement.[15] The programme lays out two options for participants: they are either integrated into the FARDC or demobilised and reintegrated into civilian life.[16] The PNDDR process was nationally run through the *Commission Nationale de la Démobilization et Réinsertion* (CONADER); however, following concerns over accounting for international funds, CONADER was abolished and replaced by the *Unité d'Execution du Programme Nationale de DDR* (UE-PNDDR) in 2008. It was originally estimated that CONADER would deal with 300,000 individuals, but by 2006, when the first stage of the programme ended, only 186,000 had gone through the programme, including 2,610 women and 30,219 children.[17] A second phase has been affected by shifting political priorities and insecurity.

Disarmament and community reintegration process. The DCR was conceived to support the ex-combatants who did not fall under the PNDDR because they belonged to armed groups that were not signatories to the national-level peace agreements. In May 2003 Ituri militia leaders gathered to discuss a non-military solution to the violence that had erupted in the region. Out of this meeting, seven militia leaders signed the Dar es Salaam Accords and committed themselves to the Ituri DCR Programme.[18] The process emphasised community support as opposed to focusing solely on ex-combatants. DCR mainly took place in Ituri and was supported by UNDP, alongside other partners. When the programme ended in June 2005, after having demobilised approximately 15,800 combatants, the PNDDR assumed work with the remaining active armed groups in the region.[19]

SSR overview

SSR in the DRC has also faced a number of challenges. First and foremost, SSR has been hampered by the political context. Efforts to support a broad approach to SSR that encompasses a governance dimension have been sidestepped in favour of a narrower approach. In this context, SSR is generally understood as including only police, defence and judicial reform.[20] This is reflected in the focus of the national coordinating mechanisms that have been set up to support SSR: *Comités de suivi* have been established in the areas of army integration, police and judicial reform.[21]

National security forces are generally perceived by the local population as unable to provide adequate protection and are often the perpetrators of serious crimes.[22] A narrow approach to SSR does not take into account the fact that there is a strong link between the crimes committed by members of the security forces and the poor pay and conditions for soldiers.[23] This emphasises the importance of an SSR process capable of addressing these underlying issues. However, there is a lack of political will to develop the governance component of SSR.

Army reform has been a primary focus of SSR. The reform of the FARDC has been a difficult process given the military's traditionally influential role in Congolese politics.[24] The FARDC's concept of operations stems from its experience during the Mobutu era, when soldiers were encouraged to fend for themselves. This mentality is reflected in the Congolese saying '*civil azali bilanga ya militaire*', meaning 'the civilian is the [corn] field of the military', a mindset that has proven resistant to change over time.[25]

In September 2005 the *Plan National Stratégique d'Integration des Forces Armées* was issued as the reference document for the future organization of the armed forces, as well as for the execution of the integration and DDR processes.[26] The *Plan Directeur Global de la Réforme de l'Armée*, presented by the government at an SSR roundtable held on 25–26 February 2008, also details the government's approach to defence reform.[27] The vision for the future army is based on the creation of infantry brigades (*forces de couverture*), a rapid reaction force and the establishment of the main defence force by 2010. An integrated military structure was created in 2004 to conduct the *brassage* and *recyclage* of ex-combatants in view of forming integrated brigades.

Recent reverses demonstrate that the main challenge the FARDC faces is from rebel groups in the east.[28] The newly integrated brigades have in some cases proved ineffective.[29] Lack of discipline and serious command and control problems are additional challenges. Many weapons are defective, and the integrated brigades have not been able to conduct live-firing training since 2004. In addition, 45 per cent of the troops understand only Lingala *or* Swahili, while 50 per cent are illiterate.[30] The integrated brigades also suffer from poor social conditions and infrastructure.

The Congolese National Police faces similar challenges. The police force was created in 1997 and replaced the previous gendarmerie. It was formed without a clear structure and recruited candidates without defined criteria in terms of background and training. The police force is perceived as inefficient and has a record of human rights abuses.[31] Without adequate pay, police officers are also known to resort to extortion. This is particularly visible in the eastern part of the country, where many police officers are not registered and therefore do not receive a salary.[32]

Increasing the overall human and financial management of the police and contributing to their professionalization is a major SSR challenge. As of September 2006, after a two-year consultation period between donors, international experts and the Congolese authorities, as part of the *Groupe Mixte de Réflexion sur la Réforme et la Réorganization de la Police*

Nationale Congolaise, a draft law on police reform in the DRC was finalised. The law draws on 'the provisions of Articles 182 to 186 of the Constitution that the PNC (*Police Nationale Congolaise*) should function at the genuine service of the Congolese people, be apolitical, subject to the control of civil authority and not be diverted for personal ends'.[33] The draft law aims to establish transparent, unitary lines of command as well as continuing the demilitarization of the police.[34] However, there have been continuous delays in the adoption of this law by parliament.

Reform of the justice sector has benefited from having a coordinating commission since 2005 (*comité mixte de justice*) as well as a single justice reform programme. Nonetheless, the five-year plan for justice sector reform is said to lack 'a strategic vision for reform or an analysis of needs'.[35] Moreover, considerable challenges remain. Perpetrators of sexual violence and other atrocities are often not prosecuted and have in some cases been protected from prosecution by local authorities. Only 7 per cent of victims of sexual violence reportedly receive judicial support if they choose to pursue legal action.[36] Since perpetrators are also found within the security forces, this erodes the trust of local communities and perpetuates a culture of impunity.[37] A robust judicial system would exclude those who have committed atrocities against civilians from joining the FARDC.[38] Judicial reform is therefore an important priority in stabilizing and promoting peace in the DRC.

Key actors

The United Nations is a key actor in the DRC: its peacekeeping mission is the UN's largest and most expensive field mission, with an annual budget exceeding US$1 billion and a total of 20,819 uniformed personnel.[39] Numerous UN programmes, funds and agencies also play a major role. UNDP, for instance, has over 140 staff members and several offices across the country.

The various peace agreements give significant responsibility to the United Nations in supporting the national DDR and SSR processes, particularly in the area of DDR-RR. The Lusaka Ceasefire Agreement sets out disarmament and repatriation in strong terms describing it as 'peace enforcement'. This has since led to confusion with respect to the UN's mandate to disarm and repatriate combatants on a voluntary basis on Congolese territory.[40] The Pretoria Agreement of 2002 stated that 'MONUC, acting together with all relevant UN Agencies, should be requested to immediately set up processes to repatriate all Rwandese, ex-FAR and

Interahamwe to Rwanda, in coordination with the governments of Rwanda and the DRC.'[41]

MONUC was formally established by Security Council Resolution 1279 in 1999, and was initially mandated to provide technical assistance to the Joint Military Commission in the implementation of its functions under the Lusaka Ceasefire Agreement and to plan for the observation of the ceasefire and the disengagement of forces.[42] In 2000, MONUC was mandated to develop an action plan for the overall implementation of the ceasefire agreement, with particular emphasis on:

> the collection and verification of military information on the parties' forces, the maintenance of the cessation of hostilities and the disengagement and redeployment of the parties' forces, the comprehensive disarmament, demobilization, resettlement and reintegration of all members of all armed groups referred to in Annex A, Chapter 9.1 of the Ceasefire Agreement, and the orderly withdrawal of all foreign forces.[43]

MONUC was also called on 'to contribute to the disarmament portion of the national programme of disarmament, demobilization and reintegration (DDR) of Congolese combatants and their dependants' and to 'facilitate the demobilization and voluntary repatriation of the disarmed foreign combatants and their dependants'.[44] The mandate therefore indicates that the mission's priority was DDR-RR, where it was mandated to support the entire process, as opposed to DDR where MONUC was only mandated to support the 'disarmament' portion. This was reflected in the relative staff numbers attributed to DDR and DDR-RR, as well as the comparatively large field presence of the DDR-RR section.[45] This was not the case for the other major UN actor in this field: UNDP played a strong role in DDR, contributing to the disarmament and community reintegration process and supporting CONADER in the demobilization of ex-combatants.

In 2003, SSR language was explicitly included in Security Council Resolution 1493, which mandated MONUC to assist in 'the reform of the security forces'. In 2004, Security Council Resolution 1565 went further by mandating MONUC to support '[s]ecurity sector reform, including the integration of national defence and internal security forces together with disarmament, demobilization and reintegration and, in particular, the training and monitoring of the police, while ensuring that they are democratic and fully respect human rights and fundamental freedoms'.[46] Thus, SSR was explicitly linked to DDR in the mandate.

Beyond the United Nations, international actors supporting DDR, SSR and related activities include Angola, Belgium, China, France, South Africa, the UK, the United States and the European Union. The EU established the European Union Police Mission in Kinshasa (EUPOL-Kinshasa, later replaced by EUPOL RD Congo) and the European Union Security Sector Reform Mission (EUSEC). EUSEC provides advice and assistance for SSR, mostly in the area of defence sector reform.[47] EUPOL supports police reform by providing advice to the national police reform monitoring committee, supporting the link between police and justice and supporting the border police directorate. In the area of DDR, the Multi-Country Demobilization and Reintegration Program (MDRP) of the World Bank has played a key role in supporting the PNDDR, with most DDR financing channelled through this mechanism.[48]

The DDR/SSR Nexus in the DRC

The experience in the DRC highlights how DDR can impact on SSR and vice versa. A key example is the relationship between DDR and army reform. On the DDR side, late payments at the orientation centres resulted in setbacks for the SSR process as ex-combatants refused to leave the centres without collecting their allowances.[49] The formation of the integrated brigades – a key component of army reform – was therefore partly stalled until room was made in the centres for further ex-combatants to enter and select integration. On the SSR side, disagreements over the modalities for army reform – linked to Nkunda's demand that the CNDP troops remain in the Kivu region without undergoing *brassage* – resulted in delays in advancing the DDR process. Many ex-combatants that had spontaneously assembled in view of joining the DDR process gave up and returned to the bush.

In practice, efforts to think in terms of a DDR-SSR nexus are undermined by the siloed approach to DDR and SSR. This is compounded by a short-term focus which is often justified by the non-enabling security environment. This section considers how, despite the difficult environment, opportunities to link DDR and SSR do exist. It therefore examines the different dimensions of the DDR/SSR nexus, identifies key entry points and opportunities, and also highlights areas where harmful gaps between DDR and SSR have persisted. It goes beyond what are considered to be the core components of SSR in the DRC (army, police and justice) to touch on other aspects of the broader SSR agenda essential to overall efforts, including oversight and management, gender, small arms, etc.

DDR and army reform

The most obvious linkage between DDR and SSR in the DRC is the integration of ex-combatants into the army. During the first phase of the PNDDR programme approximately 83,000 ex-combatants were integrated into the FARDC.[50] Ex-combatants were transferred from the responsibility of the national DDR commission to that of the integrated military structure. This required coordination between these two structures to ensure that ex-combatants were moved for training in distant *brassage* centres, thus seeking to break the chain of command with their former armed group. While innovative approaches were adopted (i.e. the *tronc commun* outlined below), many areas that required harmonization between DDR and army reform were overlooked (i.e. data collection, complementarity of benefits, and dependents of ex-combatants).

Tronc commun. The key nexus between DDR and army reform can be found in the *tronc commun* (dual track in English). The *tronc commun* represents the intersection of the DDR and defence reform programmes, and is jointly managed by two structures: the national DDR commission (CONADER, later the UE-PNDDR) and the integrated military structure (SMI).[51] The *tronc commun* was a concept originally developed to overcome funding restrictions on army reform. By agreeing that the military status of all combatants was suspended while they went through the *tronc commun* process, independently of whether they were combatants from armed groups or members of the former armed forces, the World Bank was able to show flexibility in the use of funds for joint activities such as transporting individuals to orientation centres.[52] Candidates would undertake a series of common activities before choosing integration or reintegration.[53] Those opting for integration into the army were then transported from orientation centres to *brassage* centres to undergo military training.

The *tronc commun* has offered an innovative approach to dealing with the challenges of linking DDR and SSR; however, the experience has not been flawless. Despite the development of a joint operations plan, lack of coordination has been cited as a major problem. For example, military authorities have changed the location of *brassage* centres without first consulting with CONADER, regardless of the implications this may have on the positioning of the orientation centres run by the latter.[54] Despite efforts to recognise the potential for fostering synergies in the area of the *tronc commun*, support to DDR and SSR could have been better coordinated.

DDR/SSR data collection. Army reform should begin with the screening and identification of ex-combatants who are seeking integration into the army at the demobilization centres. Data collected on ex-combatants, including qualifications and weapons specializations, can be used to support human resource management within the army by facilitating the identification of gaps to be filled through recruitment. Collecting and sharing this data can also strengthen the information management system and help avoid multiple payments to ex-combatants registering for both integration and reintegration programmes. Finally, this can also provide a useful basis for a census of the armed forces as a key entry point for security sector reform. Data collection is therefore an important way that DDR and SSR may intersect.

Since data was not transferred to military authorities in the DRC, an opportunity was missed to use information generated through the DDR process in support of SSR. Collecting this information would have provided a baseline for army reform, particularly useful given the widespread problem of ghost soldiers. The incentive to inflate the numbers of ex-combatants entering the DDR process – arising from the influence (and money) granted to commanders according to troop numbers provided to DDR authorities – has resulted in lost revenues. While this underlines the need to set more demanding criteria for entry than the number of people a group can assemble, it also points to the importance of data collection as a means to address this challenge. Efforts in this direction have only recently been taken with the conduct of a census of the FARDC in 2008. This had an impact in reducing fictitious payments and redirecting savings to raise overall salaries. A chain of payments system to prevent money from being derouted before it reaches the soldiers has also proved a useful initiative.[55] Ultimately, there is a need to establish proper information management systems and raise awareness of what information is useful for both stakeholder groups, and how it can be shared while respecting guidelines on confidentiality.

Reintegration and integration. In the DRC ex-combatants were provided with a voluntary choice between reintegration in society and integration in the army. This approach did not take into account how integration would affect the size and nature of the army, and led to disproportionate numbers of officers and sub-officers entering the army compared to other ranks, many of whom lacked qualifications or basic training.[56] Contrary to expectations, the majority of ex-combatants preferred to enter the demobilization process rather than choosing integration.[57] The main reason appears to have been the reputed dire social conditions in the army, as well as a comparatively low salary of US$10 per month, as opposed to the reinsertion package of US$25 per month plus a bulk payment of US$110 if ex-combatants chose demobilization.[58] The fact that a large number of military personnel have not been receiving their salaries at all – funnelled off during the payment process – has also been influential.[59]

This imbalance has had a negative impact on the reintegration process. More ex-combatants than could be absorbed by national budgets have applied for reintegration. There is also a significant backlog in the payment of reinsertion benefits. Generating jobs for ex-combatants is a major challenge. Moreover, government officials have raised the security concern that too many ex-combatants reintegrating into communities may have a destabilizing effect. Providing clearer guidance to ex-combatants on the choice between a military career and community reintegration could have mitigated the resulting challenges. The sensitization at the beginning of the DDR process was acknowledged to have been minimal, causing ex-combatants to choose reintegration while being unaware of the difficulties of finding sustainable employment.[60] Enhanced coordination between DDR and SSR stakeholders could also have helped ensure that the benefits offered for demobilization did not outweigh those provided through integration.

Voluntary integration has costs for SSR. It was offered as an act of good faith to ex-combatants in order to 'buy the peace', but the size and capacities of the armed forces are not being defined by a clear vision of its role, objectives and values. Discussions on controlling the number of ex-combatants of each rank to be integrated through stricter criteria for entry were abandoned because the human resources management system was not able to support such filtering, recalling the lack of attention that has been given to supporting management capacities for the security sector.

Dependants of ex-combatants and army reform. Dependants of ex-combatants were not adequately planned for in the area of army reform. Ex-combatants were transferred from orientation to *brassage* centres away from their families and then deployed to other regions of the country. The need to build orientation centres in the vicinity of *brassage* centres was not considered, resulting in increased travel across the country, higher costs and logistical problems.

This has had a detrimental effect on the training of soldiers. As provision was not made for families at *brassage* centres, ex-combatants often chose to give their food rations to their families, thereby creating difficult conditions for them during training.[61] This contributed to a sentiment among soldiers that their needs were not taken into consideration by their superiors. It is acknowledged that this encouraged desertions as well as undermining discipline and respect for the chain of command.[62]

The failure to see a connection between the dependants of ex-combatants and the need to build a professional army points to the consequences of incoherence across DDR, SSR and the broader peacebuilding project. For example, the humanitarian community focuses on vulnerable populations as a whole and not just the special category of military dependants. On the other hand, from a DDR perspective, it was considered that family needs were something the humanitarian community should address.[63]

DDR and police reform

Unlike the army, until 2009 there was no system of direct integration of ex-combatants into the police through the DDR process.[64] This did not, however, prevent the entry of ex-combatants into its structures. National authorities did not perceive this as a significant problem because at the time entry was *ad hoc* and only happened in certain areas. Moreover, the police force was scheduled to undergo training which would result in greater harmonization. In practice, the fact that ex-combatants entered the police through diverse routes meant they had not received a minimum level of training. The absence of a *brassage* process for these components also suggests that command structures could potentially be left intact, raising the question of whether a concentration of ex-combatants remaining in one area with a new policing function may pose a potential security risk.[65]

These challenges have been compounded since 2009 with the integration of CNDP ex-combatants into the police. It has been noted that the number of ex-CNDP combatants currently integrated into the police structures in North Kivu outweighs other components, and many of these ex-combatants failed to hand over a personal weapon during the integration process.[66] Given the central role of the police in providing security to individuals and communities, the vetting and training of such police officers remains an important but neglected nexus between DDR and SSR (see below on transitional justice). Another area that was overlooked was the targeting of police reform to support DDR efforts.

Police support to DDR. An important aspect of the DDR-SSR nexus is the role of SSR in creating a sustainable environment for DDR. In the DRC, police reform could have played a greater role in supporting DDR by factoring security provision for vulnerable communities affected by the process into training and resource allocation for police deployments. For instance, security vacuums created by the departure of ex-combatants to demobilization centres was often overlooked, leaving these communities vulnerable to attacks by other armed groups. Communities were also affected by heightened insecurity when other demobilised combatants were in the vicinity.[67] In areas without an active militia presence, demobilised fighters (and civilians) are said to have been 'commonly or increasingly responsible for both economic and violent crimes'.[68] Such problems linked to the presence of ex-combatants affects the ability of DDR programmes to succeed.

Lack of effective community policing in the DRC has resulted in the absence of a stable environment permitting the secure return of ex-combatants. This has been particularly devastating in the case of former child soldiers: it is reported that more than half of those reunited with their families in North Kivu 'have since been re-recruited by the armed groups'.[69] The alternative of keeping children in transit centres is prohibitively expensive. The vulnerability of disarmed children to re-recruitment by armed groups underscores the important role of the security sector in providing security to communities. Supporting the capacity of the police to protect these children could be enhanced through greater emphasis on their specific risks. However, police capacities will only be focused on this priority if support to the DDR process is factored into planning, training and resource allocation.

If the police force is to be in a position to fill these gaps, information on potential security vacuums must be identified and shared in time for the police to adapt. Efforts to increase coordination between police and DDR authorities have only been made since the February 2008 roundtable, which raised awareness on this issue. The police have now asked to be present at the PNDDR, which would represent a significant step forward. Ultimately, although a holistic SSR process may not be feasible before the DDR programme is finalised, it is none the less possible (and desirable) to target certain key areas of the SSR process that support a sustainable environment for DDR.

DDR and judicial aspects

DDR/SSR and transitional justice. Security Council Resolution 1794 (2007) calls upon the Congolese authorities 'to establish a vetting mechanism to take into account when they select candidates for official positions – including key posts in the armed forces, national police and other security services – the candidates' past actions in terms of respect for international humanitarian law and human rights'.[70] Vetting should therefore not only be considered an important activity related to DDR, but also part of a holistic approach to SSR. As of yet, this has not been the case; at most, there has been a screening process meant to eliminate ex-combatants who have committed human rights abuses or who do not have proper 'moral values' from the integration process. This falls short of a vetting procedure predicated on thorough background checks for the ensemble of personnel to avoid targeting only those associated with former rebel groups.

It is recognised that such a comprehensive vetting process would need to rely on effective human resource and information management systems, which have been lacking to date. In practice, however, vetting has not been pushed strongly because it was not considered feasible in the face of so many urgent and competing priorities. One major dilemma is that if vetting were conducted, senior stakeholders on all sides would probably be found guilty of wrongdoing. Vetting has thus been delayed in an effort to stabilise the overall security situation. The risk of delaying this process, however, is that a culture of impunity is perpetuated. The human rights section of MONUC has tried to raise awareness on this issue, but it did not have an appropriate forum in which to do so until its inclusion in the SSR coordination group created in July 2008. Communication within the UN mission and country team is important to tackle such sensitive issues which require an extensive understanding of the political and security situation as well as a coordinated approach between DDR and SSR stakeholders.

DDR and housing, land and property rights. The issue of access to land has been recognised as one of the root causes of the conflict. In this context, lack of clarity over housing, land and property (HLP) rights is an important issue with security dimensions, especially for internally displaced persons (IDPs) and ex-combatants looking to return to their local communities. Distrust, continued violence and 'the uncertain pace of disarmament' are making it difficult to plan and implement returns.[71]

Clear HLP rights, procedures and mediation mechanisms, it is hoped, will increase confidence in those returning to their local communities and support the stabilization of eastern DRC. IDPs and ex-combatants have been returning to their communities for several years now without receiving support in this area. Ensuring that the proper mechanisms are put in place to deal with possible land disputes is key to avoiding renewed tensions within receiving communities. However, support to this issue was lacking until September 2008, when UN Habitat developed the Housing, Land and Property Interventions in Eastern DRC Programme, in line with the UN Security and Stabilization Strategy.

DDR/SSR and gender

Gender has not been mainstreamed into either DDR or SSR in the DRC, despite efforts by the United Nations.[72] In particular, female combatants have not been adequately taken into account within the DDR process. The common definition of ex-combatants does not incorporate women associated with a rebel movement because they do not possess a weapon.[73] In the rare cases where female combatants have been considered as a separate category with their own needs, as was the case in Kisangani, they were automatically demobilised without being offered the choice of a military career.[74] MONUC's gender section has raised these problems in numerous forums, but has been told that the reason women are not specifically targeted in DDR programmes is because of the low number of registrations compared to men (only one woman for every 40 men). This ignores the reality that a large number of women do not register for fear of stigmatization.

Creating adequate incentives for women to enter the DDR process and supporting efforts to destigmatise these women is of key importance. The absence of women from the security sector is not just discriminatory but represents a lost opportunity to benefit from the different skills sets and approaches offered by women as security providers.[75] Gender mainstreaming in the security sector needs to start with DDR, because if female ex-combatants are not given adequate consideration in DDR processes it is very unlikely they will be able to enter the security forces through the path of integration.

DDR/SSR and SALW

Poor management of government weapons stockpiles allowed the seizure of weapons by armed groups, thus creating a disincentive to join the DDR process.[76] This is an issue that has also been raised in the recent report of the Group of Experts on the DRC, which notes that 'the poor condition of stocks and control mechanisms within FARDC and the national police, coupled with poorly disciplined and paid troops, poses a serious risk of continued diversion of military equipment to armed groups'.[77] The market for these stolen weapons is not only armed groups, but also ex-combatants wishing to enter the DDR process. The combination of the 'one man one weapon' approach and the substantial financial rewards offered by the DDR programme has created a market for purchasing such weapons.

Incentive structures need to be clarified to prevent cases where the cash value of the reinsertion package greatly outweighs the market price of a weapon. Inadequately managed military and police weapons storage facilities also show the importance of supporting oversight and control capacities. Thus, the absence of complementary disarmament and stockpile management programmes represents a missed opportunity to link DDR and SSR.

DDR and private security companies

The vacuum created by ineffective national security institutions has created a market for private security companies (PSCs). The private security industry has come to play a prominent role in the DRC and has 'engaged in the provision of security and crime prevention, guarding and response, security advice and risk assessment'.[78] Overall, PSCs are considered much more professional than the national security services.[79] They have even been considered as a possible solution for securing orientation centres for ex-combatants, as they are considered more professional than the police.[80]

Official data does not exist on the numbers of ex-combatants seeking employment in the commercial security sector in the DRC. There is therefore no proven correlation between DDR and the growth of private security companies. However, the potential significance of this relationship is exemplified by one PSC that 'declared that it had employed a small number of ex-combatants who had been through the DDR programme, based on a special arrangement with the Ministry of Interior and CONADER'.[81] Considering the private security sector as a source of employment for ex-combatants merits further analysis. However, there is also a clear need to monitor the state of regulation of PSCs and to ensure that strict vetting and certification procedures are in place.

DDR-RR and SSR

DDR-RR and border security. As reflected in the 2007 Nairobi communiqué, the need to tighten border controls is widely acknowledged due to the unregulated flow of minerals, arms and foreign combatants across the DRC's borders. Part of the challenge is that the DRC has over 10,000 kilometres of border.[82] The International Organization for Migration has only recently started to support a border security programme. Activities will take place in strategically sensitive areas in the east renowned for arms-trafficking problems. Within the Security and Stabilization Strategy developed by MONUC, there is also a proposal to establish 32 border posts in North and South Kivu.

Despite the clear connection between DDR-RR and the transit of foreign combatants over borders, there are no plans for the border security programme to address transiting foreign combatants. Expertise to address these issues from a DDR-RR perspective is lacking and there has been a reluctance to address border security as a joint DDR-SSR planning issue.

DDR-RR, SSR and the exploitation of natural resources. A recent report of the UN Group of Experts on the DRC reaffirmed the links that exist between the activities of armed groups and the exploitation of natural resources.[83] The exploitation of natural resources by armed groups provides the motivation and resource base to prolong violence. It was further recognised that SSR is essential to end this problem.

MONUC and the FARDC have developed an operational plan to increase the military pressure on the FDLR 'in areas where it controls commercial activities and the illegal exploitation of natural resources'. However, this cannot be done in isolation from activities in DDR-RR; the first phase of action must be to reduce the FDLR's control over 'major routes and sites of economic activity'.[84] This is an area where DDR-RR and SSR support could be better coordinated, combining training of the security forces with a communication strategy to encourage repatriation.

Challenges and Lessons

DDR and SSR in the DRC take place within a highly challenging environment. This is reflected in the language surrounding this process, characterised by the Minister of Defence as 'stabilizing the parameters of reform'. In practice, this has meant that the focus of national authorities and the allocation of resources are directed towards operational activities. Strategic analysis of the longer-term consequences that DDR may have on SSR and vice versa is lacking. Opportunities and gaps identified in the previous section point to the difficulties of identifying and operationalizing the DDR/SSR nexus in the DRC. This section highlights some of these challenges, and suggests lessons which serve as a basis for the recommendations laid out in the conclusion. Challenges are divided into three categories: the political and security context; strategic and operational challenges; and institutional challenges specific to UN support.

Political and security challenges

Shifting political and security priorities. In the DRC, DDR and SSR were approached as activities that could be translated into fixed sequencing and timelines, with DDR starting first and SSR beginning only once DDR had been completed. The guiding logic for these activities was the urgent need to stabilise the east of the country. The creation of a professional army was seen as a necessary precondition for the government's goal to secure the national territory – notably in the Kivu region.[85] In order to provide the human resource base for the new army, the first step in this process would be DDR in order to provide a pool of ex-combatants that could integrate the army. However, this intended sequencing created a dilemma as it soon became apparent that in order to support the DDR of the remaining armed groups, targeted army reform would first be necessary to enable offensive action against the armed groups, as well as to ensure the troops could better protect individuals and communities in the vicinity of the fighting through targeted capacity-building. Therefore the cut-off between the end of DDR and the beginning of SSR became more ambiguous than was originally envisaged.

Initially, the integration of ex-combatants into the national army and the reintegration of ex-combatants were planned to be completed before the elections scheduled for June 2005. The argument was that SSR would be able to start once DDR had been terminated, and that the newly elected government would make the political decisions necessary for SSR, thus enhancing the national ownership of the reform programme. The timelines outlined in the peace agreements for troop withdrawals and tracking and cantoning armed groups, however, are acknowledged to have been 'so short as to be nonsensical'.[86] This was compounded by the fact that demobilization was perceived to be an uncomplicated, short and technical project.[87] In practice, lengthy delays in the DDR process meant that sequencing did not work out as planned; consequently, the national authorities were forced to address DDR and SSR simultaneously.

Delays in the DDR process have led to the question of whether the objective to finish DDR before the elections may have been based on the wrong premise.[88] While unsure of the political outcome, it is unlikely that rebel groups would be inclined to put their best soldiers into the DDR process. Politically motivated violence after the elections has been cited as an illustration of this effect.[89] Ultimately, without DDR and DDR-RR finished and in the face of fluctuating security and political conditions, SSR has been conducted very much from a short-term perspective, focusing on the immediate aim of stabilizing the east of the country. This has meant that efforts to support the development of the national security sector governance framework have been sidelined. This points to the need for flexibility in programming; mitigation strategies to deal with shifting political and security priorities; and, ultimately, the need to recognise that both DDR and SSR are essentially political processes that depend on political circumstances.

DDR and DDR-RR. A specific challenge in the DRC has been the need to tackle both DDR and DDR-RR simultaneously at the operational level, while keeping the two processes separate at a political level. The presence of foreign combatants has strengthened the support base of Congolese militias such as the CNDP. This has provided the CNDP with the excuse to disagree on the modalities of the *brassage* process, which, in accordance with the Goma Agreement, mandated that troops undergo *brassage* outside the Kivu region. Consequently, CNDP's refusal to demobilise has been one of the main reasons why the Amani programme has stalled.[90] The need to deal with two types of rebel groups has thus presented a major challenge and contributed to stalling army integration and reform. Increased dialogue between DDR and DDR-RR stakeholders is essential to overcome such challenges.

Strategic and operational challenges

Narrow approach to SSR. A key DDR/SSR challenge has been the narrow understanding of SSR adopted by the majority of national and international stakeholders. One outcome of this narrow approach has been that efforts to empower oversight and management bodies have been sidestepped in favour of more limited capacity building of security providers. This has had significant consequences. For example, the lack of a human resource management system capable of supporting a census of the armed forces has made it difficult to plan realistically in advance for the number of ex-combatants who could be accommodated within the armed forces. Moreover, the lack of financial and social auditing can in part account for the imbalance between ex-combatants registering for demobilization rather than integration into the army, which has resulted in excessive pressure on reintegration schemes. These examples demonstrate the centrality of security sector management and oversight concerns to the DDR-SSR nexus.

Stovepiping. Synergies between DDR and SSR have been hampered by stovepiping within and across DDR and SSR communities. The large number of actors engaged in SSR at national and international levels has enabled the government to deal with the international community individually rather than collectively, undermining efforts to promote coherence. A contact group, including a subgroup for SSR, was created to address this problem, but the lack of a clear 'lead' donor meant that coordination was missing at this level. In the area of DDR this has been less of a problem as fewer players are involved and the majority of funds were distributed through the MDRP. Moreover, there is a clearer sense of national ownership of the DDR process, despite the multiplicity of structures at the national level.[91]

The stovepiping that occurred in the area of SSR has been a major impediment to encouraging synergies between the DDR and SSR processes. One example is the excessive time it took to undertake a census of the armed forces. This was the consequence of the idea being 'batted back and forth between donors, each one saying that the other one was doing it'.[92] This points to the need to link the creation of structures for coordination with adequate political will to support them.

Financial resources. Securing adequate funding has been a key challenge for DDR and SSR in the DRC. Funding gaps have been particularly apparent in the area of army reform, partly due to the fear among donors of being perceived as supporting an instrument of internal repression. The close linkages between DDR and army integration in the DRC means that DDR has been dependent on a steady flow of people moving out of the *brassage* centres so that other ex-combatants can move into them. Delays in army reform due to funding gaps have blocked money earmarked for the DDR process. This has further heightened tensions in areas where ex-combatants were not able to enter the DDR process until space was made in the *brassage* centres.

Although the *tronc commun* was created to bypass restrictions on funding for military reform, keeping the funds segregated meant that the negative impact of the lack of funding could not be entirely avoided in practice. This is an important aspect of the overall coordination challenge across DDR and SSR processes, pointing to the importance of joint planning to ensure complementarity.

UN-specific institutional challenges

Strategic management. The absence of a UN system-wide approach to DDR/SSR has impacted on the ability to link, sequence and prioritise activities. For example, MONUC's vision of the DDR/SSR nexus has been limited to the obvious linkage between DDR and army integration, without taking into account the potential to tap into other areas of the security sector.[93] This is related to a lack of knowledge as to the potential benefits of synergies between DDR and SSR.

In order to reflect the DDR-SSR nexus in the field there is a need for commitment at the strategic level. The lack of a centre of gravity that promotes coherent UN support across DDR and SSR underlines the need to develop strong lines of management responsibility within the mission and a clear delineation of roles and responsibilities from headquarters. In this respect, the terms of reference of certain key positions should include the need to address the relationship between DDR and SSR through proactive coordination and planning. Including such criteria in terms of reference may encourage monitoring and evaluation on the basis of progress achieved in this area. Ultimately, the new module in the UN Integrated DDR Standards (IDDRS) on DDR and SSR should contribute to developing common UN understandings in this area.

Evolving structures for DDR and SSR. Weak and evolving institutional structures for DDR and SSR have negatively affected the ability to foster synergies. DDR was not managed by an autonomous unit within MONUC but rather by a few staff members from the DDR-RR unit voluntarily working on DDR issues. While the DDR-RR section was made up of over 30 staff, from 2002 until 2004 there were only two people working on DDR, and this was done on an informal basis since it was not part of their original terms of reference.[94] In 2004 the situation improved when a new Security Council resolution mandated MONUC to contribute to the disarmament portion of the PNDDR; however, support to DDR still remained *ad hoc* and was not translated into a unit within the mission until the 2006 decision to create a DDR/SSR section.[95]

It could be expected that merging DDR and SSR into a joint section would increase coherence, but in practice personnel continued to focus on either DDR or SSR. This may have been because the reason for creating the new structure had less to do with attempting to strengthen the linkages between DDR and SSR than with the objective to develop an SSR section within the mission.[96] This DDR/SSR unit operated with eight staff members from August 2006 until July 2008, when DDR was again merged with DDR-RR and a dedicated SSR team was created.[97]

The constant modifications to DDR and SSR structures have not been conducive to fostering synergies. A key lesson is that the choice of separate or joint DDR/SSR units is less important than ensuring that structures reflect priorities on the ground and have adequate coordination mechanisms in place. Ensuring that these priorities are reflected in the Security Council mandates is important, and could be encouraged through their inclusion in technical assessment missions.

Coordination and cooperation. Coordination and cooperation between UN structures constituted an additional challenge to operationalizing the DDR/SSR nexus in the early years of the mission. Indeed, coordination was difficult within each entity, which in turn complicated efforts at broader cooperation.[98] Improvements were only made in 2008 with the creation of new structures and mechanisms – the first time since the mission was established in 1999 that other sections of MONUC, such as gender or civil affairs, were systematically consulted on elements of DDR and SSR. In particular, an SSR working group was introduced in 2008 to improve coordination.[99] *Ad hoc* meetings on DDR under the auspices of the deputy special representative of the Secretary-General (DSRSG) have been held since the second quarter of 2008. The DSRSG, as the resident coordinator and humanitarian coordinator of the country team, ensured that other UN funds and agencies such as UNDP were clearly visible in these mechanisms.

Increased cooperation on SSR reflected the creation of the small SSR unit within MONUC, led by an adviser to the special representative of the Secretary-General (SRSG). The SSR adviser played a key role in ensuring that there was one UN voice on SSR.[100] A relatively clear division of labour was established between this SSR team and the other SSR-related sections of the mission. The SSR unit was located at the strategic level and did not support technical operational activities, which were the remit of the individual sections. Strengthening strategic management for SSR thus ensured wider support to inclusive coordination mechanisms that fostered linkages with other related components of the mission/country team.

Planning and programming of DDR and SSR. DDR and SSR concerns will not be addressed in implementation if they are not already integrated at the planning stage. However, planning and programming on DDR within MONUC have been beset by difficulties. In an audit of MONUC's DDR-RR programme by the UN Office of Internal Oversight Services (OIOS) in 2005, 'the ad hoc manner in which the Mission developed its plans' was identified as a major weakness.[101] It was also noted that the plans had never been approved by the head of mission, and contained details on the role to be played by other sections without ensuring that they had been involved in the planning process. Feedback from interviews held with the DDR team as part of this study also reflected a lack of systematic planning and coordination.

Undertaking joint assessments or conducting integrated planning could support a more coherent approach to DDR and SSR. A significant step in this direction was taken with the development in 2008–2009 of the International Security and Stabilization Support Strategy.[102] The strategy identifies five key areas of support: improving security; supporting political dialogue; strengthening the state; supporting reintegration, recovery and reconciliation; and addressing sexual violence. The strategy includes SSR components, such as support to the armed forces, police and judiciary, as well as support to DDR.[103] The plan focuses efforts within key strategic areas in the east where armed groups disband as a consequence of the Goma and Nairobi agreements. The strategy takes an integrated approach to planning by involving all sections of the mission, the wider UN family and relevant international actors. The development of an integrated strategy offers a useful tool for linking DDR and SSR.

Human resource capacities. One challenge in supporting DDR and SSR has been the common institutional problem of harnessing adequate capacity. From 2004 to 2006, MONUC's DDR team faced an additional challenge in that the team was never budgeted for nor included in MONUC's original mandate. As a result, human resource support to DDR has been mostly based on the voluntary work of staff from the DDR-RR unit.[104] Until the creation of the SSR team in July 2008 there was also limited capacity for SSR within the DDR/SSR unit that existed from 2006 to 2008. As part of the DDR unit, the SSR team consisted of eight staff (six civilian and two military), transferred to that section from the DDR-RR unit and working on both DDR and SSR issues. The creation of the SSR team in 2008 has not increased SSR capacity, although the unit was finally attributed its own staffing table within the results-based budget framework, consisting of one D1-level post, one P3-level post and one administrative assistant.

Reinforcing the capacities of DDR and SSR teams is a clear priority. It is particularly important to identify individuals experienced in supporting management and oversight structures. Skills sets that contribute to supporting the development of national capacity are equally important. The fact that there is an overlap of human resources needed for both DDR and

SSR offers an opportunity to pool resources and organise training in cross-cutting issues.

Financial resource capacities. The need to approve the mission's budget one-and-a-half years in advance has made it hard to inject flexibility into funding. This has been further compounded in the area of SSR, where army reform has been underfunded because of the reluctance of donors to support an army associated with human rights abuses. It has been noted that 'one of the greatest obstacles to security sector reform in DRC lies in the difficulties involved in mobilizing funds, especially taking into account the fact that military reform does not form part of public development assistance'.[105] UNDP staff in Kinshasa, for example, have found it hard to persuade counterparts in headquarters that equipment for the military is essential to the post-*brassage* process.[106]

Further compounding the lack of funds for the SSR process have been restrictions related to contributions from the assessed budget. This is not able to cover project-related costs (with the exception of quick-impact projects) and is generally restricted to the payment of personnel costs, infrastructure, logistics and transportation.[107] Financial constraints are not only a problem for SSR: in the area of DDR there has been a lack of development partners willing to support reintegration for the numbers of ex-combatants who need it. This points to the need for innovative solutions. The establishment of the Stabilization and Recovery Fund facility in 2009, which is a flexible mechanism for managing and disbursing international funds in support of the International Security and Stabilization Support Strategy, is an important step in this direction although it is yet to be determined what impact this will have in practice.

Monitoring and evaluation. The lack of effective monitoring and evaluation of DDR and SSR in the DRC has hampered the ability of the United Nations to use this as an entry point for linking DDR and SSR concerns in planning. While monitoring and evaluation of DDR programmes is usually more developed – in part due to the compendium of best practices for monitoring and evaluating DDR programmes developed within the IDDRS framework – this was not the case in the DRC. In an audit of MONUC's DDR programme conducted by the OIOS in 2005, it was noted that the programme was in dire need of an evaluation after having been in operation for over three years.[108] This was reiterated by a senior official of the DDR team, who stated that in terms of monitoring and evaluation there was a '*vide totale*'.[109] The reason for this was said to be the rapid pace of events in the DRC, which made it impossible to track progress.

Despite the lack of comprehensive monitoring and evaluation, all areas of the mission must report to some extent on results. Therefore, according to the results-based budget framework, achievement in the DDR process may be based on the indicator of 'the number of remaining disarmed Congolese ex-combatants demobilised'.[110] The indicators for the SSR team are mainly political such as 'adoption by the Government of a comprehensive strategy and action plan for reform of the defence sector'.[111] In this sense, the performance indicators evaluate *compliance* of the government, but not *effectiveness* of the international community's support, or of the United Nations for that matter. Greater emphasis needs to be given to monitoring and evaluating DDR and SSR programmes in order to provide for a more structured approach to recognizing and operationalizing the linkages between DDR and SSR.

Conclusion and Policy Recommendations

The environment within which the UN integrated mission in the DRC operates is significantly different to many other peacekeeping contexts. The country's size, ongoing security challenges, shifting political dynamics and the vulnerability of its geographical position have had a profound impact on DDR and SSR. Since the mission was established in 1999, the United Nations has faced numerous crises in the country, including prolonged fighting in Ituri and the Kivus, the seizure of Bukavu in 2004 and the Gatumba massacres in the same year. Vast challenges were also associated with the organization of the national elections in 2006, which required significant resources, both political and material. In this sense, the setting has never been a clear-cut post-conflict environment but rather a constant state of emergency, requiring the United Nations and the wider international community to adapt rapidly to changing political and security conditions.

In this context, the first priority for the mission has been stabilization. Consequently, the importance granted to DDR and SSR has shifted according to the requirements at the time. During the months prior to the elections, election security was the key priority and emergency efforts were put into supporting the capacity of the police. Currently, given the risk of renewed fighting among rebel groups, DDR and DDR-RR are a first priority. However, these shifts should not mean that one activity is neglected over the other: progress in one area may contribute to supporting a conducive environment for the other. Ensuring that linkages between key components of DDR and SSR programmes are not overlooked is therefore of critical importance.

In the DRC, linking certain parts of the DDR and SSR processes could have contributed to greater overall effectiveness of the mission. Equally important, however, is the recognition that sometimes the two areas of activity need to be delinked to contribute to greater flexibility in responding to emergency situations. Ultimately, political will and ownership of the DDR and SSR processes are key to success, not only on the government side but also in dealings with rebel groups.[112] UN support to DDR has been hampered by the fact that 'many rebel groups have done everything possible to hinder their disarmament and *brassage*'.[113] This reinforces the point that DDR should not be seen as just a technical activity but as part of the broader political process.

Recommendations

The recommendations listed below are based on the context of the DRC; however, a number may also be relevant to other peacekeeping and development contexts where DDR and SSR activities are supported by the United Nations.

Broaden the understanding of the DDR-SSR nexus. The understanding of the potential linkages between DDR and SSR should be broadened beyond the obvious relationship between DDR and army reform to include issues such as DDR and police reform, DDR and border security management, DDR/SSR and gender, etc. This case study shows how adopting a narrow approach to the DDR-SSR nexus has resulted in missed opportunities to deliver on common goals. Awareness needs to be raised on these issues through training. The new DDR-SSR module in the IDDRS will be an important vehicle to promote this understanding.

Increase support to the governance component. Security sector governance issues need to be supported from the outset, as they are equally crucial to effective DDR and SSR. Efforts to reinforce the national governance framework should not be sidestepped by dealing solely with short-term security priorities. Target issues should include financial and social auditing of the security sector; the development of a human resource management system within the security sector capable of supporting a national census; and efforts to professionalise, oversee and manage security sector personnel.

Encourage a consultative process of national dialogue on SSR. National dialogue processes can increase the legitimacy of DDR and SSR decision-making. Decisions on the size and capacities of the armed forces should reflect an informed understanding of their role, objectives and values. Consideration must be given to the sustainability of resource commitments, including salary payments and future pensions of armed personnel, when considering integration. A strategy that reflects experiences from both rural and urban areas and incorporates the views of civil society, academia and parliamentarians is necessary in order to reach out to different groups and interests.

Identify priorities for SSR based on DDR concerns. Priority setting for SSR should be linked to fundamental needs in the area of DDR. This implies that support to the DDR process is factored in to planning, training and resource allocation for SSR. This includes the use of data generally collected during DDR but not properly exploited and the development of up-to-date contextual security analysis. Comprehensive assessments of the capacity of national actors to support these processes should also be conducted to identify where focused support would be of most use.

Recognise the need for coordination across DDR-SSR. Improved dialogue between DDR and SSR stakeholders is necessary to support coordination on key issues. These include: complementarity of funding; harmonization of benefits between reintegration and army integration; the location of orientation and *brassage* centres; acting on possible security vacuums in the vicinity of DDR programmes; identifying data collected during DDR registration that could support SSR planners; coordinating requirements for the vetting of ex-combatants and security sector personnel. Coordination is also essential to develop mitigation strategies that foresee and deal with delays in each process and their consequences.

Optimise existing forums. DDR/SSR working groups or steering committees should ensure coherence across support to DDR and SSR. Existing national commissions (such as those for DDR) can also encourage dialogue between DDR and SSR stakeholders. The utility of such forums depends on effective awareness-raising and communication; it was only when representatives of the national police attended an SSR roundtable in 2008 that attention was given to the positive impact targeted police support could have for the DDR process.[114]

Encourage gender-responsive DDR and SSR. If female ex-combatants are not given adequate consideration in DDR processes, it is very unlikely they will be able to enter the security forces through the path of integration. There is a need to enhance the support to, and incentives for, women to enter the DDR process. Likewise, conditions within the security sector must be improved to ensure that integration is a real option. This should be encouraged by addressing gender-based violence as well as providing access to psychosocial support and sensitization. The same consideration of the specific challenges faced by female ex-combatants during reintegration (e.g. stigma, non-conventional skill sets, reproductive health needs) should be given to the challenges they face during integration into the security sector.

Support awareness-raising on the DDR-SSR nexus. There is a need to raise awareness on the DDR-SSR nexus. A first step in this direction would be to provide training to relevant field and headquarters staff. Providing for cross-participation in DDR and SSR training may also be considered so as to highlight mutual constraints and opportunities for cooperating together and foster a culture of exchange between DDR and SSR stakeholders. Second, the need for addressing DDR-SSR linkages should be included in the terms of reference of relevant personnel to ensure that they are tasked and measured against this requirement.

Notes

1. In accordance with UN SC Resolution 1925, 28 May 2010, MONUC was renamed the UN Organization Stabilization Mission in the Democratic Republic of the Congo (MONUSCO), to reflect the new phase reached in the country. This case study mainly refers to MONUC as it focuses on events that occurred until 2010.
2. The detailed field research for this report was conducted in September 2008 and involved interviews in Kinshasa and Goma. The author is extremely grateful for the support of Mr. Yves Bouchard in the research conducted for this case study.
3. In response, the DRC government received support from Angola, Namibia and Zimbabwe, among others.
4. The DRC ranks 176 out of 182 on the Human Development Index (2007/2008). UNDP, *Human Development Report* (UNDP, 2009). Available at http://hdr.undp.org/en/statistics/.
5. D. Kampf, 'The Democratic Republic of Congo: Beyond the Elections', *African Security Review* 16, no. 1 (2007): 111. Available at www.ssrnetwork.net/doc_library/document _detail.php?id=3693.
6. The Interahamwe is a Hutu militia particularly active in Rwanda during the genocide. After the liberation of Kigali, thousands of these rebels fled to the DRC.
7. The CNDP was a rebel group led by General Laurent Nkunda that claimed to fight for justice for the people and protection of the Congolese Tutsis.

8 'Mayi Mayi' is a term used to describe Congolese rebel groups that were created to defend their territory against other armed groups, particularly those from neighbouring Rwanda.

9 *Brassage* (commonly known in English as 'mixing') refers to the process of intermingling individuals from different rebel groups in order to break former chains of command before army integration.

10 The Amani programme was replaced by the STAREC (Stabilization and Reconstruction Plan for War-Affected Areas) programme in 2009.

11 In October 2008 the leader of the rebel movement CNDP, Laurent Nkunda, announced his withdrawal from the Goma peace agreement.

12 The government negotiated two military agreements with Rwanda and Uganda to remove foreign Rwandan and Ugandan combatants from Congolese soil, and joint military operations were conducted in early 2009. In parallel, the CNDP leader, General Nkunda was arrested in January 2009. On 23 March 2009 the Congolese authorities signed a series of peace agreements with the CNDP, and the armed groups of North and South Kivu. The agreements provide for the integration of these elements into the security sector, as well as for their transformation into legal political parties. At the time of writing, the implementation of these agreements has been stalling. Moreover, problems concerning the accelerated integration of these elements, including the lack of payment of their salaries, have contributed to further escalating tensions in the east.

13 The UN Integrated DDR Standards (IDDRS) has noted that the United Nations uses the concept and abbreviation 'DDR' as an all-inclusive term that 'includes related activities such as repatriation, rehabilitation, reconciliation and so on that aim to achieve reintegration'. However, in this case study a distinction is made between DDR and DDR-RR, as they have been conducted as two entirely separate programmes in the DRC.

14 The joint military operation was pushing combatants to leave, while the DDR-RR programme was offering them a way out. See 'Briefing on the Eastern DRC: Repatriation of FDLR Combatants and Their Dependants from DRC to Rwanda' (Woodrow Wilson Center, March 2009). Available at www.wilsoncenter.org/index.cfm?topic_id=1417 &categoryid=09b716eb-65bf-e7dc-4f396daec6ad4f99&fuseaction=topics.events_item_ topics&event_id=512007.

15 This includes the *Forces Armées Congolaises* (FAC), the *Rassemblement Congolais pour la Démocratie – Goma* (RCD-Goma), the *Rassemblement Congolais pour la Démocratie – Nationale* (RCD-N), the *Rassemblement Congolais pour la Démocratie-Kisangani/Mouvement de Libération* (RCD-K/ML), the *Mouvement de Libération Congolais* (MLC), Mayi Mayi and other *autodéfense* militias, as well as the Ituri armed groups.

16 Plan d'Intégration des Forces Armées de la République Démocratique du Congo, (SMI, February 2006), 11.

17 Interview with UE-PNDDR official, Goma.

18 These militia groups were: the Popular Armed Forces for the Congo (FAPC), the Nationalist and Integrationist Front (FNI), the Revolutionary Front for Ituri (FPRI), the Popular Front for Democracy in Congo (FPDC), the Party for Unity and Safeguarding the Integrity of Congo (PUSIC), the Union of Congolese Patriots (Thomas Lubanga) (UPC-L) and the Union of Congolese Patriots (Floribert Kisembo) (UPC-K).

19 Hans Rouw and Rens Willems, 'Connecting Community Security and DDR: Experiences from Eastern DRC' (April 2010). Available at http://unddr.org/docs/Community _Security_and_DDR_-_DRC_case_study_-_final-April_2010.pdf.

[20] These are the three components of SSR examined in the meetings of the SSR/DDR contact group.

[21] While the committees for police reform (*Comité de Suivi sur la Réforme de la Police*) and justice reform (*Comité technique pour la Réforme de la Justice*) have worked fairly well, a similar structure for army reform was lacking until the creation of the *Comité politique pour la réforme de l'armée*, which is presided over by the minister of defence. See Henry Boshoff, 'Demobilisation, Disarmament and Reintegration in the Democratic Republic of Congo: A Never-ending Story', *Africa Security Review* 16, no. 2 (2007): 59–62.

[22] For example, population surveys have affirmed that only 8.1 per cent of respondents in North Kivu and 11.9 per ent in South Kivu reported they felt protected by the police. Patrick Vinck, Phuong Pham, Suliman Baldo and Rachel Shigekane, 'Living With Fear' (August 2008), 27. Available at www.ictj.org/images/content/1/0/1019.pdf.

[23] Oxfam, 'Protection Assessment – OGB and Partners North Kivu, South Kivu and Ituri' (Oxfam, May/June 2008).

[24] Amnesty International, 'DDR and Reform of the Army' (January 2007), 9.

[25] Maria Eriksson Baaz and Maria Stern, 'Making Sense of Violence: Voices of Soldiers in the Congo (DRC)', *Journal of Modern African Studies* 46, no. I (2008): 57–86, at p. 65.

[26] Plan d'Intégration des Forces Armées de la République Démocratique du Congo, February 2006.

[27] This plan received a lukewarm reception from the international community.

[28] See for instance the capturing of the Rumangabo army base by the rebels loyal to Laurent Nkunda. BBC News, 'DR Congo Rebels Capture Army Base', *BBC,* 9 October 2008. Available at http://news.bbc.co.uk/2/hi/africa/7660592.stm.

[29] In September 2008, while the seventh integrated brigade was fighting the CNDP, the force disintegrated under pressure and some government soldiers switched sides.

[30] Interview with MONUC Deputy Chief of Staff for SSR.

[31] Interviews with civil society and MONUC officials.

[32] International Crisis Group, 'Security Sector Reform in the Congo', Crisis Group Africa Report No. 104 (ICG, 13 February 2006), 5.

[33] Amnesty International, 'DRC: Torture and Killings by State Security Agents Still Endemic' (Amnesty International, October 2007), 9. Available at www.amnesty.org/es/library/asset/AFR62/012/2007/en/dom-AFR620122007en.pdf.

[34] Ibid.

[35] United Nations, 'UN Secretary-General Report', UN Doc. S/2008/218, 13.

[36] Ibid., 11.

[37] Vinck et al., note 22 above: 27.

[38] Amnesty International, 'Democratic Republic of Congo: DDR and Reform of the Army' (Amnesty International, January 2007), 43–44. Available at www.amnesty.org/en/library/asset/AFR62/001/2007/en/domAFR620012007en.pdf.

[39] Figure as of April 2010. The category of uniformed personnel includes military contingents, military observers, and MONUC Police. See http://monuc.unmissions.org/.

[40] Lusaka Ceasefire Agreement, Chapter 8, Annex A. See also Peter Swarbrick, 'Avoiding Disarmament Failure: The Critical Link in DDR', Working Paper (Geneva: Small Arms Survey, February 2007).

[41] Pretoria Agreement, 30 July 2002.

[42] UN SC Resolution 1279, 30 November 1999. The disengagement of forces is the language used in the DRC to refer to the withdrawal of armed forces from their positions.

[43] UN SC Resolution 1291, 24 February 2000.

44 UN SC Resolution 1565, 1 October 2004.

45 However, this also reflects the strong national ownership of the DDR programme with direct funding support from the World Bank.

46 UN SC Resolution 1565, 1 October 2004.

47 EUSEC RD Congo Factsheet, June 2008.

48 For an overview of the coordination mechanisms relevant to the international community in the area of SSR, see Renner Onana and Hannah Taylor, 'MONUC and SSR in the Democratic Republic of Congo', *International Peacekeeping* 15, no. 4 (2008).

49 Caty Clément, 'Security Sector reform in the DRC: Forward to the Past', in *Security Sector Reform in Challenging Environments*, eds. Hans Born and Albrecht Schnabel, 104 (Munster: Lit Verlag, 2009).

50 Henri Boshoff, 'Completing the demobilisation, disarmament and reintegration process of armed groups in the Democratic Republic of Congo and the link to security sector reform of FARDC', Situation Report (Institute for Security Studies, November 2010).

51 The SMI was formed in 2004 to operationalise the relevant provisions of the 2003 Global and All-Inclusive Agreement.

52 Nicole Ball and Dylan Hendrickson, 'Review of International Financing Arrangements for Disarmament, Demobilization and Reintegration: Phase 2 Report to Working Group 2 (Stockholm: Stockholm Initiative on Disarmament, Demobilization and Reintegration, 26 September, 2005), 20.

53 These activities include sensitisation, encampment, disarmament, identification, storage or destruction of combatants' weapons and the transfer of disarmed combatants to orientation centres for identification.

54 Ball and Hendrickson, note 50 above: 16.

55 This was supported by EUSEC.

56 It must be acknowledged that this was designed as a mechanism to 'buy the peace' by occupying these ex-combatants.

57 An informal working paper on UNDP and SSR in the DRC cites 70 per cent as the percentage of ex-combatants preferring to enter civilian life.

58 The basic salary of soldiers was increased from US$10 to US$25 per month in 2006.

59 This is set to change with the completion of the census, and the subsequent raise in salaries.

60 It has been recognised that despite the existence of *centres d'orientation*, the 'time and space for individual combatants to consider their options for remaining in the new national army' needed to represent 'a discrete stage in the DDR process'. Swarbrick, note 40 above.

61 Interview with MONUC gender unit.

62 This emerged in numerous interviews. For a discussion on the views of soldiers on the reasons behind pillaging and lack of discipline, see Baaz and Stern, note 25 above, pp. 76–77.

63 The IDDRS, however, does underline the need to consider the dependants of ex-combatants in DDR programmes.

64 This has only just changed with the recent decision to integrate elements of the CNDP into the national police following the Goma agreements of 23 March 2009.

65 This was the case in Bunia, for instance, where the numbers of the police went from 8,000 in 2003 to 15,000 in 2008 mainly through the integration of ex-combatants. Interview with UNDP official.

66 See UN Security Council, 'Interim Report of the Group of Experts on the Democratic Republic of Congo', UN Doc. S/2009/253.

67 Interview with MONUC police commissioner.

68 Oxfam, note 23 above.

69 Amnesty International, 'No End to War on Women and Children: North Kivu DRC' (Amnesty International, September 2008), 15. Available at www.amnesty.org/en/library/asset/AFR62/005/2008/en/bbe6934a-9f60-11dd-9e51-afa0a8282a50/afr620052008en.pdf.

70 UN SC Resolution 1794, 21 December 2007.

71 UN Habitat, 'HLP Interventions in Eastern DRC to Facilitate Returns of IDPs and Refugees and Improve the Land Administration', HLP Project Document (2008), 3.

72 This includes appointing a senior adviser on sexual violence reporting directly to the DSRSG responsible for developing a strategy for linking SSR and sexual violence.

73 This narrow approach has been influenced by budgetary considerations. See the IDDRS.

74 Interview with MONUC gender section.

75 Megan Bastick and Kristin Valasek, Kristin, eds., 'Gender and Security Sector Reform Toolkit' (DCAF, OSCE/ODIHR and UN-INSTRAW, 2008). Available at: www.dcaf.ch/gender-security-sector-reform/gssr-toolkit.cfm?navsub1=37&navsub2=3& nav1=3.

76 A key example occurred in 2008 when the CNDP seized a number of heavy weapons from the FARDC military base at Rumangabo.

77 UN Security Council, note 64 above.

78 Meike de Goede, 'Private and Public Security in Post-war Democratic Republic of Congo', *The private security sector in Africa*, ed. Sabelo Gumetze, Monograph No. 146, 37 (Pretoria: Institute for Security Studies).

79 Ibid., p. 46.

80 Interview with EU Commission official.

81 de Goede, note 77 above: 47.

82 This would imply the creation of about 1,000 border posts to attempt to secure the border. Interview with Ministry of Interior official.

83 Interim report of the Group of Experts on the Democratic Republic of the Congo, pursuant to Security Council Resolution 1698 (2006), S/2007/40, 9.

84 United Nations, 'UN Secretary-General Report', UN Doc. S/2008/433, 7.

85 Interview with Ministry of Defence officials.

86 Zoe Marriag, 'Flip-flop Rebel, Dollar Soldier: Demobilisation in the Democratic Republic of Congo', *Conflict, Security and Development* 7, no. 2 (2007): 281–309, at p. 295.

87 Ibid., pp. 289 and 295.

88 Interview with UK official.

89 Interview with UK official. Jean-Pierre Bemba was the main opponent of Kabila in the elections.

90 Interview with UN official. Paradoxically, this has also resulted in the direct entry into the army of numerous ex-combatants who were not given the opportunity to choose between the two options through the DDR process. This was the case in the east, where some ex-combatants wishing to be integrated into the army were promptly accepted in transit centres for direct entry into the army, without going through orientation centres. Interview with SMI in Goma and visit to transit centre to meet ex-combatants integrating into the army directly.

91 MDRP Progress Report and Work Plan, January–March 2005. Available at www.mdrp.org/PDFs/progreport_2005_q1.pdf.

92 Swarbrick, note 40 above: 56.

93 For instance, communicating potential security vacuums to those responsible for training and deploying the police was not considered important despite the support the police could have provided in filling these vacuums. Similarly, the impact of possible security vacuums was not considered to be a priority for SSR but rather was underlined as an issue for the DDR section. Interviews with MONUC SSR team, UNPOL and DDR staff.

94 Interview with MONUC DDR unit official. Please see the discussion on MONUC's mandate earlier in this chapter.

95 UN SC Resolution 1565, 1 October 2004.

96 Interview with former head of DDR/SSR section. The niche for the new unit was identified in the area of defence reform, in particular the intersection of DDR and army integration. It should be noted that this was before evolution of the UN SSR policy, when the in-house understanding of SSR was primarily in the context of defence sector reform. Also, a rule of law section and police section (UNPOL) already existed within the mission, which meant that the niche to be filled in SSR was in the area of defence reform.

97 The new SRSG in 2008 took this decision in order to strengthen ties between DDR and DDR-RR. In practice, the impact of merging these two sections has been limited, in part because the majority of the DDR team is based in Kinshasa, while DDR-RR is based in Goma. Interviews with MONUC DDR and DDR-RR staff.

98 For example, the absence of 'a systematic and structured approach to coordinating disarmament and demobilisation activities with other sections and components within the Mission' was noted by the UN Office of Internal Oversight Services in its 2005 audit. See: UN Office of Internal Oversight Services, 'Audit of the DDRRR programme in MONUC', 8 December 2005 (AP2005/620/08).

99 The SSR working group consists of an adviser each in political affairs, human rights, military, EUSEC, EUPOL, UNDP, DDR, the Integrated Office, sexual and gender-based violence and gender, as well as other interested observers.

100 Interview with MONUC SSR adviser.

101 UN Office of Internal Oversight Services, 2005.

102 The strategy builds on the UN Stabilisation Strategy developed in 2008 following a request from the UN Security Council in May 2007, but implementation was delayed because of difficult security conditions.

103 Interview with Stabilisation Plan team leader. Also see ISSSS factsheet. Available at http://monusco.unmissions.org/LinkClick.aspx?fileticket=IDgo1m%2fCcRw%3d&tabid=4520&mid=4882.

104 The DDR-RR unit, on the other hand, had 43 approved posts in 2007–2008, including a large field presence. The creation of a DDR/DDR-RR unit in 2008 is set to increase this capacity to 50 posts and will also include DDR-specific posts.

105 Xavier Zeebroek Fride, 'The United Nations Mission in Congo: Searching for the Missing Peace', (July 2008). 7-8. Available at www.globalpolicy.org/security/issues/congo/2008/07missingpeace.pdf.

106 Interview with UNDP official.

107 See IDDRS, chapter 3.41 on Finance and Budgeting.

108 UN Office of Internal Oversight Services, 2005, note 99 above.

109 Interview with MONUC DDR official.

110 Report of the Secretary-General on the budget for the United Nations Organisation Mission in the Democratic Republic of the Congo for the period from 1 July 2008 to 30 June 2009, A/62/755.

111 Ibid.

[112] For example, the ex-FAR and Interhamwe were not part of the negotiations leading to the Lusaka Ceasefire Agreement or the Pretoria Agreement, despite the fact that these agreements provided the framework for the DDR-RR process these groups were meant to engage in voluntarily. It has been noted that 'the cost of such an approach has been an outright rejection of the process by the FDLR, Interahamwe and ex-FAR armed groups'. Nelson Alusala, 'Armed Conflict and Disarmament: Selected Central African Case Studies', ISS Monograph No 129 (Pretoria: Institute for Security Studies, 2007). Available at www.ssrnetwork.net/doc_library/document_detail.php?id=3394.

[113] Fride, note 104 above.

[114] The national police has since then requested to attend meetings of the *Commission interministérielle du programme national pour le désarmement, la démobilisation et la réinsertion*, in order to be kept abreast of developments in the DDR process.

PART III

CONCLUSION

Chapter 6

The DDR-SSR Nexus: Turning Practical Experience into Good Practice

Alan Bryden and Vincenza Scherrer

Introduction

Interested academics, policy makers and practitioners recognize that disarmament, demobilization and reintegration (DDR) and security sector reform (SSR) are closely inter-linked. A central assumption underpinning this volume is that the relationship between the two can only be properly understood through combining findings from the policy literature with empirically grounded analysis of how, in practice, DDR and SSR processes have played out. Drawing on diverse experiences in Afghanistan, Burundi, the Central African Republic (CAR) and the Democratic Republic of the Congo (DRC), this chapter identifies opportunities for approaches to programming that take into account the nexus between DDR and SSR.

As ever, form should follow function. In other words, a prerequisite for identifying *how* DDR and SSR may be linked is some level of consensus on *why* this objective is being sought in the first place. This volume contends that the nexus between DDR and SSR is found in the need to integrate early measures that address ex-combatants in the aftermath of conflict with long term efforts to build an effective, well-managed security sector within a framework of democratic governance. While many technical activities may be pursued that can link DDR to component parts of the SSR agenda, these efforts should be understood as part of an inherently political, civilian-led process of national reconstruction and development.

As discussed in Chapter 1, this volume emerged as part of a guidance development project undertaken on behalf of the UN Department for Peacekeeping Operations (DPKO) and the United Nations Development Programme (UNDP) under the auspices of the Inter-Agency Working Group (IAWG) on DDR. While the purpose of this work was primarily to distil insights from UN experience with a view to developing guidance for the future work of UN actors in this area, lessons could have a much wider application. This concluding chapter builds on the four case studies that fed into this process in order to derive insights that can support DDR/SSR policies and programmes.

The four cases explored in this volume highlight the opportunities and challenges of the DDR-SSR nexus in practice. They also demonstrate that despite unpredictable security dynamics, challenging political environments and resource gaps characteristic of many post-conflict contexts, opportunities exist to foster synergies between DDR and SSR. This chapter considers these issues in two dimensions. First, it sets out an approach that helps to understand DDR-SSR linkages at policy and programming levels. It then identifies specific entry points to embed the nexus in DDR and SSR programmes.

The DDR-SSR Nexus in Policies and Programmes

Common DDR-SSR concerns need to be addressed in both policies and programmes. While acknowledging the diversity of actors and approaches involved in each set of activities, the overriding objective should be to avoid stovepiping and enhance overall coherence and effectiveness. The work of practitioners can be facilitated through situating efforts within a comprehensive approach that is then reflected in different programming options. Table 6.1 summarises the policy-practice issues explored in this section.

1) The policy framework

Policies that take into account the DDR-SSR nexus need to avoid narrowly technical approaches. As benchmarks for successful DDR and SSR, improved physical security therefore goes hand in hand with trust and confidence building. This requires sensitivity to context-specific politico-security dynamics. It also means embedding activities within a broader national political process.

Consider DDR-SSR during peace negotiations. Peace negotiations can potentially frame DDR and SSR decisions and targets within a coherent approach to peacebuilding and statebuilding. Agreements often set parameters for DDR, and SSR-related concerns are also increasingly

Table 6.1: The DDR-SSR nexus in policies and programmes

Level	Objectives
Policy	• Address DDR/SSR concerns in peace negotiations. • Ensure DDR decisions are consistent with a national vision of the future security sector. • Build ownership around DDR and SSR processes. • Harmonise DDR and SSR initiatives.
Programming	• Support a joined up approach to assessments; link DDR programmes with related SSR activities in programme design; improve monitoring and evaluation. • Ensure that data collected during the DDR process can be useful for enhancing SSR planning and vice versa. • Consider the resource implications of the DDR-SSR nexus.

prevalent as part of peace negotiations.[1] Trade-offs will almost certainly be necessary in order to fulfil the terms of a political settlement. A starting point is to meet at least the minimum expectations of those sitting around the table. This is particularly challenging in a context such as Burundi where the fragmentation of the different armed groups led to a multiplicity of agreements. The interests of ethnic groups and armed factions that signed peace agreements at different times had to be weighed. As Rumin (Chapter 3) points out, this juggling act led to a massive increase in untrained and under-qualified security sector personnel, admitted at the expense of experienced police and gendarmes who were forced to demobilise. The resulting frustration as well as the loss of capabilities could have been mitigated if the cumulative effect of these deals for the security sector had been better thought through at the negotiation stage.

DDR and SSR can potentially provide an opportunity to acknowledge and address underlying ethnic, political, religious or other tensions found within the security sector. In Burundi, the army was used from early post-colonial times as an instrument to maintain the authority of the Tutsi elite over the majority Hutu population. Defence reform was therefore a key requirement for Hutu groups negotiating terms for DDR. In contrast, Afghanistan conspicuously lacked a negotiated political settlement addressing DDR and SSR.[2] With no overarching political framework for these issues there was little incentive for armed groups to join the DDR process nor could roles and responsibilities for DDR and SSR be easily attributed. As Sedra (Chapter 2) notes, an agreement that mandated the demobilization of these groups and made specific reference to the establishment of security sector oversight mechanisms would have contributed to a more coherent, integrated and enforceable process. Moreover, some demobilised armed groups in Afghanistan retained both internal staff structures and their small arms and light weapons. The lack of commitment to demobilization shown by certain groups was compounded by the narrow approach adopted to reforming the Afghan National Army – the process did not seek to integrate militias but rather rebuilt the army from scratch.

Failing to take into account interests and dividing lines between different stakeholders can thus contribute to programmes that are insensitive to root causes of conflict and insecurity. Peace agreements should therefore be considered as an important entry point to establish basic principles for DDR and SSR. But this opportunity can only be exploited if participation is widened to include the range of national actors with a stake in the outcome of negotiations. This will contribute to more inclusive settlements that embed diverse interests in new security sector governance arrangements.

Build on a national vision of security. If DDR and SSR may emerge from highly charged political bargaining processes, programmes should seek to fit within or support the emergence of a coherent vision that reflects national security priorities, needs and constraints. The source of this vision may be found in a national security policy or strategy, or a poverty-reduction strategy paper developed through a consultative and inclusive process. A major outcome of such a process can be to address the blurring of lines between different security actors that is a common dynamic of armed conflict. According to N'Diaye (Chapter 4), because it did not serve as a prop to regime security in CAR, the police force was neglected and under-funded in comparison to the army. In this respect, DDR *is* security sector reform. The process offers an opportunity to clarify and agree roles and responsibilities within the security sector as part of a wider political transition. Yet from a security sector governance perspective, it is evident that the reach of state security institutions is limited. A genuine national vision from which to derive security sector reforms in the CAR should therefore acknowledge the prominent de facto roles in providing security played by different armed non-state actors.

An important re-balancing that can occur through both DDR and SSR is the shift in emphasis from external to internal security provision. While integrating ex-combatants in order to strengthen law enforcement capacities may be desirable, using former soldiers in policing roles will be counter-productive without proper screening and appropriate training. Practical consequences include applying military approaches to tasks that require sensitivity and restraint or undermining trust in reformed policing structures by engaging ex-combatants with an abusive past.

This requirement presupposes that a wider security sector governance framework is itself based on a collaborative relationship between the state, security sector and citizens. In reality, for the contexts discussed in this volume as for many other post-conflict states, national security architectures and policies are outdated or founded on inappropriate, externally imposed models. At the same time, security sector management and oversight remains a mechanism of regime security that is closely guarded by political and security elites.[3] A major challenge is therefore to support programmes that not only acknowledge these governance deficits but also contribute to moving beyond them through developing more affordable, appropriate and responsible security institutions.

In practice, DDR decisions that represent important milestones in a wider security sector reform process are often made well before national security policymaking frameworks can even start to be re-evaluated. The difficulty of balancing longer term peacebuilding objectives with responding to immediate security requirements is best exemplified in stabilization contexts – such as Afghanistan and the DRC – where conflict remains a reality on parts of the national territory. In both cases, activities designed to address direct security threats have emphasised training and equipping security forces. The requirement to build a sustainable, responsive security sector has been downplayed. The quality of DDR in these contexts has also suffered. DDR as a post-conflict tool has proven to be much less effective in the absence of certain pre-conditions, notably a definitive ceasefire.

Yet examples do exist of states that have transitioned through stabilization to peacebuilding then developmental orientations. Such examples tend to eschew fixed templates in favour of process-based approaches that link DDR and SSR. In Rwanda and Sierra Leone, for example, early emphasis on 'security first' measures shifted to an integrated approach to DDR and SSR that was grounded within the wider political transition.[4] Common to both cases was a strong commitment to dialogue at national, regional and community levels as a means to bind (in principle opposing) constituencies to a process of change. This helped to demonstrate that violence was not the best way to advance group or individual interests while contributing to the wider goal of national reconciliation.

Rather than force specific policies or strategies where political space is lacking, an inclusive national dialogue process can help elaborate a shared vision of the priorities, threats and values that ought to mould legal and policy frameworks for the security sector.[5] A wide range of national stakeholders, including parliamentarians, civil society actors and local community figures would set out their own security needs, objectives and values. The outcome of these deliberations would then help to determine reforms affecting the shape and missions of the security sector and how they should relate to DDR. For example, while the national seminar held in the CAR between 14–17 April 2008 was primarily an effort to develop a common framework for supporting SSR, DDR and SSR were addressed together in order to encourage synergies and enhance the understanding that these two activities are closely linked. This contributed to providing locally generated understandings of security threats and needs, and laid out a roadmap to clarify future steps in the reform process. Despite evident (ongoing) problems of political will at the national level, a new window has opened following the 2011 presidential elections to better integrate national and international support for these processes.[6]

Foster ownership around DDR-SSR. Although distinct activities, both DDR and SSR concern the military, the security sector more broadly, as well as overlapping groups responsible for their management and oversight. As part of efforts to promote transparent and participative decision-making, security sector management and oversight bodies are well placed to address the question of who should be demobilised, how reintegration should be conducted and what should be the shape and size of the reformed security sector. However, the challenges to broadening the political space for DDR/SSR decision making can be substantial. A lack of political commitment from national and international stakeholders around participatory approaches to DDR and SSR can prove costly. For example, in Burundi the National Commission for Demobilization, Reinsertion and Reintegration does not represent a meaningful example of local ownership due to its narrow military composition. This profile constrains its ability to reach beyond the Ministry of Defence to work across government or to allow access for expertise across other Ministries and in the non-governmental sector. As a result, the decision-making base is narrow and militarily-oriented.

Encouraging dialogue on security matters can be highly sensitive for national elites. But it is an important means to foster political will and build consensus around issues previously excluded from the public domain. Thus, the 2008 national seminar in the CAR should be understood as an attempt to create momentum behind a political process at a particular moment. The space for reform had not been available in the earlier *Projet de Réinsertion de Ex-combattants et d'Appui aux Communautés* (PRAC) process, which took place in the absence of a formal ceasefire with unwilling belligerents and ill-prepared national actors. N'Diaye asserts that government supported security sector reform post-2005 was understood purely as a means to professionalise the armed forces. There was no interest in a 'new deal' on security that would upset the political status quo. This analysis is born out by a major shortcoming of the PRAC: it only dealt with militias and rebel groups while leaving the police and armed forces untouched. Moreover, there was no effort to integrate the leadership of the armed groups in DDR/SSR decision making. Such an approach perpetuates conflict dynamics by giving an impression of victor's justice. A re-orientation of the military as a democratically accountable republican institution in the CAR would require a sustained effort to integrate both the leadership and rank-and-file ex-combatants from armed groups into a reformed national army. This underlines the importance of creating ownership at different levels. Reaching out to marginalised segments of society can help ensure the success of DDR and SSR efforts.

At the political level, commitment needs to be cemented in specific agreements, such as a memorandum of understanding confirming DDR and SSR aims between relevant political stakeholders. An approach utilised by the World Bank's Multi-Country Demobilization and Reintegration Program (MDRP) has been to require that a national DDR plan submitted for funding is accompanied by a letter of demobilization policy outlining explicit links to SSR.[7] If followed up, such agreements can facilitate work at the operational level by providing a baseline and set of agreed commitments that can be referred back to when challenges arise.

Harmonise initiatives. Mainstreaming the DDR-SSR nexus requires a certain degree of harmonization. One example is the issue of rank. This is a sensitive integration issue that should not be ignored in contexts where state and non state actors are brought together within reformed security institutions. Differences in age, education, social status, religious or ethnic background can exacerbate tensions between former conflict parties. In order to deal with actual or perceived inequities, fair treatment should be visibly demonstrated in approaches to rank harmonization. This balancing act should not unwittingly undermine the effectiveness of security institutions nor should it run counter to budgetary realities. The recurrent costs of integrating and providing pensions for additional high ranking officers within the security sector would need to be sustainable and within national budget projections.

Beyond questions of rank, numerous other harmonization issues may also arise. This could include social and financial incentives offered to ex-combatants integrating within the security sector versus those electing for reintegration. The need to ensure that vetting policies for ex-combatants seeking to join security institutions are also applied to other security sector personnel may also be necessary (see below). Getting these issues right means that the various stakeholders supporting DDR and SSR adopt a long term view. For example, national institutions established to support DDR are often transitional, coming to an end once the programme is concluded. However, integrating DDR structures into security sector governance frameworks may result in important payoffs. A national DDR commission could evolve into an entity responsible for veterans and other beneficiaries, establishing links with similar processes being undertaken across the security sector. It may also provide a useful conduit to central government for community concerns. These bodies can therefore play a dual role of promoting coherence – at national level as well as with international partners – while also offering an entry point to foster more participative security sector governance dynamics. The need to work with a broad range of stakeholders could be written into the terms of reference of commissions, opening decision making to actors that may have been bypassed within government such as ministries of justice and interior, as well as parliamentarians, civil society organizations, community leaders, customary authorities, women's groups etc.

2) Programming level

Acknowledging that DDR and SSR are conceptually interconnected amounts to little if key insights are not informing programming on the ground. Yet DDR and SSR may involve different objectives, activities, timelines and stakeholders. From a UN perspective, there is a programmatic engagement with DDR across strategic/policy and operational levels. The breadth and diversity of the SSR agenda makes for a more diffuse distribution of roles. The SSR Unit provides strategic guidance. Yet depending on the context, operational roles are assumed by a range of different UN components, in conjunction with different constellations of international, regional, bilateral and non-state actors. Linkages therefore need to be pursued selectively in order to avoid blurring roles and responsibilities. Ways to nurture synergies at headquarters as well as in the field are developed in the new IDDRS module on DDR and SSR.[8] This section briefly signposts opportunities to consider DDR and SSR jointly within the programme cycle.

Support assessments that consider the DDR-SSR nexus. Assessments can provide an entry point to identify and introduce prospective synergies between DDR and SSR. Stocktaking of existing activities and mapping relevant (state and non-state) security actors, management and oversight bodies provides an important point of departure for developing or recalibrating programmes. For Sedra, understanding the various armed groups in Afghanistan, including their political as well as economic interests and influence is critical.[9] The lack of detailed needs assessments was one contributing factor to programmes designed to an unrealistic state-centric model. Activities consistently failed to take into account informal and traditional actors central to Afghanistan's security dynamics.

Supporting assessments that consider the DDR-SSR nexus can be encouraged by including this as an objective in terms of reference and disseminating them widely with DDR and SSR counterparts. In order to identify appropriate, context-sensitive programming options, needs assessments should benefit from DDR and SSR expertise as well as incorporating regional knowledge and local language skills. For more general assessments, knowledge of the political context for DDR and SSR may be more valuable than sector-specific expertise. This should lead to a realistic appreciation of the political space available for different programming options. Finally, assessments should be based on engagement with a broad selection of stakeholders – including non-state and traditional security and justice providers. Assessments should provide an opportunity to engage with communities in identifying challenges relating the DDR process and how that can impact on SSR (e.g. tensions linked to community reintegration). It can provide bottom-up perspectives on the performance of security providers and how this may be linked to DDR objectives.

Link DDR and SSR in programme design. Linking DDR and SSR concerns in programme design helps avoid duplication and ensure that activities reflect common objectives. The consequences of incoherence are well illustrated by the Afghanistan case. The Disbandment of Illegal Armed Groups Programme (DIAG) – launched in 2005 as the successor to an earlier DDR programme – laid out the requirements for voluntary, negotiated or enforced disarmament. However, the main instrument mandated to enforce compliance, the Afghan National Police, was incapable of performing its task due to systemic corruption, mismanagement and capacity deficits. This de-legitimized the programme and fuelled non-compliance.

The absence of integrated planning has been a major shortcoming in the DRC. However, attempts have been made to address this through the design of a security and stabilization strategy intended to draw together different actors and issues (e.g. SSR, DDR, political dialogue, sexual violence). Getting the strategic framework right can thus link DDR and SSR in programme design and planning, potentially minimizing duplication and enhancing coordination. The development of donor coordination matrices at country level to map all donors working in SSR-related areas can also pool knowledge and create synergies across programmes. However, implementing a coherent approach requires political will as well as coordination. It also demands determined efforts to link programmes to national planning processes.

Programmes should be designed on the basis of a close understanding of how DDR and SSR will affect local security dynamics. Synchronizing DDR and community security initiatives can be an important way to substantiate the DDR-SSR nexus. Yet a major gap in knowledge across different DDR programmes is on the security impact of reintegration. This needs to be addressed through tracking and reacting to the DDR process and its consequences. A tangible emphasis on the security needs of people can send a powerful message that 'something has changed' in the mindset of security institutions.

Improve monitoring and evaluation. Monitoring and evaluation can play a key role in gauging the impact of DDR/SSR and thus to catalyse adjustments to policies and programmes. Yet a common theme across the case studies is the absence of effective monitoring and evaluation. This represents a missed opportunity to identify the extent to which DDR and SSR programmes are planned and implemented in a joined up manner. Specific indicators may include the establishment of joint communication strategies informing integration and reintegration options; the implementation of training programmes for national DDR and SSR personnel as well as the use of data collected for DDR purposes by SSR stakeholders (and vice versa). Mid-term reviews are increasingly recognised as a useful mechanism to assess the impact of activities, reconsider priorities and make necessary changes to ongoing programmes.[10]

The case studies point to a reliance on quantitative statistics that measure implementation outputs – soldiers trained, weapons surrendered etc. – rather than quantitative and qualitative criteria that address impact and effectiveness. As Sedra points out, the Afghan New Beginnings Programme can provide detailed statistics on weapons collected or numbers of ex-combatants reintegrated but cannot state whether militias have been broken up or commander patronage networks disrupted. Similarly, Rumin questions the ability to determine reintegration 'success' in the absence of data linking the process to issues such as crime rates, prison populations or the composition of armed groups in neighbouring countries.

It is particularly important that information flows are sustained. In this respect, the lack of public surveys and focus group analysis is significant. Nuanced analysis would enable DDR and SSR activities to better respond to community needs and vulnerabilities. Instead, dynamic factors such as flows of ex-combatants, links to former armed groups and reintegration impacts at the local level may be obscured.

Systematise knowledge management. The absence of accurate and timely information to support DDR/SSR decision making is a common challenge across all phases of the programme cycle. In practice, all the case studies highlight knowledge gaps as well as the stovepiping of key data. One major problem facing the DIAG programme in Afghanistan was that information was not available on issues such as weapons holdings or the profiles of active armed groups. It was therefore difficult to verify compliance. In Burundi, a lack of information on detainees created a risk of confusing common law criminals with ex-combatants eligible for release as part of the DDR process. An early SSR focus on prison reform in order to clarify and record the status of detainees could therefore have contributed to fulfilling DDR objectives. This lack of knowledge also represented a missed opportunity to support SSR, further emphasizing the need to improve information flows.

Sharing data is one way to build a more mutually reinforcing relationship between DDR and SSR. Extensive data is often collected during the disarmament and demobilization stages using the DDR management information system (MIS). The MIS is designed to manage biometric and socio-economic information on participants, beneficiaries and partners in DDR programmes. While data captured at disarmament or demobilization points is intended to inform reintegration processes, it may be more widely relevant. Including data entries in the MIS on the weapons skills of ex-combatants, rank or command functions could guide the selection of candidates for entry into reformed security bodies. The practical utility of information may also extend beyond DDR and SSR. To take one example, systematically gathering data on individuals' knowledge of landmine use could provide valuable support to mine action efforts.

Enforcing strict guidelines on confidentiality is essential in order to ensure that data is not misused to target specific individuals or groups because of their background, affiliation or assets. Data collected during the

DDR process that builds a profile of ex-combatants can support SSR by highlighting relevant skills as well as weeding out criminals, human rights abusers or perpetrators of war crimes. The screening and identification of ex-combatants at demobilization centres generates information with multiple uses. For example, Rumin identifies pre-disarmament assembly as a valuable opportunity to gather data on ex-combatants relevant for both integration and reintegration purposes. However, a narrow focus on the DDR process *sensu stricto* meant that this opportunity was not exploited in Burundi.

Consider the DDR-SSR nexus from a resource perspective. DDR and SSR are both resource-intensive activities. Competition between DDR and SSR needs may be visible in certain cases. Former soldiers with legal rights to pensions combined with the costs of integrating ex-combatants into the security sector can generate unsustainable pressure on national budgets. But the use of national resources can be optimised with adequate planning, dialogue and coordination. This requires a mutually supportive approach to the financial, human and physical resources dedicated to these activities. Measures that improve how security budgets are managed and scrutinised should therefore be an integral part of the decision making process. This may include support to a security sector census to identify and weed out ghost soldiers thus enabling substantial savings in the national budget.

It is often overlooked that funding gaps in one area may have spillover effects leading to lost funding or delays to the overall process. Sedra makes the point that DDR/SSR funding in Afghanistan has contributed to the stovepiping of initiatives. Rather than supporting coordination, isolated funding streams have created a further barrier to cross-sectoral programming. Moreover, Scherrer (Chapter 5) describes how in the DRC funding deficits for defence reform stalled the DDR process and heightened tensions in locations where ex-combatants awaited entry into the programme. Such treatment will not encourage a move away from habitually predatory attitudes to local populations.

Investing in existing human resources and filling capacity gaps is a common DDR/SSR requirement. This is a two way street. Supporting capacity development for national staff engaged in DDR and SSR is an important way of operationalizing local ownership. Cross-cutting skills such as line management, budget and financial management will enhance the effectiveness of national programmes while building capacities with wider application beyond these processes. It also emphasises that international partners need to provide support built on a skills transfer based model.

To make the most of capacity building opportunities for international actors, trainings for international staff should where feasible encourage combined participation from both DDR and SSR communities. This will support knowledge transfer and foster common understandings. Actively identifying and supporting linkages could be included as a requirement in the terms of reference for relevant personnel. Finally, opportunities to pool resources for DDR and SSR should be pursued in areas of common interest, for example, community security or small arms collection and weapons exchange initiatives.

Investment in physical sites constructed for DDR may have an SSR role, offering substantive benefits. For example, semi-permanent sites created for the cantonment of ex-combatants can become barracks for the armed forces. Likewise, visibly linking the DDR process to the rehabilitation of security institutions signals a change in approach that can enhance confidence and build trust in communities as well as within security institutions. Of course, the creation of such sites must be weighed against the setting up of mobile demobilization sites which may offer more flexibility to DDR programmers. Nonetheless, planning with common concerns in mind can help to ensure that limited resources are not wasted on parallel structures. Similarly, the infrastructure created under the auspices of a DDR programme to collect and manage weapons can form the foundations of a weapons procurement and storage system for the security forces.

In summary, opportunities do exist to foster appropriate, context-specific linkages between DDR and SSR that can contribute to common peacebuilding goals. This requires conscious efforts to align the political framework with specific DDR/SSR initiatives. At the heart of such an approach is the need to design interventions that are consistent with and contribute to furthering the security of the state and its citizens. The following section considers different entry points in order to support these goals.

The DDR-SSR Nexus in Practice

SSR measures undertaken in all the case studies considered in this volume have tended to focus narrowly on support for state security sector providers (notably the army and police) at the expense of community safety and wellbeing. An approach predicated on how individuals and communities

Table 6.2: Entry points to operationalize the DDR-SSR nexus

Governance	Support security sector management and oversight to ensure sustainability of DDR and SSR.
The legal dimension	Consider how legal framework for the security sector can reinforce DDR objectives.
Integration/reintegration options	Balance incentives offered to ex-combatants choosing reintegration versus those choosing integration into the security sector to avoid consequences of an unintended bias. Adopt a proactive approach to the social concerns of both security sector personnel and ex-combatants.
Disarmament and weapons management	Link disarmament to firearm regulation legislation and national stockpile management. Address the relationship between civilian and military disarmament to bridge DDR and SSR concerns.
Community security	Coordinate community security activities to maximise the impact of DDR and SSR on individuals and communities.
Gender mainstreaming	Ensure women have a genuine choice between security sector careers or viable reintegration options.
Mapping security privatization	Analyse the relationship between ex-combatants and the private security sector to understand the consequences of DDR on informal/commercial security provision.
Vetting	Ensure equal treatment in vetting ex-combatants and other security sector personnel.

experience security is needed that would take into account a much wider array of issues and actors than those falling within the sphere of the state.[11] This reflects a need to better engage non-state actors that are often more visible in providing security (as well as causing insecurity) than the state in the day to day lives of individuals and communities. It also demonstrates the need to include other important dimensions, such as governance, gender, or transitional justice when seeking to operationalize the nexus.

This section identifies frequently overlooked opportunities to support a joined up approach to DDR and SSR. Moving from more general to more specific entry points, Table 6.2 summarises practical ways that synergies can be realised across support to DDR and SSR. The dimensions are then discussed in more detail drawing on insights from the case studies.

Entry point 1: Governance

Efforts to improve governance within the security sector provide a means to build important synergies between DDR and SSR. In concrete terms, the governance dimension entails understanding that security sector management and oversight functions are critical determinants of sustainable DDR. For example, SSR initiatives that strengthen national control of conflict-driving resources – from arms to precious materials – can increase the likelihood of armed groups entering the DDR process by closing down alternative options. Another important challenge is to address the corruption risks that often accompany large volumes of combatants and significant flows of money. Enhancing the transparency and accountability of national commissions and related implementation agencies can therefore increase the effectiveness of DDR support while delivering on this key SSR goal.

DDR and SSR processes need to build from shared values. Fostering a duty of care both within security institutions and in the way that ex-combatants are treated is essential if entrenched prejudices and behaviour patterns within the security sector are to be shifted.[12] This process needs to start at the political level. As N'Diaye stresses, the DDR of armed groups in the CAR will not contribute to resolving underlying conflict dynamics unless this is mirrored by political will at the national level to commit to an SSR process that brings all sides together within reformed security institutions.

A security sector census is one practical example of a measure that can be taken to enhance management arrangements and enable national authorities to balance the real size of security institutions against identified requirements and budget constraints. Early emphasis on such a process may help avoid the problem of 'double dipping' by ex-combatants registering for integration into the security sector *and* community reintegration. It can also point to civilians trying to pass for ex-combatants to improve their economic position. As seen in the DRC, a census can help reduce the erosion of security budgets by the payment of non-existent ghost soldiers. On a different level, a security sector census can demonstrate effective use of limited resources and address corruption, important goals by themselves which also foster confidence between national authorities and donors.

A key DDR/SSR outcome from a security sector governance perspective should be the lowering of barriers between the state, security sector and citizens. Awareness raising activities such as visits by officials, parliamentarians and community representatives to security installations are straightforward examples of activities that can dispel misperceptions over soldiers and their social conditions while also improving the knowledge base of actors responsible for security sector management and oversight. Allocating time to sensitization training and community dialogue should not be overlooked if programming is to go hand in hand with confidence building.

Entry point 2: The legal dimension

Revising the legal framework for the security sector can institutionalise the relationship between DDR and SSR. For example, in Afghanistan the new law on 'Fire Weapons, Ammunitions, and Explosive Materials' mandated the Afghan National Police to enforce a countrywide registration system intended to support the demilitarization of ex-combatants. However, while the legal framework was successfully introduced, the police lacked capacity to enforce the law. This highlights the importance of ensuring that implementation capacity can match up to legal and policy initiatives.

Another important concern is that legal mechanisms need to be established or simply applied in order to resolve potential land disputes linked to the internally displaced and other returnees, including ex-combatants. Scherrer points out that while access to land has been a driver of conflict in the DRC, a focus on this issue only came at a late stage, despite the risk of significant tensions as a result of land tenure disputes. An early focus on clarifying the legal status of returnees and ensuring the deployment of law enforcement capacities in sensitive areas would have represented an opportunity address a community security concern linked to DDR through making it an SSR priority.

Entry point 3: Integration/reintegration options

Both the reintegration of ex-combatants as well as their integration into security institutions raise sensitive security issues with cultural, political and socio-economic overtones. A lack of clarity on the rationale for and implications of these two options can undermine prospects for SSR. In particular, the voluntary choice between reintegration and integration offered to ex-combatants in many contexts raises the question how this can impact on a security sector reform process.

The case studies illustrate the risks of an unintended bias emerging with respect to the incentives offered for integration versus reintegration. If incentives are not harmonized this may unbalance programmes, resulting in distortions that need to be addressed later. For example, in Burundi the disproportionate numbers of ex-combatants choosing integration led to an over-inflated army. A two-phase approach which first accepted the integration of an excessive number of ex-combatants may have satisfied all sides during negotiations but it resulted in trouble later. Enforced demobilization in a second round engendered uncertainty, tension and frustration among those concerned, with hundreds of soldiers refusing to undergo compulsory demobilization. In the DRC, a package of financial and social benefits for reintegration that at one stage clearly outweighed those for integration placed significant strain on the DDR programme. This resulted in backlogs of unprocessed payments as well as difficulties in identifying reintegration opportunities for such large numbers of ex-combatants. Moreover, the perception of more limited alternative career options led to a disproportionately high number of senior officers remaining within the military.

It is important to recognize that ex-combatants are individuals and not a homogeneous entity. The choice between reintegration and integration is more than just an economic one – decisions will reflect concerns over status, association and political affiliation. The impact on identity and future roles is very different in each case. Ex-combatants should therefore be sensitized to the challenges of re-entering civilian life while acceptable standards of treatment need to be applied within reformed security bodies. Failing to offer minimum terms and conditions can have important security implications.

Making provision for special categories such as female ex-combatants, the disabled, former child soldiers and dependants within DDR processes is one way to build integrity within security institutions. An early opportunity is provided by the cantonment of ex-combatants where a focus on improving living conditions can help lower tensions. Situating *brassage* centres in the DRC far away from orientation hubs runs directly counter to this approach. Dependents were left to struggle by themselves to follow ex-combatants, breeding low morale, indiscipline and desertion.

Prudence is necessary to ensure that the financial and social benefits for integration and reintegration do not unintentionally favour one option. Thinking through the concerns and needs of individual ex-combatants as well as placing greater emphasis on two-way communication can help address misperceptions. Ensuring that options are clearly understood, taking due consideration of dependants and offering employment counselling that is realistic about future employment opportunities are a few ways of reducing the risk of tension among demobilised combatants choosing to follow reintegration or security sector integration paths.

Entry point 4: Disarmament and weapons management

National coordination mechanisms that share responsibility for DDR and SSR can help integrate disarmament and wider efforts by the state to control weapons on the national territory. Demilitarised weapons in Afghanistan were not tracked after reaching an arms depot. Similarly, poor stockpile management and inadequate protection of transports and storage areas has facilitated the seizure of weapons by armed groups across the different contexts. In the CAR, looting from arms dumps has been a significant problem. N'Diaye suggests that poor pay and conditions are the primary cause with the military selling on the weapons they were supposed to be guarding. The negative consequences of disarmament in the DRC are also highlighted by Scherrer with the market for arms boosted by the rewards offered to ex-combatants returning weapons. In all these cases, the achievements of the disarmament process are at least partially undermined because they contradict the SSR objective of improving control over armouries and stockpiles.

A focus on the community level demonstrates the close relationship between success and failure in the disarmament of ex-combatants and civilian disarmament. One aspect of the civil war in Burundi was the tit-for-tat self-arming of Hutu and Tutsi civilians as well as local militias by successive governments. The lack of success in gathering weapons from ex-combatants has been mirrored in the paltry results of civilian disarmament efforts. Both reflect a lack of confidence in the ability of the police and army that is exacerbated by continued mistrust across the ethnic divide. In Afghanistan, certain groups continued to exert authority over local populations following demobilization via the collection of taxes and exploitation of natural resources. The strategy of offering development incentives to communities in order to undermine support for armed groups was based on a false premise of positive community-armed group relations. Instead, armed groups were by and large predatory and criminally motivated so other approaches would have been required. The disarmament dimension should therefore be considered an important opportunity to build coherence across DDR and SSR.

Entry point 5: Community security

Community security should be a central concern for DDR and SSR.[13] The successful reintegration of ex-combatants can promote reconciliation. It can also generate trust in the police and other state security actors through recasting their image as a positive force capable of assuring the protection of the population. Beyond the direct security pay offs, community security initiatives should therefore be considered as a mechanism for encouraging communities to accept ex-combatants and at the same time enhance the status of local law enforcement actors.

Confidence will only be built around tangible improvements in how individuals and communities experience security. A reintegration process can serve as a catalyst to redefine police-community relations through jointly developing local security plans. In this way, security provision for communities can be improved through planning and resource allocation for local law enforcement capacities that is linked to DDR activities. Police training at regional centres through the District Development Programme has created more effective, interoperable Afghan police at the local level. However, the overall benefits could have been increased through thinking about disarmament and police reform together. As Sedra points out, linking this process to weapons collection initiatives in the concerned areas would increase the likelihood of disarmament success as a result of greater confidence in local law enforcement capacities.

Drawing on insights from communities can help ensure that reintegration ambitions are matched by local employment opportunities. Otherwise, important distinctions between urban and rural settings (e.g. availability of jobs, housing costs, peer pressure/prestige issues) may be missed. At a different level, perceptions of DDR as 'rewarding' ex-combatants may be nuanced through engagement with local authorities. Greater dialogue can also point to specific challenges such as the vulnerability of ex-child soldiers to re-recruitment of the continued existence of patronage networks among ex-combatants.

Entry point 6: Gender mainstreaming

Gender concerns represent an important aspect of the DDR-SSR nexus. As noted in the IDDRS, 'the involvement of women is the best way of ensuring their longer-term participation in security sector reform and in the uniformed services more generally, which again will improve long-term security.'[14] If female ex-combatants are not provided adequate incentives, it is very unlikely they will be able to enter the security sector through the path of integration. This is not just discriminatory but can be a missed opportunity to benefit from the different skill sets and approaches offered by women as security providers.[15] Providing women with the means and support to enter the DDR process should therefore be linked to encouraging the full representation of women in the security sector and thus to meeting a key goal of Security Council Resolution 1325.

In practice, the case studies highlight multiple ways in which women face discrimination. This is apparent in lacunae such as the absence of specialized demobilization kits or failing to acknowledge the stigmatization caused by being labelled an ex-combatant as a major disincentive for women to join a DDR programme. In the DRC, the common definition of 'ex-combatant' failed to incorporate women associated with a rebel movement unless possessing a weapon. More generally, in cases where female combatants were considered as a separate category with their own specific needs, female ex-combatants were automatically demobilised without being offered the choice of a career in the security sector.

Gender mainstreaming within the security sector can start with DDR. The four case studies point to a number of specific measures that contribute to this goal. First, women need to be notified of their options under the DDR and SSR processes. Dialogue and communication campaigns can play an important role in explaining the choices that need to be made but also can help de-stigmatise female ex-combatants. Second, measures should be tailored to the needs of women. Appropriate facilities during disarmament and demobilization, specialised reinsertion kits and appropriate integration/reintegration options are all important requirements.

Entry point 7: Mapping security privatization

An important way in which DDR and SSR can be more closely aligned to 'real' security dynamics is through tracing the influence of DDR processes on the private security sector and how this in turn impacts on the security of individuals and communities. A lack of emphasis on informal security (and justice) systems presents a major challenge. First, the non-state security providers prevalent in many settings are invisible to national elites as well as international actors operating in these contexts. And second, these actors are far removed from the state systems responsible for security at the national level.[16] They may benefit from significant legitimacy through filling security gaps left by a non-responsive state. But for this very reason non-state and informal entities represent a threat to central government and therefore a source of tension for internationally supported programmes.

A phenomenon that may have particular resonance for DDR and SSR is the growth in commercial security provision. This issue has multiple faces. In Afghanistan there is evident concern over the conduct of international private security companies. In the DRC the focus is on nationally-owned companies. If anecdotal evidence suggests some relationship between the national authorities responsible for DDR and private security companies in the DRC, in reality there is no official data available on the link between ex-combatants and a burgeoning private security industry. While such knowledge gaps are not unusual in states emerging from conflict, it is of particular concern given the significant security implications that may result from ex-combatants joining the private security sector without adequate vetting or certification.

There may be little that can be done from the supply side to stop ex-combatants taking their skills to the private sector. But mapping the phenomenon is a necessary first step to managing its consequences. Gauging the extent and nature of the privatization of security should therefore be a common DDR/SSR concern. Subsequent SSR initiatives may include regulation of commercial companies or practical measures at the community level to align the roles and objectives of state and non-state security providers.

Entry point 8: Vetting

Vetting within the framework of DDR and SSR can enhance the legitimacy of security sector institutions. Echoing the 'train and equip' approach adopted to rebuild the Afghan National Army, the reform of the Afghan police was conducted without a parallel vetting process to remove inappropriate candidates. In the DRC, there are no formal procedures or tracking mechanisms for ex-combatants entering the police. This has raised the possibility of regional police capacities filled by unsuitable candidates that may retain their old affiliations to armed groups. These approaches undermine public confidence and can create new insecurities. In this sense, vetting should be perceived as part of a broader process of institutional reform and not as a means of targeting or excluding certain ex-combatants from entry into the security sector. This implies the need for an agreed approach between DDR and SSR stakeholders on how vetting is designed and implemented.

The fact that vetting remains very sensitive in many post-conflict contexts means that programmes should be carefully considered in relation to minimum political conditions being met. These include sufficient political will, adequate command and control over the security services as well as national capacity to implement measures. Vetting therefore needs to be accompanied by complementary measures. This can include the development of ethics codes, provision for independent oversight, and providing capacity building support to institutions responsible for the vetting process.

Conclusion

This volume demonstrates how a focus on the nexus between DDR and SSR can potentially contribute to more effective DDR and SSR interventions. There is no blueprint for linking DDR and SSR; the potential for synergies is context-specific. DDR and SSR processes may run autonomously with little obvious relationship between them. In some cases, DDR provides an entry point for SSR or vice-versa. In others, DDR can play a critical role in shaping an SSR agenda. Evidence-based assessments can help to 'do no harm' in operationalizing this relationship. Although the four case studies highlight numerous challenges, they also illustrate how these impediments can be mitigated by adopting politically-sensitive, coherent policies, plans and programmes.

Two key messages emerge from this volume. First, international efforts need to more closely engage with context-specific political and security dynamics. And second, a red line running through DDR and SSR interventions should be the underlying (if sometimes unstated) goal to re-centre security institutions on the needs of individuals and communities. Neither political awareness nor a human security focus should be abstract goals. Rather, as discussed in this concluding chapter, contextually-grounded analysis points to concrete entry points at policy and programming levels that can foster meaningful synergies between DDR and SSR.

The imperative to locate DDR and SSR within a security sector governance framework is compelling. It builds on a commitment to integrated approaches across the post-conflict peacebuilding agenda. This drive for greater coherence is not about blurring lines between distinct activities or simplifying complex relationships between stakeholders with different approaches and objectives. Rather, it recognises the need to work towards certain common outcomes. And while many technical activities may be involved, this process is inherently political in nature. But changing behaviour is seldom easy. By relying on key individuals rather than knowledge management strategies, inadequate institutional memory has often constrained the international community's ability to learn from past experience and adapt accordingly. Integrating a focus on the DDR-SSR nexus into guidance and related training packages for programme managers as well as other relevant field and headquarters staff would be an important step forward. The networking dynamics that are increasingly apparent within and across different strands of the peacebuilding community offer real opportunities to break down stovepipes and convert experience into good practice.

This volume demonstrates that opportunities do exist – even in difficult stabilization contexts – to develop approaches in which DDR and SSR can jointly contribute to improving security sector governance dynamics. Early efforts to build national management capacities or to support the oversight roles of marginalised stakeholders may realise common DDR/SSR goals. But more importantly they can provide a foundation of dialogue and trust. This is the only way to move beyond deep-rooted cleavages between the state, security sector and citizens that lie at the root of insecurity and under-development.

Notes

1 See Eboe Hutchful, *Security Sector Reform in Peace Agreements*, African Security Sector Network (2009).

The 2001 Bonn Agreement contains only very general provisions relating to the establishment and training of new Afghan defence and security forces (Annex 1.3) as well as the integration of mujahadin into these forces (Annex 3.3).

3 Alan Bryden and 'Funmi Olonisakin, 'Enabling Security Sector Transformation in Africa', in *Security Sector Transformation in Africa*, eds. Alan Bryden and 'Funmi Olonisakin, 225-7 (Munster: Lit Verlag, 2010). Available at: www.dcaf.ch/publications.

4 A useful comparative analysis of DDR and SSR in Burundi, DRC and Rwanda can be found in: Martin Edmonds, Greg Mills and Terence McNamee, 'Disarmament, Demobilisation and Reintegration and Local Ownership in the Great Lakes: The Experience of Rwanda, Burundi and the Democratic Republic of Congo', *African Security* 2, no. 1, 29-58. For an analysis of SSR in Sierra Leone that offers a balanced approach from both Sierra Leonean and international perspectives, see Peter Albrecht and Paul Jackson, eds., *Security Sector Reform in Sierra Leone 1997-2007: Views from the Front Line* (Munster: Lit Verlag, 2010). Available at www.dcaf.ch/publications.

5 Although the level of international support was much higher in the former case, this approach was a feature of SSR in Sierra Leone and South Africa – two reform processes generally held as examples of SSR good practice.

6 The opening up of political space was the catalyst for a July 2011 UN DDR/SSR assessment mission to the CAR. The mission included a wide range of UN DDR and SSR experience drawn from DPA, DPKO sand UNDP. As a point of departure, the mission recognised that an inclusive national political framework is a precondition for progress on DDR and SSR.

7 See MDRP, 'Position Paper: Linkages between Disarmament, Demobilisation and Reintegration of Ex-Combatants and Security Sector Reform' (2003) paragraph 16. Available at: http://www.mdrp.org/PDFs/ssr-paper.pdf.

8 IDDRS Module 6.10, Section 9. pp. 17-22.

9 This is also a central conclusion of Michael Bhatia and Robert Muggah, 'Demobilisation and Reintegration Dilemmas in Afghanistan' in *Security and Post-Conflict Reconstruction: Dealing with Fighters in the Aftermath of War*, ed. Robert Muggah (Routledge: London, 2009).

10 O.J. Greene and Simon Rynn, 'Linking and Coordinating DDR and SSR for Human Security after Conflict: Issues, Experience and Priorities' (Center for International Cooperation and Security, July 2008), 49.

11 For an empirically rich analysis of gaps between SSR 'design' and how people actually experience security, see Judy Smith-Höhn, *Rebuilding the Security Sector in Post-Conflict Societies: Perceptions from Urban Liberia and Sierra Leone*, (Munster: Lit Verlag, 2010). Available at www.dcaf.ch/publications.

12 See Hans Born and Ian Leigh, *Handbook on Human Rights and Fundamental Freedoms of Armed Forces Personnel*, (Warsaw: DCAF/ODIHR, 2008).

13 See UNDP, 'Community Security and Social Cohesion: Towards a UNDP Approach', UNDP, Bureau for Crisis Prevention and Recovery, (December 2009). Available at: http://www.securitytransformation.org/images/documentos/687_UNDP_BCPR_CSSC_Concept_Paper_Final.pdf.

14 IDDRS, Module 5.10, p.10.

15 Megan Bastick & Kristin Valasek, eds., *Gender & Security Sector Reform Toolkit*, (DCAF, OSCE/ODIHR, UN-INSTRAW, 2008).

16 See 'Funmi Olonisakin, Eka Ikpe and Paschal Badong, 'The Future of Security and Justice for the Poor', *CSDG Policy Studies*, no. 21, Conflict, Security and Development Group (March 2009).

Annex

IDDRS Planning and Design Checklist

The following is an indicative checklist for considering DDR-SSR linkages. Without being exhaustive, it summarises key points emerging from the module relevant for policy makers and practitioners.[1]

1) General

- Have measures been taken to engage both DDR and SSR experts in the negotiation of peace agreements so that provisions for the two are mutually supportive?
- Are a broad range of stakeholders involved in discussions on DDR and SSR in peace negotiations including civil society and relevant regional organizations?
- Do decisions reflect a nationally-driven vision of the role, objective and values for the security forces?
- Have SSR considerations been introduced into DDR decision-making and vice versa?
- Do assessments include the concerns of all stakeholders, including national and international partners? Have SSR experts commented on the terms of reference of the assessment and participated in the assessment mission?

---

1 Source: Integrated Demobilisation Disarmament and Reform Standards (IDDRS) Module 6.10: 'DDR and Security Sector Reform'. Available at: http://www.unddr.org.

- Is monitoring and evaluation carried out systematically and are efforts made to link it with SSR? Is M&E used as an entry-point for linking DDR and SSR concerns in planning?

2) Programming and Planning

SSR/DDR dynamics before and during demobilization

- Has the potential long-term use of demobilization and disarmament sites been factored into planning for DDR?

- Have disarmament programmes been complemented by security sector training and other activities to improve national control over stocks of weapons and ammunition?

- Has a security sector census been considered/implemented to support human and financial resource management and inform integration decisions?

- Have clear criteria been developed for entry of ex-combatants into the security sector? Does this reflect national security priorities as well as the capacity of the security forces to absorb them? Is provision made for vetting to ensure appropriate skills and consideration of past conduct?

- Have rank harmonization policies been introduced which establish a formula for conversion from former armed groups to national armed forces? Was this the result of a dialogue which considered the need for affirmative action for marginalised groups?

- Is there a sustainable distribution of ex-combatants between the reintegration and integration programmes? Has information been disseminated and counselling been offered to ex-combatants facing a voluntary choice between integration and reintegration?

- Have measures been taken to identify and address potential security vacuums in places where ex-combatants are demobilized, and has this information been shared with relevant authorities? Are security concerns related to dependents taken into account?

- Have efforts been made to actively encourage female ex-combatants to enter the DDR process? Have they been offered the choice to integrate into the security sector? Has appropriate action been taken to ensure that the security institutions provide women with fair and equal treatment, including realistic employment opportunities?

- Is there a communications/training strategy in place? Does it include messages specifically designed to facilitate the transition from combatant to security provider including behaviour change, HIV risks and GBV?

SSR/DDR dynamics before and during reintegration

- Is data collected on the return and reintegration of ex-combatants? Is this analysed in order to coordinate relevant DDR and SSR activities?

- Has capacity-building within the security sector been prioritised in a way to ensure that security institutions are capable of supporting DDR objectives?

- Have ex-combatants been sensitised to the availability of housing, land and property dispute mechanisms?

- In cases where private security bodies are a source of employment for ex-combatants, are efforts actively made to ensure their regulation and that appropriate vetting mechanisms are in place?

- Have border management services been sensitised and trained on issues relating to cross-border flows of ex-combatants?

3) Communication and Coordination

Coordination

- Have opportunities been taken to engage with national security sector management and oversight bodies on how they can support the DDR process?

- Is there a mechanism that supports national dialogue and coordination across DDR and SSR? If not, could the national commission on DDR fulfil this role by inviting representatives of other ministries to selected meetings?

- Are the specific objectives of DDR and SSR clearly set out and understood (e.g. in a 'letter of commitment')? Is this understanding shared by national actors and international partners as the basis for a mutually supportive approach?

Knowledge management

- When developing information management systems, are efforts made to also collect data that will be useful for SSR? Is there a mechanism in place to share this data?

- Is there provision for up to date conflict and security analysis as a common basis for DDR/SSR decision-making?

- Have efforts been made to share information with border management authorities on high risk areas for foreign combatants transiting borders?

- Has regular information sharing taken place with relevant security sector institutions as a basis for planning to ensure appropriate support to DDR objectives?

- Are adequate mechanisms in place to ensure institutional memory and avoid over reliance on key individuals? Are assessment reports and other key documents retained and easily accessible in order to support lessons learned processes for DDR/SSR?

4) Funding

- Does resource planning seek to identify gaps, increase coherence and mitigate competition between DDR and SSR?

- Have the financial resource implications of DDR for the security sector been considered, and vice versa?

- Are DDR and SSR programmes realistic and compatible with national budgets?

5) Capacity Development, Pooling Resources and Training

- Have efforts been made to sensitise staff on the DDR/SSR nexus through training or other activities?

- Has the need for personnel to link DDR and SSR concerns been clearly agreed at Headquarters and included in the ToRs of relevant personnel?

- Has cross-participation in DDR or SSR training been implemented to foster knowledge transfer and build relationships?

- Have key skills sets been identified and provision made for the availability of a multidisciplinary resource pool? Are linguistic and 'knowledge transfer' skills adequately represented in order to support national capacity development?

- In the area of national capacity-building, has the development of cross-cutting skills such as human resources and financial management (common requirements for both DDR and SSR) been encouraged?

- Has pooling financial and physical resources for DDR and SSR been considered, for example, in the area of community security initiatives or SALW initiatives?

- Are UN personnel aware of available SSR Resources, including through the UN Inter-Agency SSR Task Force (e.g. policy guidance, resources, gap analysis, backstopping)?

Contributors

Alan BRYDEN is Deputy Head of Research at the Geneva Centre for the Democratic Control of Armed Forces.

Boubacar N'DIAYE is an associate professor of political science and pan-African studies at the College of Wooster, Ohio.

Serge RUMIN is Programme Manager of the Security Sector Development programme in Burundi.

Vincenza SCHERRER is Programme Manager of the United Nations and Security Sector Reform programme at the Geneva Centre for the Democratic control of Armed Forces.

Mark SEDRA is a Senior Fellow at the Centre for International Governance Innovation (CIGI) and a research scholar in the University of Waterloo's Department of Political Science.

About the Geneva Centre for the Democratic Control of Armed Forces (DCAF)

The Geneva Centre for the Democratic Control of Armed Forces (DCAF) is an international foundation whose mission is to assist the international community in pursuing good governance and reform of the security sector. To this end, DCAF develops and promotes appropriate norms at the international and national levels, determines good practices and relevant policy recommendations for effective governance of the security sector, and provides in-country advisory support and practical assistance programmes to all interested actors.

Detailed information is available at www.dcaf.ch

Geneva Centre for the Democratic Control of Armed Forces (DCAF)
Rue de Chantepoulet 11
PO Box 1360
CH-1211 Geneva 1
Switzerland
Tel: + 41 22 741 77 00
Fax: + 41 22 741 77 05
E-mail: info@dcaf.ch